PREPARING FOR

WORLD WAR III

A Global Conflict That Redefines Tomorrow

PREPARING FOR

WORLD WAR III

LTC ROBERT L. MAGINNIS

DEFENDER
CRANE, MO

Preparing for World War III: A Global Conflict That Redefines Tomorrow
By LTC Robert L. Maginnis

Defender Publishing
Crane, MO 65633

©2024 Defender Publishing

All Rights Reserved. Published 2024.

ISBN: 978-1-948-014-85-4

Printed in the United States of America.

A CIP catalog record of this book is available from the Library of Congress.

Cover designer Jeffrey Mardis
Interior designer Katherine Lloyd

This book is dedicated to my grandchildren Campbell, Hudson, and Liberty. It is my prayer that you grow old in a free country and never have to experience war. Keep your hearts right with the Lord and remember to keep looking up, for as He promises in Matthew 28:20 (NASB): "I am with you always, even to the end of the age."

CONTENTS

ACKNOWLEDGMENTS

I gratefully acknowledge…

…my wife, Jan, who supports these writing projects and my thinking out loud about tough topics. She is a comfort and supporter through these challenging times.

…my friend Mark Shaffstall, a historian and military expert, who provided valued recommendations, edits, and keen insights about a possible future war.

…finally, my Lord Jesus Christ, who gave me the opportunity, skills, and breath to complete this work, and I pray it serves His purpose. All the glory is to Him.

—Robert Lee Maginnis
Woodbridge, Virginia

PREPARING FOR WORLD WAR III:

A Fight That Could Radically Change the World We Know

I know not with what weapons World War III will be fought, but World War IV will be fought with sticks and stones.[1]

—Albert Einstein, German-born theoretical physicist, developer of the theory of relativity

The world is on the cusp of a global, unimaginable war unlike any past conflict, thanks to a host of rogue leaders armed with incredible technologies. Unless mankind is very careful, as Albert Einstein warned above, World War III could rob our future of the trappings of modern civilization, forcing us back into the Stone Age and perhaps ushering in the prophetic end times.

Of course, the specific geopolitical circumstances that might trip us into a global armed conflict are hard to predict. However, be assured, given the present level of international tension, radical "leadership," and especially the growing instability in the West, these factors could very well trigger widespread conflict that rapidly engulfs all humanity.

Numerous indicators of the coming conflict will likely be like what we've seen previously in history. Specifically, in the first half of the twentieth century, the two world wars (World War I, 1914–1918, and World War II, 1939–1945)—and even, to a more limited extent, the global Cold War (1948–1991) between the Soviet Union and the West—provide signals of possible war to be realized, such as a new geopolitical polarization and the realignment of nations. That is in part why danger signs are now flashing red across the world, warning of something giant on the horizon.

World War III presents challenges that are genuinely frightening.
Photo by Somchai Kongkamsri on Pexels[2]

Spark from China?

Foreign powers—a growing cohort of true American enemies—are seeking to take advantage of a weakened West led by the United States. Communist China, under the iron-fisted grip of leader Xi Jinping, is building a global network through a variety of alliances and worldwide programs such as its Belt and Road Initiative that now touches 150 nations. No doubt Mr. Xi is succeeding, considering the expanding influence of the People's Republic of China given its world-class economy; its ever-growing, giant-sized and sophisticated military; and its intimidating diplomacy; as well as its all-of-government, "unrestricted warfare" doctrine now operationalized against the West. Further, President Xi's frequent hegemonic public pronouncements paint a troubled future of conflict, which will not be limited to retaking the democratic island nation of Taiwan, officially the Republic of China. No, the communist dictator Xi sees a renewed "Middle Kingdom" on the horizon, which raises Beijing's stature to govern a new world order that leaves the US and perhaps much of the democratic West in the trash bin of history.

The breadth of Xi's ambitions truly knows no bounds. In 2023, the

China Aerospace Science and Technology Corporation, the maker of Beijing's main rocket-building effort, Beijing's moon launcher company, hosted a conference to announce its two hundred-year program to occupy our solar system. Evidently, the communist regime aims to extend its control first to our moon, next to Mars, and then to the balance of our solar system. Why? Richard Fisher, a senior fellow at the Virginia-based International Assessment and Strategy Center, answers: "In order to reinforce their control on Earth."[3]

Spark from Russia?

Russia's President Vladimir Putin saw weakness and tested President Joe Biden with his 2022 war of choice to reclaim control of the nation of Ukraine. That war might have momentarily rallied the North Atlantic Treaty Organization (NATO) nations, but it has also become a geopolitical anchor around Europe's neck. Besides, the alliance's arsenals are almost emptied by Ukraine's fight, and their citizens are angry at their bickering politicians, which could mean the balance of Western Europe, beginning with the Baltic states (Latvia, Estonia, and Lithuania) could well become Putin's next target. That is assuming the Kremlin restocks its arsenal and takes to heart the many combat lessons learned from the Ukraine battlefields—something the evidence suggests is happening.

Spark from the Islamic Republic?

The Islamic Republic of Iran, which seeks to be the Middle East's principal hegemon, saw blood in the water as a result of a weakened US beginning in 2021, to wit, President Joe Biden's debacle of a withdrawal from Afghanistan after twenty years of war, and the mullahs reveled as naïve Biden lifted former President Donald Trump's crippling economic sanctions on Iran. Now, Tehran's war coffers are full to the brim, and those funds are used to fuel a broader conflict against Israel and the West through its proxies like Hezbollah, Hamas, and the Houthis. Meanwhile, Israel became complacent, given its past security successes, and took its eyes off threats encircling the Jewish state.

Biden's geopolitical policy malfeasance and Israel's missteps gave Tehran the means and opportunity to deploy proxies like Hezbollah, Hamas, Yemen's Houthi rebels, and miscreants in Syria, which are all in step with

Iranian ambitions. Most recently, Hamas' bloody invasion of southern Israel on October 7, 2023, was the most blatant Mideast conflagration in decades. It was a savage attack funded and approved by Iran—and it will not be the last. The 2023–2024 Israel-Hamas war, with help from Hezbollah in Lebanon, suggests Tehran is just getting its second wind as its allies and ideological surrogates further weaken the West and Israel through constant attacks. Meanwhile, here in the US, anti-Israeli/pro-Hamas progressives collaborate with domestic Islamists and socialists, mostly on college campuses, to bolster Iran's radical cause and weaken support for Jerusalem.

Security Challenges Collide with Frightening Technologies: A Future Ripe for Global Conflict

Couple these security challenges—China, Russia, and Iran—with a host of sophisticated, frightening technologies now available to ambitious tyrants, and we have the real potential for global war: true tyrants armed to the teeth with deadly artificial intelligence-powered killer drones; a host of autonomous killing machines; cyber "armies" capable of crippling critical infrastructure; hypersonic systems armed with nuclear weapons that can precisely target anything on earth in minutes; the weaponization of space that can blind modern economies and defense establishments; the proliferation of nuclear arsenals; and much more. Therefore, authoritarians like Xi and Putin and their cohort of rogue allies and surrogates like Iran and North Korea can be expected to use these cutting-edge killing capabilities to advance their all-consuming thirst for global power.

Thus, and understandably, the world is rapidly becoming poised for World War III, a conflict that could quickly return the globe to the Stone Age because of the devastating power of modern weapons and the will of a cohort of authoritarians to use them. But, of course, some of the blame for that outcome is on the weakened United States, the world's last remaining erstwhile stabilizing force, for failing to deter the coming conflict. Why? Consider that in 2014, President Barack Obama failed to appropriately respond to Putin's seizure of Crimea, a former autonomous republic of Ukraine, which is a peninsula on the northern coast of the Black Sea. Had Obama done more to vigorously respond to Russia's annexation of Crimea, it is quite possible the Kremlin never would have invaded Ukraine in 2022. Further, under President Biden, America was humbled and was no longer respected by many friends and foes because of his years of corrupt policies such as open borders, rampant crime, election insecurity, asymmetrical weaponization of justice, mushroomed debt, unaccountable federal bureaucracies, disinformation, societal decay, dysfunctional foreign policies (such as the Afghanistan withdrawal debacle), destruction of trust in institutions, and a lot more.

Couple these signs of a seriously weakened US with a host of hegemonic foreign thugs armed with an arsenal of frightening weapons, and all we need is a spark or two to trigger global conflict that no nation or alliance of states will contain. That is the world we live in today.

A Glimpse of World War III

Although it's hard to predict with precision when World War III might break out, it is clear that the next global conflict will likely be the most frightening, chaotic time ever known to humankind.

We can speculate as to the triggers that spark the future global war: massed military forces on the border of neighboring states, the seizure of critical natural resources like energy fields, the arrest of a state leader in a foreign land on trumped-up charges levied by the International Criminal Court, renewed insurgencies, domestic issues that lead to civil war within key states, the destruction of satellite networks, malicious cyberattacks on critical infrastructure, the assassination of key leaders, and immeasurably more. Likely, these and similar other potential sparks will spread fear across the world, fanned by sensational media reporting that will then drive tough, emotionally loaded political decisions in multiple capitals. Then, of course, as caution is thrown to the wind by government decision-makers, hostilities spark and just as quickly spiral out of control.

Once both kinetic (the physical engagement of targets) and non-kinetic (e.g., cyber and electronic warfare) actions are launched by mostly state actors and the effects are broadly realized, follow-on responses are not easily contained; global conflict becomes a sobering reality as casualties such as critical public services and the human toll quickly mount.

Modern technologies will define that future conflict. Initially, non-kinetic efforts will blind the parties to the threats using cyber and electronic warfare that disables critical satellites and major networked communication systems. The result is the creation of information-free chaos across nation-states, which also cripples satellite-dependent military operations. Many energy grids, water systems, cellular networks, and food distribution services will all be disrupted. These casualties of war throw much of society into pandemonium, forcing nation-states to address domestic crises with their military forces just as enemies move to the next step of hostilities.

The biggest military danger in the future conflict is unplanned escalation. Command centers, in the dark thanks to disabled satellites and corrupted computer networks, will force authorities to calibrate their next moves without adequate and timely information. Will they apply minimalist or maximalist responses? At some point, artificial intelligence—AI—will aid commanders in decision-making, and response times will be cut short as violence and confusion accelerate.

Of course, AI tools will help offset enemy advantages by pairing human beings and machines to buy back a qualitative balance. The consequences will put much of the important tactical decision-making under the control of smart machines; thus, the outcomes will become less predictable and chaos will likely spread.

Meanwhile, kinetic strikes will begin to target strategic sites with hypersonic missiles—super-charged projectiles that fly worldwide many times the speed of sound and carry either conventional or nuclear warheads, striking with pinpoint precision. Some are maneuverable, making them unpredictable and hard to intercept.[4]

Soon, forward-postured conventional units will move into action. Air, ground, sea, and space forces—a mix of human and autonomous entities—will occupy their planned launch locations, ready to attack or defend. Many of their moves will be prearranged based on contingency orders, with the goal of persuading the adversary/adversaries to measure the effects and back down before the full response is operationalized.

The consequences of this series of events will be global devastation, felt in a short time—hours and days rather than months—by much of the known world. Quickly, the average citizen will be thrown back into the Stone Age with no electronic communication, electricity, water, or food; generally, chaos will rule, right down to the local street level. Our medical system will be stretched beyond its limits, and local police will be marginalized by escalating crime carried out by those who are taking advantage of the situation as much of humanity will huddle in fear because they've been denied the essence of life-supporting resources.

Is this scenario realistic? Is humanity so depraved that such a thing could happen?

Yes.

That is why preparing for and, if possible, deterring such an outcome is critical for governments and citizens of every country.

For the Christian attuned to the prophetic end-times scenarios, the above description may appear to fulfill the future foretold in Revelation, the last book of the Bible. However, what if this outcome isn't the true end times? In fact, this future conflict could be yet another global struggle like the past two world wars. Therefore, we must somehow adjust and continue to live, anticipating that the Scripture-promised Rapture of the Church and Christ's return are yet more distant, in a future age to come.

Journey through Six Sections

Preparing for World War III in six sections outlines what we face today and, if possible, how to prepare for and—if it's even doable—deter global war that appears inevitable, aimed at destroying the life we know.

Section I outlines our current situation and how, despite our collective best intentions, the world could quickly fall into a war that transforms all our lives. What is the evidence of that coming World War III?

Section II reviews the historic record of past global conflicts, both World Wars I and II. What circumstances, causes, and indicators led to those periods of mass instability, and what were the consequences? Are there lessons from those histories for us in 2025? Better, is our current crop of world leaders likely to learn from those lessons to prevent World War III?

Section III identifies the dangerous technologies modern states now have—or in the foreseeable future will come to possess—and the implications those capabilities have for global conflicts. This section takes a deep dive into the proliferation of war-fighting technologies and profiles their frightening effects. What kind of worldwide clash might result from the use of these instruments of destruction, and what are the long-term implications of that conflict for humankind?

Further, the third section digs into history to consider how technologies that were new for World War I and World War II changed the complexion of warfare. After all, the First War started with tactics from the nineteenth century, but quickly changed with the introduction of new weapons such as the machine gun, the airplane, and poison gas. The Second World War saw nations unprepared for the transition from horses to tanks as well as combined arms maneuver warfare, all new at the time. The mass use of heavy bombers, unthinkable in World War I, dramatically altered the fight in the Second World War.

Are we really seeing anything new today, or is it just more advances in existing technologies strapped to old fighting platforms? Also, although we haven't fought a nuclear war, we certainly prepared for one during the Cold War. How would World War III be different than the nuclear war we got ready to fight with the Soviets?

Section IV provides a template to make ready the US—and, by association, the entire West—for World War III; alternatively, it outlines how we must try to deter such a global conflagration. After all, we prevented a nuclear Armageddon during the Cold War with the Soviet Union by using policies like our mutual assured destruction doctrine and later President Ronald Reagan's Strategic Defense Initiative (Star Wars). Can we do the same, given the current world environment? Also, what might become the prophylaxis measures to prevent World War III?

Section V is for local government leaders and citizens who anticipate the possibility of a coming global war and want to prepare themselves, their families, communities, and nations. States and local communities ought to act now to prepare for the worst case (war) much like they take precautions in anticipation of natural disasters by stocking supplies and equipment so they can quickly respond. Meanwhile, there are many so-called preppers ready to advise us on building underground shelters, securing safe spaces, stocking up on food, learning survival skills, arming ourselves, and much more. The time for action is now because the signs of worldwide conflict are obvious.

Section VI is for those who are especially anxious about the spiritual aspects of our coming world war. Specifically, is it appropriate to ask whether the future crisis is the means for the coming Antichrist to wrestle control over the world? Is there evidence that the forces of evil are preparing for the end-times battlefields spelled out in biblical prophecy? If so, what should Christians do as the indicators of such a conflict grow more evident?

A new global war could become a reality, and soon, which gives us an outcome no rational person should want, but one we must prepare to experience if deterrence fails. Yes, prudent people around the world should rally to prevent this possible contagion of violence. However, given the current level of geopolitical instability and the rush by most nations to arm up, we must admit that averting a cataclysmic conflict of epic proportions is a high bar, especially given global uncertainty and our current host of corrupt and weak world leaders tempted to use frightening modern technologies to expand their power.

Section I
WORLD RIPE FOR COLLAPSING INTO WORLD WAR III

Yes, peace can and must be won, to save the world from the terrible destruction of World War III.[5]

—Paul L. Robeson (1898–1976), American actor, professional football player, and political activist

The first section of *Preparing for World War III* addresses our current state of global affairs and how, despite our collective best intentions and naïve sense of security, we could quickly fall into another universal war that forever transforms our lives.

Arguably, World War III has already started, and it's not like America's post-September 11, 2001, era, the so-called War on Terror. No, the coming great-power global war will be similar in scope to the kind of conflict that afflicted Europe and Asia in World War II, pitting economic and ideological rivals. Unfortunately, in the interim between World War II and the present, the West has embraced a self-righteous—"the US is always right"—foreign policy and abandoned the restraint necessary to avoid such an outcome.

Yes, the twenty-first century's great war has already started, as the giant powers support adventures across the world that could quickly trigger a global conflict. The fight today is marked by a naïve willingness among the great powers to use limited military force, believing the consequences are less dire than in the past. Why? That's simple. Few today are still sobered by or remember the West's costly triumph in the Second World War. Besides, we've become complacent and unaccustomed to enduring hardship for our foreign-policy choices—the losses of life and wealth, and experiencing other suffering that marked past great conflicts.

We have also distanced ourselves from what then President Harry Truman (1945–1953) warned about modern war. He said a future war would make America "a battlefront." In other words, the thirty-third president cautioned, "We can look forward to destruction here, just as the other countries in the Second World War." Yet, with such a threat hanging over our collective heads, all US presidents since Truman have meddled in foreign wars that ran the risk of global escalation.[6]

Initially, our fear of nuclear war that would end civilization became our prophylaxis against expansion. Yet, as we built up our atomic arsenals, we took precautions by warning the public to build bomb shelters and educate themselves about fissionable effects like radiation poisoning. However, even during the nuclear-threatening Cold War (1948–1991), we fought limited conflicts in Korea and Vietnam but stopped short of expanding those actions to avoid global war.

Consider, for example, that in 1950, President Truman sent US troops to defend the democratic South Korea against the communist north's invasion, assisted by Chinese forces. However, Truman exercised great caution to contain that conflict. After all, General Douglas MacArthur, the commander of US forces in the region at the time, recommended a nuclear attack on both North Korea and communist China, but Truman wisely feared such a move would certainly escalate the war on the Korean peninsula into a broader conflict. Instead, Truman fired MacArthur to kill his out-of-bounds advice and settled for a stalemate that continues to this day.[7]

General Douglas MacArthur (seated), Commander in Chief, United
Nations forces in Korea, and staff view pre-landing in Korean waters off Inchon.
Robert W. Porter, US Army, Public Domain[8]

Avoidance of a broader war restrained Truman in Korea, but, with time, that measure of restraint among our political class has weakened, thanks to our popular cultural influence that feeds on the faux idea that America will always win wars. After all, for decades, Hollywood gave us movies and television programs about how the US saved the world from tyranny in the prior world wars, and those Western victories promised humanity a bright future. That perspective of righteous and certain victory distorted America's psyche about history and future war-making.

Ever since, many of our leaders came to embrace that false view to justify an adventurous foreign policy. For example, presidents like Bill Clinton (1993–2001) celebrated past global victories by labeling our Second World War allies as "the stars of a majestic galaxy" that "unleashed their democratic fury." We allegedly, according to Clinton's distortion, became the saviors of the world, an untouchable lot for the good of humankind![9]

That view was infectious and created a false sense of security. For example, the "peace dividend" after the Cold War was an idea encouraged by former Secretary of Defense Robert McNamara, who testified before Congress on December 13, 1989, that the Pentagon's annual budget could be safely cut in half. "By such a shift," McNamara argued, "we should be able to enhance global stability, strengthen our own security and...produce the resources to support a much needed restructuring of the economy."[10] The same type of myopic thinking drove us to suspend the requirement for every male citizen to serve in time of war. Specifically, in 1973, we left behind the political nastiness of conscription (the draft) that marred the Vietnam conflict, which wasn't supported by the American people, to create the all-volunteer military. After all, at the time, military technologists promised that future war belonged to air power, not to conscripted grunt infantrymen. The effect of these changes on US society was predictable.

President George W. Bush used that same so-called manifest destiny to remind Americans of scenes from World War II to justify his 2003 Iraq invasion. "The scenes of the concentration camps, the heaps of bodies and ghostly survivors, confirmed forever America's calling to oppose the ideologies of death," Bush said at the National World War II Memorial dedication. However, the fact is the US did not enter the Second War because of the Jewish Holocaust, but for more sanguine reasons, such as

Japan's unprovoked attack on Pearl Harbor. Further, Bush's distortion of history was meant at the time to justify toppling tyrants like Iraq's Saddam Hussein—more hubris and yet another tragic foreign-policy mistake that cost the US 4,492 lives and more than a trillion dollars.[11]

Unfortunately, this forgotten taste of world war and the rewriting of history to serve domestic political ambitions contributed to the dismantling of our means to defend ourselves as well. Certainly, Europe led that charge after the Cold War (1991) by scuttling investment in its arsenals of war in favor of social programs. America tended to do much the same by slashing defense spending as well.

Americans soon felt safe from the horror of war. After all, we were cushioned by giant oceans on both flanks and protected by an all-volunteer military armed with the latest high-technology weapons. The thinking became: Who could threaten America? The general feeling of being secure from modern battle thus became our collective inheritance, despite our previous often-bankrupt and adventurous foreign-policy decisions.

Unfortunately, the post-Cold War era that gave us this false sense of security is now dead. The twenty-first century is a new, more dangerous era of intense great-power competition that could easily escalate to global war. We must seriously consider the consequences of today's new world.

The evidence of the death of this false sense of security, the danger of our current world, and the potential consequences of this new world order are addressed in three chapters.

Chapter 1 profiles what world leaders and average citizens think about the likelihood of a future global war. There is a general sense that the restraint that has prevented global war in the past is now gone, and the level of instability seems to be flashing red at every turn.

Chapter 2 addresses the preparations now underway for what appears to be the global fight. There is a worldwide rush to prepare militaries and, more broadly, all levers of government for conflict, and too many political leaders seem to have the will to follow through with their often naively tough, war-like rhetoric to acquire their stated ends.

Chapter 3 demonstrates the emergence of a palpable global realignment of antagonists. In fact, there is emerging a true clash of civilizations—a new world order is being realized—that is more than rhetoric and could very soon burst all restraints into worldwide conflict.

Chapter 1

A GLOBAL TINDERBOX

Four-star US Air Force general predicts US war with China: "I hope I am wrong. My gut tells me [we—US and China] will fight in 2025."[12]

—General Mike Minihan,
Head of the US Air Force's Mobility Command

A significant cross section of people believe global war is on our near horizon. This chapter profiles what some world leaders, international affairs security experts, and average citizens believe about the possibility of world war and provides evidence that the restraints on such a future conflict are waning. Certainly, the degree of global instability suggests that the likelihood of a major clash cannot be far into our future.

What World Leaders Say about the Possibility of World War III

Billionaire Elon Musk argues that world leaders are "sleepwalking into World War III." The founder of major corporations like SpaceX and PayPal explained that global war can in fact be avoided by abandoning foolish decisions, which make war more likely.[13]

Unfortunately, according to Musk, civilization is at risk because many conflicts at one time, layered on top of the other, could lead to "devastation that far exceeds World War I and World War II." Then Musk said, "Nobody wants...to have World War III," but events could "cascade out of control." In fact, he soberly posited that the US military's capability is being "overestimated," and the growing axis of Russia, China, and Iran "should be viewed as...very strong relative to the West."[14]

Then former President Donald Trump blamed America's vulnerability for global war on President Biden's many failings. Specifically, Trump said, "It truly breaks my heart to see crooked Joe [Biden]—the weakest and most incompetent president in history—ruin our country as he pushes America to the brink of World War III." Trump also boasted while campaigning for the presidency in 2024 that he is the "only one that will prevent World War III."[15]

The world is a tinderbox that could well explode at most anytime.

Photo by NASA, Hubble Image on Unsplash[16]

The West's perceived vulnerability for World War III is shared by other leaders such as Poland's prime minister, Donald Tusk. He said in 2024, with an eye on Russia's war of choice in nearby Ukraine:

War is no longer a concept from the past. It is real, and it started over two years ago. The most worrying thing at the moment is that literally any scenario is possible. We have not seen a situation like this since 1945.[17]

A similar sentiment was spoken by the British defense secretary. In January 2024, Secretary Grant Shapps said we are "moving from a post-war to pre-war world." He warned his countrymen to prepare for further wars involving China, Russia, Iran, and North Korea. Then Shapps presented a dark picture indicating that our enemies like Russia and China have redrawn battle lines against the West.[18]

Russian President Vladimir Putin appears to agree with the Polish prime minister and the British defense secretary. In May 2024, Putin warned in his reelection acceptance speech that any direct confrontation with the North Atlantic Treaty Organization (NATO) would be "one step away from a full-scale World War III." He continued, "I think hardly anyone is interested in this [World War III]."[19]

Ukrainian President Volodymyr Zelensky called out his archenemy, Putin, stating the Russian leader had become "addicted to power," which might explain the Kremlin's sustained war with Kyiv and Putin's possible willingness to grow the current conflict beyond Ukraine, something Eastern European leaders like Tusk often publicly discuss.

It is more than talk that the Ukraine war could grow to include other nations, and in fact it could lead to a nuclear exchange and worse. Since Moscow launched its "Special Military Operation," Russian President Putin's label, which began in February 2022, the Russian leader and his surrogates have frequently reiterated Moscow's willingness to deploy nuclear weapons if their country's territorial integrity and sovereignty are threatened. In May 2024, Putin backed that when the Kremlin held tactical nuclear weapons drills in Belarus, a northern neighbor of Ukraine.

Then, on August 6, 2024, Russian nuclear saber-rattling rocketed into the limelight again after Ukraine's military conducted a ground incursion into Russia's Kursk Oblast. Moscow immediately accused the West (read "US/NATO") of encouraging Kyiv's cross-border raid that seized five hundred square miles of Russian territory. Predictably, NATO denied any prior knowledge of the operation, but almost immediately and openly indicated the US and the United Kingdom would soon provide Ukraine with long-range weapons capable of striking deep inside Russia.[20]

One of the first Russians to call for a nuclear response to Ukraine's raid was the founder of pro-Kremlin media outlet Tsargrad television, Konstantin Malofeev. He wrote an article entitled "How Much Longer?" calling for Moscow to use nuclear weapons, and he cried, "We are able and must deliver a truly potent retaliation strike in a way that will force the West to curb support of Ukraine and, consequently, will put an end to the SVO [Special Military Operation, war in Ukraine]." He warned, "It is high time for Russia's tactical nuclear weapons—it must become the weapon of victory."[21]

Shortly after Malofeev and others called for a nuclear response, Deputy Foreign Minister Sergei Ryabkov announced that Moscow will amend its nuclear doctrine to set the conditions in which atomic weapons can be used. The minister said the reason for the adjustment is the Western-backed "escalation" of the war with Ukraine.[22]

Putin ally and Kremlin propagandist, Vladimir Solovyov, predicated in May 2024 that the current conflict with Ukraine could well explode into a nuclear war and then become a global conflict. That declaration is consistent with other statements spewing from Putin and his lackeys and resonates with ally China as well.[23]

Mr. Solovyov's assertion is backed by President Putin's September 2024 announcement of a refreshed nuclear doctrine. The updated concept increases the list of threats that could warrant a nuclear response. Specifically, Russia would consider any aggression by a "non-nuclear state," such as Ukraine that was backed by a "nuclear state," such as the United States, as a "joint attack," which could then elicit a nuclear reaction. Putin elaborated that the doctrine could allow the deployment of nuclear assets if the Kremlin received "reliable information" that a "massive launch of attack vehicles" had entered Russian airspace. He defined those vehicles as "strategic or tactical aircraft, cruise missiles, drones, hypersonic and other aircraft."[24]

Not to be outdone, Chinese President Xi Jinping appears to share Putin's view about the inevitability of global war. In 2023, President Xi publicly called for his nation to prepare for combat. At China's annual parliamentary meeting, he addressed the theme of battle readiness, which included a direct message to his generals: "Dare to fight," and he called on those military officials to safeguard national security by turning the armed forces into a "great wall of steel." At the time, he also announced yet another increase in China's military budget, which has more than doubled over the last decade and is now nearing in buying power the Pentagon's annual spending.[25]

On a related front, Mr. Xi called for his entire nation to become less dependent on foreign food imports, and he unveiled new military readiness laws and air-raid shelters in cities opposite Taiwan. Further, he established "national defense mobilization" offices across that country.[26]

What is clear from this summary is that our primary adversaries are focused on the coming World War III. That it will indeed happen is a foregone conclusion among average citizens as well.

What Average Citizens Say about
the Possibility of World War III

Citizens across the world sense vulnerability that the globe is collapsing once again into war. For example, a 2024 survey of Americans found that more than two-thirds (69 percent) fear the Ukraine fight will lead to nuclear war, which could mark the beginning stages of World War III.[27]

Even putting aside concern about the Ukraine war spreading, half of Americans believe the US will become involved in a world war within the next decade, according to a national survey. "In some ways it's a rather sensible position, in that the US has been at war for most of the years since it was founded," said MacDara King, chief information officer of the Foreign Policy Association and executive producer of *America's Diplomats* and *Great Decisions* television series.[28]

The sense that average citizens believe we're rapidly approaching a global war is a general response to the "end of this unipolar world" and the rise of China, King explained. "And there's also a sense that some of the post-World War II order is falling away."[29]

The shift away from the post-World War II order started with the presidency of George W. Bush, according to Gregory Payne, a professor at Emerson College in Boston, Massachusetts. "Americans have a tendency to see the world through either a black or white prism and there's a lack of sophistication by a lot of Americans to see the complexity of a lot of global issues," Payne argues.[30]

Along with concern about a coming war rising to a fever pitch, there is also strong belief that most people can identify the nations that will be involved in that fight. Specifically, almost three in four (72 percent) believe Russia will join that conflict with the West as an enemy, and, by a similar percentage (69 percent), most believe China will be party to the war as an adversary as well. Likely, Russia and China will form a new Axis-powers alliance like the Rome-Berlin-Tokyo Axis in World War II.[31]

The outcome of future war is also very much in doubt for many Americans. For a variety of reasons, citizens aren't very confident the US and its allies—the collective West—would necessarily prevail in a future contest with Russia and or China. Only 53 percent think Western nations would be victorious if the opposition involved Russia and its lesser allies. Adding

China to Russia's side means for many Americans (52 percent) that we're likely to lose such a fight.[32]

A 2024 poll by YouGov conducted in the United Kingdom found similar outcomes. Fewer than half (44 percent) believe the West would win a war with Russia, and slightly less than a third (31 percent) said Western nations would prevail over an enemy coalition of China, Russia, and others.[33]

More broadly, when looking across the planet, there exists a pervasive sense of insecurity. In fact, United Nations' Deputy Secretary-General Amina J. Mohammed said global peace "is now under grave threat." He said:

> People's sense of safety and security is at an all-time low in almost every country. Six out of seven worldwide are plagued by feelings of insecurity, the world is facing the highest number of violent conflicts since the Second World War and 2 billion people—a quarter of humanity—live in places affected by such conflict."[34]

Do We Lack the Restraint to Prevent Global War?

The lack of a sense of global security is traceable to the absence of restraint on war-making. Experts surmise we are living in a pre-war era marked by preparations for global conflict.

Sky News asked security experts about the possibility of World War III and whether we are really living in a pre-war world.[35] Dr. David Wearings, a lecturer in international relations at the University of Sussex, England, said:

> In one sense the situation now is far more perilous than it was in 1914 and 1939 [pre-World War I and pre-World War II] because the major powers all have nuclear weapons.
>
> The danger here is not that one side takes the pre-meditated decision to spark the apocalypse, but rather that a conflict or area of tension escalates to a certain point, one party makes a move that another party misinterprets, and then a nuclear exchange begins despite the fact that no-one was looking for one."[36]

Dominic Waghorn, *Sky News*' international affairs editor, said we need to act to avoid war:

We are probably closer than we have been since the end of the Cold War to WWIII, but do not be alarmed. There is no need to stock the basement with bullets and beans quite yet.

Hotspots are hotter than for a long time, fault-lines increasingly tense and war seems to be proliferating. But the alarm being raised by generals and spooks is a bit of a red herring and, let us face it, they are keen to make the case for bigger budgets and bigger roles.

The fact is that conflict with Russia is entirely avoidable if Putin can be persuaded there is no margin in continuing his madcap misadventure in Ukraine.[37]

Simon Diggins, a retired British colonel and military analyst, told *Sky News*: "In one sense, we are always in a 'pre-war' world, as wars can start from miscalculation, from hubris, or misunderstandings as well as deliberate design." He continued, "The presumption against the use of force—which was the basis for the post-WWII world order, for anything other than defence—has been lost."[38]

Colonel Diggins also said:

The West sees that expansion [of war such as in Ukraine] as a natural and reasonable choice by individual nations. The Russians, who have long regarded themselves as a surrounded people, believe they need a bulwark of friendly, or at least, compliant countries to protect "Mother Russia" [thus the Ukraine war to provide that buffer]....

It is this disconnect of world view, combined with the willingness to use force, that makes the situation in eastern Europe so very dangerous.[39]

There are numerous other risks atop the lack of sufficient restraint for war, however.

Risks Flashing Red across the World

Even though instability is high, as indicated above, war isn't necessarily certain. However, the crises facing today's governments are incredibly destabilizing, making global conflict more likely.

The left-leaning World Economic Forum published a *Global Risks Report 2024* that indicates the world is plagued by dangerous crises such as significant levels of conflict and back-dropped by accelerating techno-logical change and economic uncertainty. These findings are the result of the opinions of 1,500 experts from academic, business, government, and the international community.[40]

According to the report, "Optimism among respondents was in short supply." Specifically, it found that half (54 percent) "anticipate a signifi-cant degree of instability and a moderate risk of global catastrophes." In fact, "almost two-thirds (63 percent) predict a stormy or turbulent world order."[41]

A major contributor to that instability, states the report, is the rapid, worldwide spread of misinformation and disinformation that often results in rising civil unrest and could drive government censorship and domestic propaganda, as well as stifle the flow of information.[42]

The free flow of information across the global Internet is just one aspect of the challenges feeding instability. Consider five other tests most readers will acknowledge.

New Political and Economic Competition

The post-World War II stability is challenged by the establishment of an alternative geopolitical and economic forum. Specifically, the creation of an alternative to the Group of Seven (an intergovernmental politi-cal and economic forum organized around shared values of pluralism, democracy, and representative government) is what is known as BRICS, an acronym for the original member states of the group: Brazil, Russia, India, China, and South Africa. That confederation of economic and political powers expanded in 2024 to include Egypt, Ethiopia, Iran, Saudi Arabia, and the United Arab Emirates. This consortium represents nearly half of the modern world's population and a third of global gross domestic product.[43]

BRICS expands trade networks that are less dependent on Western markets and a common currency, the US dollar. In fact, nations sanc-tioned by the West, such as Iran and Russia, are free inside of BRICS to evade international constraints. Further, the creation of BRICS is another indication of the emergence of a new world order—arguably, one that is much less democratic, the antithesis of the post-World War II order led by the United States.

Global Elections

The recent global election cycle may encourage less stability. Certainly, the reelection of Donald Trump returns the US to what some have labeled a policy of "global engagement abstention" such as the potential disengagement from NATO, support for the Ukraine war, and a focus on isolationism—"Make America Great Again."

Certainly, the 2024 reelection of President Vladimir Putin for a fifth term sustains his war of choice with Ukraine and his undisputed move to authoritarianism. Many Western leaders believe Putin is readying his armed forces to expand their reach into former Warsaw Pact nations such as the Baltic and Nordic countries as well as Poland.

Chinese President Xi Jinping, 71, was "reelected" for a third five-year term in 2023, which put him on a track to remain in power for life. That vote by the ceremonial National People's Congress was a foregone conclusion, with a tally of 2,952 to 0 by the NPC, members who are all appointed by the ruling communist party. Mr. Xi has the undisputed power to achieve a "national rejuvenation," his coined expression to displace the United States as dominant power in the region, control access to the South China Sea, bring Taiwan under Beijing's control, and, more broadly, return China to global dominance.[44]

The global trend of elections among many of the world's leading nations is moving away from post-World War II liberal democracy to more authoritarianism and isolationism. That shift is evident among smaller nations across the globe, with more than fifty countries—half the planet's population—holding national elections in 2024, which tested the most robust democracies and unfortunately strengthened the hands of many leaders with authoritarian leanings.[45]

Middle East Barometer

Tensions in the Middle East, such as the 2023–2024 Israel/Hamas war, predictably caused ripples of instability across the world. Certainly, the ongoing risk of new escalation of that conflict could quickly encompass Iran, Lebanon, Jordan, Syria, and other nations. Regional conflict inevitably brings major powers into the fight, at least as supporters. Economically, these battles almost always disrupt the flow of oil from the Persian Gulf, destabilizing the global energy market and thus the world's economy.

China's Economic Challenges

The fiscal pressures facing China's economy are serious and further destabilizing because of global interdependency. Some world leaders, like President Biden in 2024, labeled China's economic situation a "ticking time bomb" thanks to slow growth, high youth unemployment, the property-sector crisis, lower foreign direct investment, and weakened exports. These factors unavoidably lower consumer confidence at home and feed domestic instability, as well as impact foreign trade and thus global growth. The problem for the outside world is that President Xi may ratchet up tensions abroad to distract attention from his domestic challenges.[46]

Aging Global Populations

The risk associated with aging populations in countries like China, Japan, Germany, and America represent a serious and destabilizing challenge as well. After all, by 2050, the global over-age-sixty population will increase from 12 to 22 percent just as life expectancy increases. The impact of that graying cohort should be obvious for national economies, especially in terms of healthcare costs. In this scenario, the ratio of workers to pensioners falls, which puts tremendous pressure on the sustainability of current programs like Medicare and Social Security in the United States.[47]

Conclusion

World War III may not be on the near horizon, as many believe. However, the material in this chapter demonstrates that the issue is on most everyone's mind. That's understandable, because of the significant instability—rank risks—across every region and the growing challenges outlined above.

The next chapter profiles the global rush to prepare for conflict.

Chapter 2

NATIONS' PREPARATIONS FOR WORLD WAR III

We must be ready for war by 2029.
—German defense minister Boris Pistorius
to the German parliament, June 2024[48]

Aggressive postures by disruptive states like Russia, China, Iran, and North Korea are driving global preparations for war, according to a 2024 report by the Stockholm International Peace Research Institute (SIPRI), an international institute based in Stockholm, Sweden. For example, Russia's war of choice in Ukraine contributed to the more-than-doubling arms sales across Europe in recent years; that's likely because many Europeans expect that Moscow will not stop advancing into Western Europe if it eventually defeats Ukraine.[49]

That view is shared by notable European leaders, which explains their rush to prepare for war. German Defense Minister Pistorius' (quoted above) call to be "ready for war by 2029" is echoed by the German army's chief inspector general, General Carsten Breuver, who speculated it would take five to eight years for Russia to reconstitute its armed forces after the grinding war in Ukraine before Moscow is ready to launch into a new war with the NATO states.[50]

Unfortunately, General Breuver's estimate is likely off by years. After all, Putin has already put his defense industry at a wartime pace, which means Russia can build more tanks and artillery at an accelerated rate. Of course, that nation's major challenge will be to keep manning large armed forces because its manpower pool is shrinking, but there are six times more Russians than Ukrainians, meaning unless NATO joins the fight, the Kremlin will eventually wear out Kyiv as it exhausts its supply of able-bodied warriors.

Poland's Prime Minister Donald Tusk announced a similar view in April 2024:

War is no longer a concept from the past. It is real, and it started over two years ago [with Russia's 2022 invasion of Ukraine]. The most worrying thing at the moment is that literally any scenario is possible. We have not seen a situation like this since 1945 [the last year of World War II].[51]

Some of Europe's other uniformed military leaders shout warnings about Russia as well. In early 2024, General Micael Byden, head of the Swedish armed forces, said the Swedes need to "prepare themselves mentally" for war with Russia. In fact, the leadership in the Nordic and Baltic countries is particularly concerned about Putin's goal of expanding Russia's borders, which might first include quick land grabs in their regions.[52]

General Eirik Kristofferson, Norway's top general, said in 2024 his country must ramp up defense spending for a potential war with Russia, which could come in three years.

"The current window of opportunity will remain open for a year or two, perhaps three, which is when we will have to invest even more in defense," General Kristofferson said. He continued, "We do not know what will become of Russia in three years. We need to prepare a strong national defense to be able to meet an uncertain and unpredictable world." The general noted Moscow was building up its arsenal much faster than NATO allies.[53]

Unfortunately, the angst among Europeans about an aggressive Russia is rivaled by the stir communist China is seeding across the Asia-Pacific region. That area accounts for 37 percent of all global arms purchases, according to SIPRI. Of course, those purchases are driven by concern over China's aggression, especially toward Taiwan and against countries around the South China Sea, according to Pieter Wezeman, a senior researcher at SIPRI's arms transfer program.[54]

United Kingdom Foreign Secretary James Cleverly expressed a common concern about the People's Republic of China (PRC). He called on Beijing to be more transparent about its rapid military expansion to avoid a "tragic miscalculation." He acknowledged that "China is carrying out the biggest military build-up in peacetime history," but without justification. Specifically, today the PRC boasts the world's second-largest military budget, and, according to Cleverly, Chinese President Xi Jinping ordered the development of a "world-class military" that can fight and win wars.[55]

Mr. Xi's call for a "world-class military" is sending shock waves across the Asia-Pacific region. Already, China's navy has at least 370 ships and submarines, including more than 140 major surface combatants. That number is expected to grow to 395 ships by 2025 and 435 ships by 2030, compared with the US Navy's current total of 239 commissioned with 66 additional support vessels. Further, Beijing is increasing its nuclear warhead arsenal to more than 1,000 by 2030, according to the Pentagon's 2023 report on China, and it already has an extensive fleet of ballistic missiles capable of delivering those weapons. In fact, Richard Fisher, a senior fellow at the International Assessment and Strategy Center, suggests that "China is on the path to achieving nuclear superiority over the United States probably by the early 2030s."[56]

The People's Liberation Army (PLA) has the world's largest active military of more than two million strong and a giant, sophisticated air force equipped with more than 3,500 aircraft, including fifth-generation fighters (Shenyang FC-31 Gyrfalcon), as well as hypersonic weapons that can fly many times the speed of sound and maneuver in flight, thus making them difficult to counter. Those forces are also on the path to a conventional power-projection capability to achieve not only military primacy, but perhaps military political primacy on earth, claims Fisher.[57, 58]

President Xi, now in his third five-year term of office, has also demonstrated a willingness to brandish his armed forces on disputed borderlands from India to Taiwan, as well as across the expansive South China Sea, contesting the region with countries like the Philippines and Vietnam. No wonder nations from Australia to Japan are nervous and making war preparations, given that Xi is evidently willing to employ China's sophisticated military to realize his ambitions of once again making China the regional, if not the world, hegemon.

Predictably, many Asian nations are responding to China's aggressiveness in tangible ways. For example, in 2023, Australia's government recommended sweeping changes to its defense forces because its military is not "fit for purpose." Australia's Defense Minister Richard Marles said the suggested changes will " provide for an Australian defense force befitting of a much more confident and self-reliant nation." That conclusion is based on the "radically different" strategic environment, which means China's military buildup is "the largest and most ambitious" of any country since World War II.[59]

Japan, like Australia, is remaking its armed forces thanks to China. It is rapidly moving away from decades of pacifism in the wake of World War II to build an offensive capability and bolster its defense budget to fuel a far more aggressive national security strategy. Evidently, Tokyo concluded that action was required, given the worsening security environment with China's assertiveness, North Korea's unpredictable aggression, and neighbor Russia's war in Ukraine—as well as its close collaboration with Beijing.

In fact, the alignment between Moscow and Beijing prompted Japan's then prime minister, Fumio Kishida, to visit Ukraine's capital in March 2024, just as President Xi met with Russia's President Putin in Moscow, a signal to the world that one deadly conflict, albeit in Europe, can become knotted up with another battle thousands of miles away.[60]

Much the same can be said about the tensions that continue to spark conflict throughout the Middle East. Clearly, the 2023–2024 Israel-Hamas war is only the latest flashpoint with the Islamic Republic of Iran pulling the strings of its proxies to destabilize that region. Preparations for war across the Mideast have not dissipated one iota since the radical Islamists overthrew the Pahlavi dynasty in 1979. Further, now that Iran is closely aligned with China and Russia, the jockeying for power across the Mideast is expected to accelerate.

This chapter extends the above analysis by summarizing some of the financial and other investments/changes select allied and partner nations across the globe are making to prepare for war, especially given the significant threatening steps taken by China, Russia, Iran, and North Korea.

Increased Defense Budgets, Other Changes Address Possible Global Threats of War

In 2023, global military expenditures reached $2,443 billion, an increase of 6.8 percent in real terms over 2022, according to SIPRI. "This unprecedented rise in military spending is a direct response to the global deterioration in peace and security," said Nan Tian, a SIPRI researcher.

"States are prioritizing military strength, but they risk an action-reaction spiral in the increasingly volatile geopolitical and security landscape," wrote Tian.[61]

As expected, the world's leader in defense spending is the United States, which grew its security investment from $721.5 billion in fiscal 2020 under President Trump to a proposed fiscal 2025 national defense budget of $926.8 billion, or a 28.5 percent increase. Meanwhile, defense stocks have risen 48 percent, according to the SPADE Defense Index.[62]

Similar investments in defense are evident across the world.

Most every major country is rushing to prepare for World War III.
This is a picture of a nuclear-tipped intercontinental ballistic missile.
Photo by Stephen Cobb on Unsplash[63]

Europe Arming up for War with Russia

In 2023, the thirty-one (before Sweden joined) members of NATO accounted for $1,341 billion spending, which is equal to 55 percent of the world's military expenditures. That security investment reflects the "fundamentally changed" security situation in Europe, opined SIPRI's Lorenzo Scarzzato. He explained, "This shift in threat perceptions is reflected in growing shares of gross domestic product (GDP) being directed towards military spending, with the NATO target of two percent increasingly being seen as a baseline rather than a threshold to reach."[64]

Today, twenty out of thirty-one NATO member nations have met or surpassed the alliance's 2 percent of GDP target for military spending.

Perhaps more telling is NATO's target directing at least 20 percent of all military spending be invested in new "equipment," which was met by twenty-eight members in 2023, up from just seven in 2014.[65]

Consider several notable examples of change among European countries in the wake of Russia's invasion of Ukraine.

The United Kingdom was the largest military spender in the subregion in 2023, at $74.9 billion, which was 79 percent higher than in 2022. The British military's burden was 2.3 percent of GDP in 2023, which will continue to rise to 2.5 percent of GDP in the coming years. Also in 2023, the British joined the US and Australia in a trilateral security partnership for the Indo-Pacific region known as AUKUS for Australia, United Kingdom, and United States. Notably, that partnership involves Australia acquiring nuclear-powered submarines as well as improved cooperation on advanced cyber mechanisms, artificial intelligence, and other innovative technologies.[66]

Poland's military spending was $31.6 billion after an increase of 75 percent between 2022 and 2023, the largest increase by any European country. That is 3.8 percent of GDP, still below the government's goal of 4 percent of GDP in 2023. Warsaw has indicated it plans to transform its armed forces away from the old Soviet model to something more akin to the US' joint forces, meaning a focus on more effective capabilities. Meanwhile, Warsaw enthusiastically welcomes US forces to its territory, such as stationing the US Army's V Corps Headquarters at Camp Koscuszko, Poland. Also, much of the country's defense investment is going into the purchase of sophisticated weapon systems like the M1A2 Abrams tank and Patriot missile batteries from the US and the Chunmoo rocket artillery launchers from South Korea.[67]

Finland became the thirty-first member of NATO in April 2023, and in that year, Helsinki spent $7.3 billion, 2.4 percent of the country's GDP. Those funds tripled that nation's procurement spending to buy much-needed military capabilities like the F-35A Joint Strike Fighter (Block 4), upgraded air defense systems, and improved weapons platforms such as updates for their guided multiple-launch rocket system.

In 2022, Germany launched a major military rebuild to infuse its beleaguered armed forces to once again make it Europe's strongest. Berlin was second behind England by 2023 in terms of military spending, $66.8

billion, which was up 48 percent over the previous decade. The German government also committed to meeting NATO's military spending target of 2 percent of the GDP "as an average over the multi-year period" by 2025.[68]

Jana Puglierin with the European Council on Foreign Relations said Russia's invasion of Ukraine became a *Zeitenwende* for Germany, a historic turning point. "It was mind-boggling for me to see this because for many of the things that he [Chancellor Olaf Scholz] had basically decided overnight, I had fought [for] years and I was sure to never see them materialize," she said. After all, Berlin's defense spending wasn't even an issue just months prior to that announcement.[69]

"And I think the main reason for it [the increase in defense spending] was because German citizens did not feel threatened for a very long time," she said. "They never saw that their security was actually a fragile thing." Of course, all that changed with Russia's 2022 invasion of nearby Ukraine.[70]

Allocating a lot of new money for Germany's military isn't going to instantly fix the country's security shortfall, however. After all, it suffered so many deficiencies in the recent past to the point that, in 2015, during NATO training, its troops used broomsticks painted black instead of guns due to equipment shortages.[71]

Today, the Bundeswehr, Germany's armed forces, must play catch-up for years, said Thomas Weigold, a German journalist based in Berlin. "Funny enough, this [the latest surge in fresh defense funding] does not mean increasing the size," said Weigold, who focuses on defense and security affairs. Nor does it "mean to add completely different capabilities." All it means at this point is "to finance what actually should be there already."[72]

Asia-Pacific Reacts to Growing Chinese Threat

Every Asia-Pacific nation is watching China's military expansion, which explains why their collective military expenditure (excluding Beijing) grew by 6.2 percent in 2023, to $411 billion. Growth in military spending was significant across all countries, especially in East Asia as well as India. Meanwhile, across the entire region, there was also a discernable increase in multinational joint training, weapons manufacturing, and the building of a more combat-ready infrastructure.[73]

The evidence of a widespread military buildup is not just attributed to China's aggression. It's also about the decline in confidence in the United States' ability to adapt and stop the PRC's advances, a troubling development that could factor into future geopolitical calculations.

Consider three Asian countries' investments in anticipation of conflict with China.

1. **Japan significantly grows its security forces and will to fight.**

Japan spent $50.2 billion for its military in 2023, an 11 percent increase over 2022, and 31 percent more than 2014, notably the first year of Japan's biggest military buildup since World War II. Under Tokyo's new (2022) National Security Strategy, Japan's Self-Defense Forces, also known as the Japanese Armed Forces, will bolster its counterstrike capabilities with investments in aircraft, ships, and long-range missiles.[74]

Predictably, Japan's military spending has tracked the explosive growth of China's investments in its armed forces. Xiao Liang, a SIPRI researcher, said "Japan is undergoing a profound shift in its military policy." Evidently, wrote Liang, "The post-war [World War II] restraints Japan imposed on its military spending and military capabilities seem to be loosening." Specifically, Tokyo intends to spend up to 2 percent of its GDP on defense by 2027, which reflects a dramatic shift in Japan's military policy. Previously, Japan capped military spending at 1 percent of its GDP and limited its military capabilities to only those necessary to repel an armed attack on the homeland.[75]

That government has identified the perceived worsening security environment around Japan as the main justification for ramping up the country's military spending. It considers China's growing assertiveness, North Korea's unpredictable military activities, and Russia's aggressiveness, as exemplified by the invasion of Ukraine, as the three major threats in the surrounding region that pose serious security concerns for Japan.[76]

Japan is also stepping up its efforts to assist other Asian partners to prepare to face a threatening China. For example, it's now the largest bilateral donor of aid in Asia, and domestically, perhaps most revealing is that the country's government wants to reinterpret its constitution, adopted in 1947, to abandon the pacifism theme imposed on the country by the US after Tokyo lost World War II.[77]

2. **India is becoming a major security partner.**

India ranks fourth in the world for military spending. In 2023, it allocated $83.6 billion, a 44 percent increase over 2014. However, almost 80 percent of those funds are for personnel and operations costs, not for new and sophisticated weapons needed for its armed forces.[78]

New Delhi seeks to strengthen its military's operational readiness, given increased tension with China and archrival Pakistan. However, as indicated above, it is stingy regarding capital outlays for new procurement, which remained constant in 2023 at 22 percent of the annual defense budget; most of those funds went exclusively to domestically produced equipment and arms.[79]

India has also increased its security cooperation with both regional partners and, especially, the United States. In fact, New Delhi was one of the first countries to alert the region to China's expansion across Asia with its building of airstrips and ports, such as the military facilities it has on islands and reefs in the South China Sea. Recognition of China's growing footprint across the area persuaded the Indians to sign agreements with Japan and other partners to grant access to each other's bases for supplies and services and ease restrictions on cooperation in military hardware manufacturing.[80]

3. Australia responds to Chinese aggression with increased security investment.

Australia is making sweeping changes to its armed forces in the face of the rapidly changing Indo-Pacific region, primarily because of Chinese aggression as well. That government's 2023 Defense Strategic Review found significant deficiencies and recommended purchasing long-range missiles and drones, as well as boosting domestic defense manufacturing.[81]

Defense Minister Richard Marles said the dramatic shift recommended by his government's review was the first true recasting of the military's mission in thirty-five years. In fact, this transformation includes not just protecting the Australian continent, but also denying "any adversary [think "China"] that seeks to project power against Australia or its interests" and "with partners [like the US], to provide for collective security of the Indo-Pacific."[82]

Noteworthy is Australia's nuclear submarine deal, a joint effort with the United States and the United Kingdom. But also, Australia's army will buy extended-range weapons that can reach more than 500 kilometers

(310 miles), said Defense Industry Minister Pat Conroy. This is a radical extension of capability from the current 40-kilometer (24-mile) capability.[83]

Mideast Reacts to Iran and Its New International Partners

Military budgets across the Middle East rose 9 percent to $200 billion in 2023. That increase is mostly thanks to the threats posed by the Islamic Republic of Iran, and the largest spenders among those countries were, in order, Saudi Arabia, Israel, and Türkiye. However, China and Russia have strategic and trade relationships with the mullahs in Tehran, which further complicates tensions across the Mideast. In 2021, for example, Beijing signed a "comprehensive strategic partnership" agreement with Tehran.[84, 85, 86]

Kingdom of Saudi Arabia a Regional Counter to Iran

In 2023, Saudi Arabia was the globe's fifth biggest investor in security by spending $75.8 billion, or 7.1 percent of its GDP. Those funds are split across three security entities: Ministry of National Guard, Ministry of Defense, and Ministry of Interior. Most of the military hardware the kingdom has comes from the United States, such as aircraft (F-15 fighter, AH-64D attack helicopter, and UH-60 utility helicopter); missiles like Hellfire; air-defense systems like the MIM-104 Patriot; and armored vehicles like the M1A2 Abrams tank.

The Saudis are a counterbalance to their ideological enemy, Shia Iran, which sits on the opposite side of the Persian Gulf. In 2023, by comparison, Iran spent an estimated $10.3 billion on military hardware, and much of that went to the elite Islamic Revolutionary Guard Corps (IRGC), which manages its network of proxies used to advance Tehran's foreign policy across the Mideast. It is noteworthy that all the rocket and missile systems belong to the IRGC, and Iran has a robust domestic military production capability, as evidenced by its ability to supply the Russian military with a variety of arms, such as drones and ballistic missiles used in Ukraine as well as Tehran's proxy groups fighting Israel.

Israel Making Fresh Efforts to Secure Its Future

Israel is the only democratic state in the Mideast and a key ally of the United States. In 2023, it grew military spending by 24 percent to $27.5 billion, mainly because of its large-scale offensive in Gaza, a response to the terrorist group Hamas, which attacked southern Israel in October 2023. Going forward, expect Jerusalem to increase defense spending to modernize its forces and replace battlefield losses in the wake of the war in Gaza and because of more flagrant threats from Iranian proxies such as Hezbollah in Lebanon and the Houthis in Yemen. But also, in the wake of the April 13 and October 2, 2024, strikes on Israeli territory by missiles launched from Iranian soil, the shadow war between those nations is taking on the prospects of a new and more dangerous future.

In fact, the situation across the region might become even more volatile if Iran moves closer to possessing a deliverable nuclear weapon. Although, at this juncture, Tehran is close to having sufficient enriched uranium and the technical knowhow to make a bomb, whether there's been a decision to move forward on that project is still unknown. However, that regime could decide to field a nuclear weapon thanks to Russia.

In mid-September 2024, top Russian security official Sergei Shoigu visited Tehran with the task of cementing a nuclear deal. US Secretary of State Antony Blinken said at the time that Iran supplied Russia with short-range ballistic missiles for the Ukraine war, and in exchange, "Russia is sharing technology that Iran seeks—this is a two-way street—including on nuclear issues as well as some space information."[87]

Although it is not clear whether Tehran has made a decision to build nuclear weapons, if it moves forward with such a determination, then region-wide defense spending and tensions would likely skyrocket, and major outside allies, partners like Russia and China, might enhance their presence as tensions inevitably mount. Further, if that decision is confirmed, Jerusalem may very well launch a preemptive strike to destroy Iran's atomic program.

Türkiye: The Mideast's Sleeping Giant

The third-largest Mideast spender for security is Türkiye, which disbursed $15.8 billion in 2023. That country occupies the intersection of two seas and two continents and plays a double game. Specifically, it enjoys the benefits of NATO membership, yet in 2019, it imported S-400 air-defense systems from Russia, which resulted in the US removing Ankara from the F-35 Joint Strike Fighter Program. That government is also two-faced because it supports Ukraine while helping Moscow evade Western sanctions. Exactly where the government of President Recep Tayyip Erdogan might land in a broader war is hard to know. However, Türkiye fields a large and capable armed forces that could become a significant player in any future global war.[88]

Africa Tends to Keep Fighting among Itself

Africa's fifty-four nation-states spent $51.6 billion on their militaries in 2023. That was 22 percent higher than in 2022 and 1.5 percent higher than in 2014. That continent is known for internal conflicts from Somalia in the east; a variety of terrorist groups disrupting the peace from Sudan across the Sahara to Niger; pirates and civil wars on its west coast such as in Nigeria; and instability in the south. However, the continent is rich in minerals and thus attractive to China, which has invested heavily through its Belt and Road Initiative, and Russia, which seeks access as well to that mineral wealth and has a variety of private and government security forces throughout the continent.[89]

Much of African security investments are focused inward; therefore, few, if any, of those nations would contribute to projecting power outside the continent, much less participate in a tangible way in any future world war.

Two North African countries, Algeria and Morocco, spent the most on security in 2023, accounting for 82 percent of North African military expenditures. Algeria alone invested $18.3 billion, a 76 percent increase, largely due to an increase in revenue from energy exports to Europe. In contrast, Morocco's military spending decreased for the second consecutive year. It fell by 2.5 percent in 2023 to $5.2 billion.[90]

Military expenditures in sub-Saharan Africa were $23.1 billion in 2023, which was 8.9 percent higher than in 2022. Much of the increase is attributed to a 20 percent hike in spending by Nigeria, the region's biggest defense investor, which is embroiled in an insurgency with Islamic groups. Other countries such as the Democratic Republic of the Congo and South Sudan also had notable increases in defense expenses for the year, all to battle internal insurgencies.[91]

The Americas' Two Worlds

The Americas, except for the US and Canada, are arguably not likely to be involved in a global war as combatants, but certainly their resources and lands could very well become involved by virtue of outsiders using them as staging areas for attacks on the United States.

Some key American countries gravitate to Beijing and Moscow. Specifically, South American states such as Venezuela, Ecuador, and Bolivia are already very much aligned with China, which has commercial and emergent military basing relationships. By contrast, Russia's influence in the region is with existing autocratic regimes, such as Cuba, Nicaragua, and Venezuela, and, to a lesser extent, with Bolivia and Peru. Those relationships must be closely monitored and could become a serious obstacle in any future global war.[92]

North America: Military expenditures by countries in the Americas reached $1,009 billion in 2023, which was 2.2 percent higher than in 2022 and 10 percent higher than in 2014. Of course, the United States accounted for 93 percent of that total. By comparison, Canada's spending for its small military (68,000 active personnel) rose 6.6 percent over 2022 and was 49 percent more than in 2014, or 1.3 percent of the GDP in 2023, which is short of NATO's target of 2 percent of GDP.[93]

Central America and the Caribbean: Military investments in Central America and the Caribbean fell in 2023 to $14.7 billion. Most of those funds were for military forces to fight criminal gangs, and Mexico allocated the most at $11.8 billion.[94]

South American countries spent $50.7 billion in 2023 with Brazil outlaying almost half, at $22.9 billion, which included an increase of 3.1 percent over the previous year. The region presents a complex array of threats and challenges. However, the lion's share of the national military efforts across the region tends to be focused against transnational criminal organizations and violent extremist groups. Of course, as indicated above, the US and its partners in the region face a rapidly growing threat from China, Iran, and, to a more limited degree, Russia. Therefore, that outside influence would likely put the region in play to an unknown extent in the event of global war.[95]

Specifically, consider the Sino-Russian-Iranian influence in South America outlined by Joseph Humire, the executive director of the Center for a Secure Free Society and a visiting fellow at the Washington, DC-based Heritage Foundation. "We have this issue in Latin America where the region is going towards a much more autocratic direction," he said. "Democracy is kind of dying in the darkness, and Russia, China and Iran are positioning themselves to take advantage of all that."[96]

"If you think China is simply doing this for economic ambitions, you're not reading the tea leaves on how China operates," explained Humire. "They're buying a country. They're buying the sovereignty of this country," he said. "Fundamentally, China is making Latin America a region more inhospitable to the United States."[97]

Chinese commercial activities in South America are also a front for its military and defense industry, according to Humire. It harvests critical minerals like lithium and coltan from those countries for its defense industry, and Beijing has built forty ports in the region; some are obviously best suited for military vessels like submarines and aircraft carriers.[98]

China also collaborates with Iran in South American countries like Venezuela, which, beginning in 2006, covertly started to build military drones. In fact, much of Beijing's military projects are veiled behind other enterprises like Venezuela's state-owned oil industry, PDVSA, which shields the Iranian transfer of military technology to Caracas.[99]

Conclusion

It is quite evident, given the rush to fund significant military capabilities across Europe and Asia and the rapid move to transform armed forces elsewhere, that most nations share concern about the real possibility of future war. Part of that concern drives most countries to align themselves with like-minded nations vis-à-vis mutual defense relationships that testify to the widespread angst about the threats. Those growing alliances, relationships, and coalitions are the subject of the next chapter.

Chapter 3

GLOBAL REALIGNMENT

The world is on a bumpy journey to a new destination and the
New Normal.[100]

—Mohamed El-Erian, President of Queens' College,
University of Cambridge

This chapter demonstrates that the post-World War II period to the present, also known as the "American century," is now in crisis because there is an emerging alternative to the pro-West international order, which should be palpable for the West. In fact, the developing new network of anti-Western nations is expected to create a multipolar world, which could very soon burst all restraints pushing toward global conflict.

In four parts, this chapter describes the ongoing process of global realignment that might lead to world war. First, it profiles the world order created by the victors in World War II and the Cold War, which constructed a new, US-led international order that accelerated after the Soviet Union faded away (1991). Second, I outline the growing objections from especially authoritarian states to the US-led unipolar world order. Third, we consider the evidence that a multipolar world order is in fact reemerging due to a weakened international system and an aggressive host of authoritarian nation-states. Finally, I propose, based on objections to the current order, that a new order is surfacing that will compete with the existing international system and may quicken the world's pace toward a possible global war.

Part I: The Post-World War II
and Cold War International Order

There are numerous books, including one by former Secretary of State Henry Kissinger, *World Order,* that describe the post-World War II and Cold War international world order. My intent in this part of the chapter is to reference such related works that define the current world order before presenting evidence of the global transformation to a new, polycentric order that just might usher in the next world war.[101]

What Is Meant by World/International Order?

After World War II and particularly the Cold War, the US pursued its global interests by working with other, mostly Western, nations to construct alliances, economic institutions, security organizations, and political norms, which came to be known as the "world order" or "international order." That "order" created rules, standards, and organizations that govern relationships among key international players. The byproducts of that order were mostly stable, structured relationships among nation-states by way of an instrumented rules-based free trade system; strong security alliances backed by sufficient military capabilities to maintain peace; multilateral cooperation and international law to address global problems such as the nonproliferation of weapons of mass destruction; and the spread of democracy.[102]

The world is experiencing a realignment
not seen since the end of the Cold War.
Photo by Vladislav Klapin on Unsplash[103]

The US was the key player in the creation of the twentieth century's international order, and it embraced the leadership task of being the responsible agent to maintain world peace, whereby allowing the ideals of democracy to flourish. To protect that order, the US used its oversized influence to underwrite the rules-based environment by applying its hard, mostly military, and, to a lesser extent, soft, mostly economic powers.[104]

Today, that international system is challenged by rising powers, like communist China, that perceive the existing world order constrains it and perpetuates US global hegemony. After all, the current order relies on individual nation-states to embrace the view that the system benefits them directly, a perspective that appears to be waning among a growing list of mostly authoritarian-led countries. That list of dissatisfied players is represented by three types of governments: absolute monarchies like Saudi Arabia; military regimes like Burma; and ideological-based regimes like the People's Republic of China, the Democratic People's Republic of Korea (North Korea), and the Islamic Republic of Iran. Arguably, the Russian Federation under Putin, on paper, is a federal democratic state, but in practice, it is a dictatorship built around one man, as are others, like Laos, Eritrea, Uzbekistan, Libya, Angola, Kuwait, Niger, Algeria, and more.[105]

Currently, the international order appears to be at a turning point, according to G. John Ikenberry, a professor of politics and international affairs at Princeton University. The professor explains that by "turning point," he means the post-World War II rules and institutions are eroding. In fact, some experts like Ikenberry assert that the entire West is in crisis, and fundamental transformation of the international order is ahead.[106]

Dr. Ikenberry makes four observations about the transforming world order. First, the American-created, postwar order is a "historically novel political formation." It is built on "'liberal hegemonic' bargains, diffuse reciprocity, public goods provision, and an unprecedented array of inter-governmental institutions and working relationships." He points out that this order is not an "empire" led by the US, however. Rather, it is "an American-led open-democratic political order." It is fundamentally at odds with some of the governing philosophies of its opponents like modern communist China and the authoritarian Russian Federation.[107]

Second, "transformations in the global system are making it more difficult to maintain some of the liberal features of this order," states Ikenberry. Therefore, "the stability and integrity of this old American order are increasingly at risk." In fact, he claims the postwar alliance system, which is "so crucial to the stability of American political and economic relations with Europe and East Asia," are today "rendered more fragile and tenuous."[108]

Third, "shifting global circumstances mean that both liberal and neo-imperial logics of order are put in play," according to Ikenberry. These logics "are deeply rooted in American political culture and both have been manifested in American diplomacy over the past century," especially within the Atlantic community with expressions that include the creation of the defense alliance the North Atlantic Treaty Organization.[109]

Finally, Dr. Ikenberry states the US "is not doomed to abandon rule-based order" because "alternatives are ultimately unsustainable." Therefore, the US will continue to "try to organize unipolarity around [the existing] multilateral rules and institutions." However, "the rising power of China, India, and other non-western states presents a challenge to the old American-led order that will require new, expanded, and shared international governance arrangements."[110]

Serious observers of the international order understand that significant change is coming because of so many objections to the status quo; the aging unipolar US system is growing threadbare.

Part II: Objections to the West's Unipolar International Order

There are growing objections to the established US-led international order that threaten its foundations existentially. This part of the chapter calls out some of its principles that earn some of the most troubling challenges.

Stewart M. Patrick, a senior fellow and director of the Global Order and Institutions Program at the Carnegie Endowment for International Peace, writes that "contemporary analyses of world order tend to fall into two camps: 'the sky is falling!' and 'what, me worry?'" He continues to state that "a torrent of tomes over the past decade have documented the 'decline' of the west and the rise of the 'rest.'" That decline and rise are directly related to a growing list of objections to international rules.[111]

The nation-states that object to some of the order's rules, according to Patrick, "are determined to alter fundamental principles and standards of international conduct." He argues that these conflicts could eventually lead to a "resurgent ideological competition" and, worse, a global war (my conclusion).[112]

Not all international order scholars agree that we're heading to a "resurgent ideological competition," however. Patrick points out that a 1989 essay by political scientist Francis Fukuyama at Stanford University, "The End of History," argues that the "major ideological debates that had convulsed the twentieth century had been settled definitively in favor of democratic capitalism." Further, Princeton's Dr. Ikenberry, cited above, "has insisted that the Western liberal world order [what he labels the "Liberal Leviathan"] laid down in 1945, and which emerged victorious in the Cold War, is here to stay."[113]

Dr. Ikenberry's "Liberal Leviathan" prophecy is rather optimistic about the staying power of the pro-West international order. He declares it will survive criticism because "capitalist democracies still hold a majority of global power"; the order's rules, institutions, and networks make it "easy to join and hard to overturn"; "rising powers will never align into a cohesive, counter-hegemonic bloc, given their distinct histories, identities, and interests [a view that appears to be undermined by the rise of communist China]"; and all major powers "have a status quo orientation [also a view seemingly refuted by communist China]," which means they "attain greater voice and weight within" the order.[114]

There is a fundamental problem with Ikenberry's optimistic prophecy, however. Keep in mind, as Patrick wrote, "This order originated in Europe but achieved full expression only with the U.S. rise to global leadership." In fact, there are a growing host of objections to such optimism about the survivability of the current world order, such as what Patrick states "on how ongoing shifts in the distribution of material power affect the substantive content of the world order including its regnant norms, rules, standards, and institutions."[115]

Keep in mind that, until the present, the post-1945, US-favoring world order and the history of international politics had been multipolar or "oligopolistic," wrote Patrick. He meant that, at the time, multiple great powers competed for influence and then collectively tended to set the rules. However, today, the current international order was primarily shaped by the United States. Therefore, and predictably, the US "constructed, managed, and defended the regimes of the capitalist world economy" or what some scholars labeled the "theory of hegemonic stability," which today faces numerous serious challenges.[116]

Thus, the US-favoring world order, as Harvard professor John Ruggie wrote, became a function not only of US power but also of US purpose, what he called "American hegemony." And that's the issue. After all, as Patrick wrote:

> Had an illiberal power along the lines of Nazi Germany, the Soviet Union, or (even) imperial Britain acted in the United States' stead, it would have pursued a very different order—and had more difficulty attracting followers to its project. This insight— that world order visions inevitably bear the imprint of national purposes, historical legacies, ideological predispositions, domestic institutions, and political culture—is useful in considering whether any other power (China, say) might plausibly assume the U.S. mantle.[117]

The fact that "American hegemony" is at the heart of the current order explains many objections today. After all, America set in place certain pro-democratic bedrock principles for world order. Some of those "principles" or "rules" are identified below and demonstrate the source of a growing chorus of objections that, if abandoned, could potentially alter the world's course; change the world order; recreate a new, multipolar order; and/or lead to lethal global conflict.

The Principle of Sovereign Border Violations

History records changes in national borders by force. However, the current order puts in place rules to stop imperialism by the sword. Those rules have consistently failed to stop powers like Russia from invading the Republic of Georgia (2008), then seizing Crimea (2014), and trying to do much the same beginning in 2022 with Russian President Vladimir Putin's war of choice against Ukraine. "To justify these actions," wrote Patrick, "President Putin invoked the nationality principle, asserting an inherent right to protect not only Russian citizens but Russian-speaking 'compatriots'" who live in Ukraine. Then Patrick rightly concludes, "This opens a Pandora's Box, since globally countless minority populations could become targets of irredentism."[118]

The Principle of Not Using Force without UN Security Council Approval Consistently Violated

The new order established the United Nations' charter that prohibits military force without UN Security Council authorization. However, this rule has consistently been violated, with an assortment of excuses proffered. Parenthetically, according to the Center for Strategic Studies, the "U.S. has been involved in 393 military interventions in other nations since 1776. More than 200 of those have been since 1945, and 114 in the post-Cold War era (after 1989)." Some of the most recent foreign incursions violated the UN's mandate.[119]

Consider a couple of violations of the UN's requirement for permission and the associated excuses. NATO intervened in Kosovo in 1999 without a UN mandate to "prevent a genocide from Serbia."[120] According to President George W. Bush, the US-led coalition into Iraq in 2003 was justified based on the doctrine of "preemption." He argued that the US and its allies faced imminent attack by Saddam Hussein. Perhaps, as these and other examples of the use of military force demonstrate, the UN Security Council has become a toothless tiger when it comes to stopping the use of military force.[121]

Even though the UN seldom stops the use of military force, it does provide a venue for the world to air grievances. Remove that forum and the world's authoritarian regimes might become more aggressive.

The Principle of Nonproliferation of WMDs Violated

This principle has a spotty record of compliance as well. Yes, during the Cold War, the US and the Soviet Union agreed to limit the development and spread of nuclear weapons. Today, because of world-order rules designed to limit the spread of weapons of mass destruction (WMDs), there has been some success due to instruments such as the Non-Proliferation Treaty (NPT) and the UN's International Atomic Energy Agency; the Chemical Weapons Convention; the Biological Weapons Convention; and the UN Security Council Resolution 1540, which prohibits the transfer of WMDs and related technology.[122]

The US government has closely monitored the proliferation activities of the communist Chinese for decades, according to the Congressional

Research Service (CRS). A 2024 CRS report indicates that "Official U.S. government sources indicate that the Chinese government has ended its direct involvement in the transfer of nuclear- and missile-related items, but China-based companies and individuals continue to export goods relevant to those items, particularly to Iran and North Korea." Specifically, according to the CRS report, the US has sanctioned China-based entities for proliferation activities associated with Pakistan, Iran, and North Korea.[123]

Although there has been some success, a few nations refuse to cooperate with WMD institutions. They include India, Pakistan, and Israel, which are not signatories to the NPT. Other nations, such as Iran and North Korea, are in violation of the Fissile Material Cut-off Treaty that prohibits production of nuclear weapons material. There is also reason to believe China and Russia may still have chemical and biological agent programs, obviously in violation of agreements to which they are party. (See the notes at Appendix B.)[124]

The Principle of Maintaining an Open, Nondiscriminatory World Economy Violated

Rules and institutions that regulate the global economy have earned a broad-based commitment. After all, most national economies are "members of the main multilateral bodies governing monetary, financial, and commercial relations including the International Monetary Fund (IMF), World Bank, and World Trade Organization (WTO)." The broad-based membership in these organizations "implies acceptance of the standards and rules embodied in the international financial institutions' (IFI) articles of agreement as well as the jurisdiction of the WTO's dispute resolution mechanism."[125]

In 1999, after a series of significant international debt crises, the major nations that represented more than 80 percent of the world's economic output were elevated to the so-called G20 (Group of 20) "leaders' level and designated it the premier forum for global economic coordination." That group created a Financial Stability Board to "improve regulation of large cross-border financial institutions and approved certain standards on capital account requirements." However, soon, noteworthy fissures became evident among nation-states.[126]

Evidently, some of the objections that erupted among nation-states, according to Patrick, include "the IFIs' dollar's role as the world's reserve currency; the…scope of regional trade agreements; the right standards that should govern development cooperation; the wisdom of capital market controls; and the proper role of the state in the market." These objections became rather self-evident over the recent decade.[127]

Further, there are multiple "lightning rod issues" related to the "order's" failure to respond to these objections, which led quarrelling nations to create alternatives. Specifically, according to Patrick, the "perceived Western foot-dragging in overhauling IFI governance is an impetus behind recent 'mini-lateral' initiatives led by major emerging economies, including BRICS (Brazil, Russia, India, China, and South Africa) Bank and Contingency Fund, as well as the Asian Infrastructure and Investment Bank (AIIB)."[128]

Another crack in the world economic governance system has to do with currencies. There is no procedure or standard to adjudicate "accusations of currency manipulation." Further, Patrick explains, "There is widespread uncertainty about the long-term role of the [US] dollar."[129]

Finally, another representative objection is related to "divergent standards of development cooperation, differences between the Beijing Consensus v. Washington Consensus [see explanation at endnote],[130] and disagreements over capital controls present other problems." Specifically, Patrick calls out China's "no-strings attached" approach, which is labeled "rogue aid" by critics who view the practice as "a strategy of resource mercantilism and corrosive of good governance."[131]

The Principle of Safeguarding Access to the Open Global Commons Violated

A major ongoing challenge is preserving access to the global commons, domains not under nation-state sovereign control that have become "congested, contested, and competitive." Obviously, the most important global commons are the maritime, air space, outer space, and cyberspace domains.[132]

Since 1776, freedom of the seas has been an important US national security objective enshrined in the UN Convention on the Law of the Sea. Unfortunately, the stable governance of the maritime domain is in crisis,

primarily thanks to the communist Chinese. Beijing has become especially assertive in the East and South China Seas, for example, with the
creation of its infamous "nine-dash line," according to Patrick; China has
a questionable historical claim that argues "for sovereignty over virtually
the entire South China Sea." That view is widely rejected, including by the
United Nations.[133]

The outer-space domain faces similar pressures. An international
Outer Space Treaty (OST) provides rules over sovereignty claims. However, that 1967 document fails to address a host of issues such as orbital
debris, vehicle collisions, and the militarization of space. Both Russia and
China are pushing the international community to embrace a treaty to
prevent the weaponization of outer space, albeit while they continue to test
anti-satellite weapons. Meanwhile, China is taking many steps to weapon-
ize its space forces, and arguably already has in place such a capability.[134]

In 2021, for example, China tested its Fractional Orbital Bombardment System (FOBS) that could deliver a nuclear warhead from space.
Richard Fisher, a senior fellow at the International Assessment and Strategy Center, a specialist on the Chinese Communist Party and the Asian
military balance, indicates Beijing has unspecified number of FOBS "now
residing in silos or in missile bases and storage." He indicates that "China
has five space launch bases" where FOBS are likely stored and then could
be quickly rolled out to nearby launchers.[135]

Another critical domain is cyberspace, which needs more regulation.
This domain is rife with conflict: disagreements over cyber-governance;
cybercrime, which compromises global supply chains; increases in the use
of state-sponsored cyber systems as a weapon of war; and use of cyber
technology to surveille unsuspecting populations. The Chinese and Russians are among the worst violators of cyberspace officially through their
state-sponsored cyber-units and by allowing cybercriminals to operate
unhampered within their country and mostly against Western entities.[136]

In October 2024, to illustrate the challenge, the cyber threat led
the Biden administration to create a multiagency task force to address
extensive Chinese cyberattacks on US telecommunications companies.
Evidently, a Chinese-linked group named Salt Typhoon compromised
Internet service providers (ISPs) and telecommunications companies in
the US including Verizon and AT&T. The report in the *Washington Post*

indicates that Chinese groups "have successfully infiltrated broad swaths of U.S. networks, including critical infrastructure systems and sensitive government agencies, posing significant intelligence and intellectual property theft risks."[137]

The Principle of Protecting International Institutions Violated

The post-World War II order established a host of institutions grounded in principles and norms for the global arenas. These organizations altered the previous manner by which nations pursued their sovereign interests. However, they're at risk today, because, in part, these institutions aren't keeping pace with the growth and redistribution of wealth, a view expressed by Patrick.[138]

The power transitions across multiple regions in terms of economic size and political clout are upsetting the global status quo. For example, in 1990:

> [The] advanced market democracies, the Organization for Economic Co-operation and Development (OECD), accounted for 62 percent of global GDP. However, today the OECD only accounts for 47 percent, despite the OECD's addition of a dozen new members including South Korea and Mexico.

The objection by rising, mostly non-Western powers is whether the legacy institutions like OECD can satisfy their demands by adjusting their voting weight and rules. That is a big ask for bureaucratic international institutions, but it's likely necessary.[139]

A major challenge and source of many objections is the "thickening" of the institutional landscape. Specifically, between 1945 and 1999, "the number of [multinational organizations] jumped more than six-fold, from 955 to 6,076." Further, the US is party to more than ten thousand bilateral and multilateral treaties on a host of matters ranging from defense to communications to trade. Any rising nation seeking to join this "thickening" international environment will find it rather daunting, if not unacceptable.[140]

In conclusion, the challenges/objections to the current international order must be addressed if we're to maintain stable and legitimate institutions and a mostly peaceful global community. That requires an appreciation for the fact that today's world is more complicated as global power is diffused and there are more major players. Further, *Pax Americana* (Latin for "American Peace," peace realized when the US dominates economic, cultural, and military power) is waning in importance, and the global community must adjust through compromise. Otherwise, the growing list of objections by rising powers like China will lead to an alternative order that may lead to open conflict.

Part III: Evidence of an Emergent Multipolar World Order

This part of the chapter considers some of the indicators of an emergent alternative to the status quo international order. Evidently, objecting nations, like communist China, reject *Pax Americana's* post-World War II order with its pro-West rules and institutions, and seeks to create an alternative to their benefit.

Below are some indicators of that emerging alternative order that appear to be creating a different structure, thus giving birth to a new multipolar era and creating stresses that could result in open hostilities.

Indicator #1: Forming a Coalition of Anti-Western World Order States

In 2016, then Chinese Vice Minister of Foreign Affairs Fu Yung claimed Beijing had "no interest" in forming "an anti-U.S. or anti-Western bloc of any kind."[141] However, there is contradictory evidence. The People's Republic of China is the leader of the anti-West order movement today. After all, Chinese President Xi Jinping made his disfavor of the current world system clear at an April 2024 meeting with US Secretary of State Antony Blinken. Mr. Xi told the American: "I proposed mutual respect, peaceful coexistence and win-win cooperation to be the three overarching principles [for the new world order], which are both lessons learned from the past and guides for the future."[142]

Those words mean something quite different than we in the West might understand. The fact is Mr. Xi rejects the principle of universal values and the West's brand of democracy that targets the legitimacy of authoritarian regimes like his communist China. President Xi and other like-minded authoritarians across the globe don't believe the West will ever accept their rise to power on the world stage, because authoritarians—especially communists like Xi—reject other nations meddling in their internal affairs. Specifically, leading members of the Western world order tend to use coercive sanctions to leverage change that violates the West's sensitivities, such as China's ongoing genocide of the Uyghurs and its organ-harvesting from Falun Gong worshippers. See the endnote for a video regarding China's organ harvesting practice.[143]

Such actions by democratic-leaning states have tended to encourage cooperation among authoritarian nations, especially China and Russia. The relationship between those nations is growing in strength and coordination, because they're united in their opposition to the prevailing world order—and especially to US leadership that consistently intervenes in what they consider their internal affairs.

The level of cooperation among objecting nations like China and Russia is beyond dispute and, as a 2022 joint Chinese-Russian statement reads, "Friendship between the two States has no limits, there are no 'forbidden' areas of cooperation."[144] For example, in May 2024, Russia's Vladimir Putin and China's Xi met for their fortieth time to consider mutual interests. That conference prompted an article in Russia's *Izvestia* by Oleg Karpovich, the pro-rector of the Diplomatic Academy of the Ministry of Foreign Affairs of the Russian Federation. He wrote that the Russia-China relationship is getting stronger "amid the collapse of the foundation of the world order," which Karpovich claims was imposed by the "golden billion"—a theory that global elites are amassing great wealth at the expense of the rest of humanity—since the end of the Cold War. Further, Karpovich wrote, "the alliance" between Russia and China is "the very embodiment of stability and common sense" and is intended "to repel" the "attacks" from the West, as well as to "turn the notorious unipolarity into a vestige of history."[145]

At the May 2024 Xi-Putin meeting, the two authoritarian leaders signed eleven agreements. One of those documents is especially significant because it pledges deeper military cooperation, such as joint drills and military-technical cooperation. Other signed pacts improve the financial infrastructure between the regimes for the uninterrupted functioning of payments between Russian and Chinese economic entities. This ensures that US sanctions on Russia don't stop Moscow at the time from purchasing Chinese goods to help with its ongoing Ukraine war.[146]

Predictably, Moscow also circumvents US sanctions by finding new ways to access vital products for its war efforts. Specifically, it sets up front companies in third countries like the United Arab Emirates, Türkiye, and a number of Central Asian countries.[147] However, one of the first examples of flagrant Chinese assistance of Moscow's war effort is associated with Russian arms producer IEMZ Kupol—which, according to Reuters on September 25, 2024, is "working with local experts to produce in China a new long-range attack drone, the Garpiya-3 (G3), for use on the Ukrainian battlefield." Reuters reports that two G3 drones were sent to Kupol's headquarters in Russia for testing.[148]

Although the Chinese government may not have sent Russia arms for the ongoing fight in Ukraine, it did directly help Moscow by ramping up its purchase of Russian oil and gas, and it sold Moscow war-fighting technology—from semiconductors and electronic devices to radar and jet-fighter parts. In fact, China has dramatically increased its trade with Russia, which has grown from 10 to 20 percent between 2013 and 2021; between 2018 and 2022, Russia supplied 83 percent of China's arms imports.[149]

Of course, the maturing relationship between China and Russia is linked with other mostly Eurasian autocracies that share a common hostility to the West's international order. Specifically, revisionist autocracies such as the Islamic Republic of Iran and the Democratic Republic of Korea (communist North Korea) are members of the emergent anti-West axis. Together, these four countries and a growing list of other nations are pushing for power and forming an interlocking strategic partnership across the Eurasia landmass, as evidenced by developing trade and transportation networks and the flow of technology and arms—all protected from the influence of the US dollar and the West's military reach, as well as the international order's many rules and institutions.[150]

Evidence of the emergent realignment includes the China- and Russia-founded Shanghai Cooperation Organization (SCO), an international group created to counter Western alliances. In October 2024, that group of mostly central Asian countries met in Islamabad, Pakistan. Chinese Premier Li Qiang and Russian Prime Minister Mikhail Mishustin attended the meeting to declare that both their countries are "increasing the volume of mutual trade and launching joint investment projects." Li also said they are "creating a new international transport corridor…and strengthening food security in Russia and China." Meanwhile, the SCO member state leaders called for "enhanced cooperation in the fields of security, trade, and health, minimizing the impacts of climate change and boosting people-to-people contact."[151]

This new axis of West-hating regimes is not yet a full-blown alliance of autocratic governments. However, it is rather cohesive and represents the most dangerous group of adversaries the West has faced since the end of the Cold War.

Predictably, Putin's war of choice with Ukraine accelerated animosity between mainstream members of the international order—much of the West—and this emergent axis. In fact, the West's sanctioning of Moscow over the Ukraine war fostered the rapidness of the formation of the Sino-Russian strategic partnership. Further, had Putin succeeded in taking Ukraine in 2022, he would have restored a significant portion of the former Soviet Union. That would have bolstered Russia's position regarding the North Atlantic Treaty Organization and Europe in general. Also, Moscow's partnership with Beijing would then seem rather ascendant: authoritarians triumphing over democracies. Although Putin failed to initially achieve his Ukraine goal, years into that ongoing war, he has certainly polarized the world, conditions are worsening for the Ukrainians, and Moscow is far from finished.

The level of cooperation among the rogue axis nations, which share opposition to the Western-dominated global order, have a common antagonism rooted in their belief that their freedom of action is severely restricted. For them, that must change, which is why they're aggressively building their bench with new members from across the world.

Indicator #2: Recruiting Other Countries That Favor a Sino-Russian Alternative World Order

The anti-Western axis is quite busy recruiting across the world. Other countries, such as Belarus, Cuba, Eritrea, Nicaragua, and Venezuela, chafe against the US-led, Western international system. As a result, they, too, are working ever more closely with the developing axis of discontent just as the primary members like China and Russia reach far and wide to recruit new affiliates.

In May 2024, for example, President Xi traveled to Europe to encourage relationships with European partners. He was enthusiastically received in Belgrade, Serbia, and Budapest, Hungary, where streets were festooned with Chinese flags; folk dancers performed at airport receptions; and speeches reflected warm, bilateral relations.[152]

Both Hungary and Serbia are major recipients of Chinese investment, which likely explains the local enthusiasm for the communist leader. During Xi's visit, he announced upgrades to their bilateral relations, an effort intended to soften European policy on China that is troubled by trade, security, and human-rights disagreements—all reflections of the pro-West world order's discontentment with the Chinese.

While in Serbia and Hungary, President Xi advanced his goal of chipping away at the US-dominated world order. Specifically, Serbia's President Aleksandar Vučić, a long-time ally of Russia, became the first European leader to commit to joining China in building a "community with a shared future," an indicator of the growing alternative world order. In fact, this effort calls for a collaboration on shared interests, what Vučić said "is the highest level of cooperation of two countries." He added, "I am proud that as a president of Serbia I had an opportunity to sign that declaration with President Xi." Inking that document came along with a free-trade agreement and Chinese pledges on expanding agricultural imports and direct flights.[153]

Mr. Xi also used his Hungary visit to advance an alternative world order with Prime Minister Viktor Orbán, whose authoritarian style of rule alarms other European Union members. At the Xi-Orbán meeting, the leaders upgraded their relations to an "all-weather comprehensive strategic partnership."[154]

Xi and Orbán signed eighteen cooperation agreements that included sectors on railways, information technology, and nuclear energy. At the time, Xi declared that their countries would further "deepen economic, trade, investment, and financial cooperation."[155]

Liu Dongshu, an assistant professor of public and international affairs at Hong Kong's City University, explained the importance of Chinese allies like Serbia and Hungary. "Being close to these countries," he said, "fits China's domestic narrative that there are 'smart countries' in Europe who really understand China and do not support the United States [the

West's world order leader]—and China is working with these countries for the good of Europe."[156]

Mr. Xi's 2024 European trip was more broadly indicative of China's efforts to recruit other Europeans. Previously, Beijing expended significant energy to deepen connections with numerous European nations, especially concerning its flagship Belt and Road Initiative infrastructure drive, which has reached 150 countries globally with agriculture development, help reconstructing economies, and increasing trade.

Other regions than Europe are tilting toward aligning with the China-Russia axis as well. Surveys in late 2023 and early 2024 of five Arab countries, all of which were previous allies of the communist Soviet Union, found that the US' standing among their citizens has declined dramatically. For example, a poll taken in Tunisia conducted after the Hamas invasion of Israel on October 7, 2023, made it clear the US' loss of support has been China's gain. "Arab citizens' views of China have warmed in our recent surveys, reversing a half-decade trend of weakening support for China in the Arab world."[157]

China's efforts to recruit partners reaches into every region of the world, including much of South Asia, Africa, Latin America, and South America. Although Beijing's success rate is tainted by some of its maligned practices, such as allegations of usury associated with its Belt and Road Initiative, it is making progress in growing allies and partners to become part of its alternative world order.

Some of that growth is attributed to the growing global dissatisfaction with the world order's pro-West economic stranglehold, especially the dominance of the US dollar.

Indicator #3: The Reordering of Economic Power

The trend among anti-Western nations toward regionalism could well lead to the creation of parallel institutions that might eventually compete with the Western-dominated international institutions, especially in the economic domain.

Arguably, there is already a fundamental reordering of economic power taking place. Specifically, as mentioned earlier in this chapter, the creation of the economic alternative to the G-7 is what is known as BRICS—again, an acronym for Brazil, Russia, India, China, and South Africa. The

October 23, 2024, BRICS summit in Kazan, Russia, welcomed thirteen new members into the consortium, which bolsters the economic and political weight of the bloc.[158] At present, that group represents nearly half of the modern world's population and a third of global gross domestic product.[159]

BRICS enlarges trade networks that are less dependent on Western markets and a common currency (the US dollar). In fact, countries sanctioned by Western nations and the order's financial institutions such as Iran and Russia, thanks to BRICS, use that network to help evade international constraints.

Indicator #4: Anti-Western International Order States Seeking Economic Independence from the US Dollar

The US dollar has been the cornerstone of the global monetary system since World War II, acting as the primary reserve currency and the world's primary medium of exchange. However, that is changing as the de-dollarization movement picks up steam, encompassing regions like Southeast Asia, the Middle East, and Latin America.[160]

The shift regarding less dependence on the US dollar has many faces. It will impact "trade invoicing, foreign exchange reserves, financial clearance methods, and debt issuances." This move reflects a widespread desire for a new, more democratic economic order as well.[161]

Predictably, the alliance of anti-Western countries leads the de-dollarization mission to become less dollar-dependent and therefore less vulnerable to the US and the order's sanctions. In fact, Beijing and Moscow seek to be less reliant on foreign inputs altogether by untethering their economies from the West's international trade infrastructure (World Bank, World Trade Organization, and International Monetary Fund), and create yet another mechanism for their forming alternative world order.

The axis is making significant progress at detaching from the US dollar. Specifically, in February 2024, it is noteworthy that the Chinese yuan overtook the US dollar as the most traded currency on the Moscow exchange. However, Alexander Gabuev, director of the new Carnegie Russia Eurasia Center in Berlin, Germany, wrote that "geopolitics will not, of course, lead to the global dethronement of the dollar" anytime soon. However, the more the West sanctions axis-related countries, the greater the likelihood they will seek alternatives to existing global financial institutions and the use of the US dollar.[162]

In fact, BRICS is leading a seismic global financial shift, as nearly twenty countries are poised to abandon the US dollar in favor of their native currencies. With BRICS' growing clout, it is redefining global economic dynamics and challenging the dollar's hegemony in international trade. In 2024, an additional sixteen countries joined BRICS' de-dollarization movement, which bolsters that growing economic alliance and weakens the dollar.[163]

Indicator #5: Axis States Opposing the US-Led International Order Because of Ideological Differences

In 2022, President Biden described the global struggle over international order as one "between democracy and autocracy, between liberty and repression, between a rules-based order and one governed by brute force."[164]

This ideological struggle was made clear also by both President Xi and President Putin in their February 4, 2022, Sino-Russian joint statement just prior to launching Moscow's attack into Ukraine. Specifically, that statement, entitled "The International Relations Entering a New Era and the Global Sustainable Development," focused on seeking "multipolarity" to end the US-led unipolar order.[165]

The declaration underlined the fact that with "multipolarity" there is no "one-size-fits-all template" guiding nations to establish democracy. Alternatively, the autocratic presidents said every nation can choose its own form of government and methods of implementing democracy, albeit based on its own history as well as social and political systems. That is quite a revealing statement from the leader of a communist regime (China) and of a former communist nation (Russia). Russia claims to be a federal democratic state, but in practice, many experts regard it as a dictatorship built around the personality cult of Vladimir Putin.[166]

The Sino-Russia statement also said, "Certain states [read "the US"] want to impose their own "democratic standards [read "ideological template"]" on other nations. It continued, noting that those states are drawing "dividing lines based on the grounds of ideology," specifically by establishing "blocs" and "alliances" among those who agree.[167]

I turned to John Lenczowski for insights regarding China's ideological battle with the West, which is far more aggressive than any launched by the United States. Mr. Lenczowski is the president emeritus of the Institute of World Politics and served as President Ronald Reagan's principal advisor on the Soviet Union. On the issue of China's use of ideology against the US, Mr. Lenczowski said that, in this country regarding Beijing's psychological warfare, "There is willful blindness. There is wishful thinking. There is mirror imaging. There is corruption."[168]

Understand that Xi Jinping "has decided to take the gloves off" when it comes to dealing with the US, said Lenczowski. After all, we've seen China rise as a strategic peer and competitor. Why? Because Xi took to heart former PRC leader Deng Xiaoping's advice on the use of strategic deception, a psychological warfare tool used first by the former Soviet Union in the Cold War and one seen in the pre-World War II era as well.[169]

In the next section of this book, you will read about a similar use of deception by Germany's Adolf Hitler. Specifically, in the period prior to the Second War, the Nazi leader convinced the Allies that all he wanted was *lebensraum*, more space for the German people, something similar to the German kaiser's (Emperor Wilhelm II, 1859–1941) imperial ambitions, what Lenczowski called "its place in the sun…alongside the other great imperial powers of Europe. Why shouldn't Germany have an empire too?"[170]

The Allied thinking in the 1930s, according to Lenczowski, was that Hitler is no different than the kaiser, "and if he has indeed limited objectives" like the kaiser, then perhaps he can be appeased. However, that approach proved not to be the case with Hitler, because "appeasement will only whet the appetite," Lenczowski explained.[171]

The same is true of communist China today, according to Lenczowski. Beijing creates the "deceptive atmospherics of peace because it will give them cover for their military buildup, for their espionage activities, for their influence operations. The Chinese have 600 front organizations operating in the United States today [2024], trying to influence all sorts of segments of our society."[172]

The Chinese are successful because they use a key element of strategic deception—psychological manipulation. Unfortunately, the Biden administration refused to move our relations with China into the realm of a cold war, according to Lenczowski. He explained, "The Chinese are conducting cold war against us and have been doing so for a very long time…. I think that we need to have some defense against this [which] means conducting some of the non-kinetic instruments of political influence and even of conflict that are totally neglected by the U.S. foreign policy establishment."[173]

Lenczowski continued, "The U.S. government is totally incapable and intellectually bureaucratically incapable of conducting ideological competition. And part of it is the result of the fact that huge parts of the American elite no longer believe in the fundamental ideas that are the basis of America and Western civilization and have bought into the same kind of relativism that is at the foundation of Marxism-Leninism. So that's a problem."[174]

Now, back to the Xi-Putin joint statement, in which the second part affirms the essence of their aim: the creation of an alternative international order. It outlines a vision for multiregional development by stating:

> The sides [China and Russia] are seeking to advance their work to link the development plans for the Eurasian Economic Union [EAEU] and the Belt and Road Initiative with a view to intensifying practical cooperation between the EAEU and China in various areas and promoting greater interconnectedness between the Asia Pacific and Eurasian regions. The sides reaffirm their focus on building the Greater Eurasian Partnership in parallel and in coordination with the Belt and Road construction to foster the development of regional associations as well as bilateral and multilateral integration processes for the benefit of the peoples on the Eurasian continent.[175]

The third part of the joint statement reaffirms the "One-China principle," a reminder that Taiwan is an "inalienable" part of mainland China and calls out attempts "by external forces"—read "the West"—to interfere in Beijing's internal affairs. It also opposes "further enlargement" of NATO (which, in fact, grew by two states, Sweden [thirty-second member, 2024] and Finland [thirty-first member, 2023], thanks to Putin's Ukraine war) and called on the West to abandon its "ideologized cold war approaches."[176]

Ideology is a factor for lesser members of the axis as well. The Shia-Islam Iranian regime describes the emergent Eurasian cooperation as the antidote to the US' "unilateralism." In fact, Putin argues that the Eurasian community, which includes 103 sovereign countries,[177] is really a haven for "traditional values" under assault from Western "neoliberal elites."[178]

Middle Eastern countries are among Eurasian nations being swayed to associate, if not outright join, the axis as well. Certainly, Saudi Arabia and the United Arab Emirates are shifting because "modernizing autocracies have more in common politically with the United States' rivals than with the United States itself," said Hal Brands, a professor of global affairs at the Johns Hopkins School of Advanced International Studies.[179]

Additionally, southeast Asian countries are electing to align with axis leader China. In 2024, for the first time in five years, Southeast Asians told a pollster they prefer China to the United States. More specifically, two thousand respondents to a Singapore-based think tank, ISEAS-Yusof Ishak Institute survey, were asked "If ASEAN [Association of Southeast Asian Nations] were forced to align itself with one of the strategic rivals, which should it choose?"[180]

The survey found that seven out of ten countries—Brunei, Cambodia, Indonesia, Laos, Malaysia, Myanmar, and Thailand—"polled higher in favor of China compared to last year [2023], with the biggest changes seen in Laos and Malaysia, which jumped by 29.5% and 20.3% respectively." These countries have troubled ideological histories, which align them more with other autocracies than the pro-democratic West.[181]

Indicator #6: Statements Calling for the Establishment of a Multipolar World Order

It might surprise the reader that even some of those at the helm of international world order organizations support revamping the present system, perhaps because they fear the rise of alternative institutions and a multipolar world order. For example, United Nations Secretary-General Antonio Guterres spoke to the 2024 Munich Security Conference in Germany. The Secretary-General admitted, "Our world is facing existential challenges, but the global community is more fragmented and divided than at any time during the past 74 years." He called for "a global order that works for everyone." Of course, Guterres promised that if all countries fulfilled their obligations under the UN Charter, then "every person on Earth would live in peace and dignity." However, that is the rub, because the axis represents a growing list of countries that have no intention of living by the liberal guidelines in the UN's charter.[182]

Many current leaders openly call for an alternative order as well. Consider that in June 2024, Putin traveled to North Korea to demonstrate his appreciation for supreme leader Kim Jung Un's support of Russia's military action in Ukraine. At that summit, the two leaders signed a comprehensive bilateral strategic cooperation treaty, which was unanimously ratified by Russian lawmakers in October 2024. The Russian leader said at the time of the summit that the two countries would continue to "resolutely oppose" what Putin described as Western ambitions "to hinder the establishment of a multipolar world order based on justice, mutual respect for sovereignty considering each other's interests."[183] Then, in October 2024, to demonstrate their new relationship, North Korean troops were sent to Russia to join the Ukraine war, such as engineers helping Russian forces with North Korean-provided missiles and ground troops from North Korea's Eleventh Army reportedly sent to eastern Russia to train in preparation to join the fight in Ukraine alongside Moscow's forces.[184, 185, 186]

Certainly, the 2022 joint statement by the Chinese and Russian leaders also called for global "multipolarity," because no "one size fits all." Further, other members of the axis, who are also authoritarians, have called for an alternative world order kinder to their interests.[187]

There are also calls for a new world order from within the ranks of the pro-US unipolar system. In 2023, Japan's trade and industry minister said the post-Cold War free trade and economic interdependence had "bolstered authoritarian regimes and the United States and like-minded democracies should counter them with a new world order." Specifically, Yasutoshi Nishimura told an audience at the Center for Strategic and International Studies in Washington, "Authoritarian countries have amassed tremendous power, both economically and militarily."[188]

"We must rebuild a world order based on the fundamental values of freedom, democracy, human rights and the rule of law," Nishimura added.[189]

Indicator #7: The West's Policy of Containment Directed at China

The West's policy of containment of China could destabilize the global liberal international order, a view expressed by Bryan Druzin, an associate professor of law at the Chinese University of Hong Kong. After all, the post-World War II international order was created to promote coordination and structure global trade, which consists of a host of key institutions. The effectiveness of this network of institutions relies upon all nations being "locked" into the system, primarily because there is no alternative. However, "the problem with monopolies [like the current order] is that it is difficult to assess their true strength because it may simply be due to the absence of competition," wrote Professor Druzin in the *Duke Journal of Comparative & International Law*. He continued by saying our unipolar institutional system may in fact be "brittle" because of the lack of competition, and it might be primed to collapse.[190]

Therefore, the risk of containing China, an accusation of the West made by Beijing, is that the effort may destabilize the liberal order it seeks to protect. As a result, as we're seeing, containment appears to be forcing China and its fellow axis members to begin establishing alternative institutions, such as BRICS. The outcome of that undertaking will weaken the "lock-in effect" of the existing order, and disaffected countries like the axis nations will begin to completely abandon those institutions, which then could become irrelevant.[191]

In conclusion, there are a host of objections from many countries regarding the international order and indicators that those objections are resulting in tangible changes that create serious challenges to global security. There is reason to believe enough of these challenges could act as a trigger that results in open conflict, the topic of the next part of this chapter.

Part IV: Why a Multipolar Global War Would Be More Likely Thanks to the Emergent Multipolar Order

"Historically, competing orders have invited conflict," wrote Professor Hal Brands with Johns Hopkins School of Advanced International Studies. He continued, "Wars arise from specific conditions, such as a territorial dispute, the need to protect national interests or the interests of an ally, or a threat to the survival of a regime." Then, he cautioned that "the likelihood that any of those conditions will lead to war increases in the presence of dueling orders." That's why, in the face of competing orders, the chance of open conflict rises.[192]

The fact is that when a single order prevails, such as the *Pax Americana* era, the balance-of-power system has maintained peace. Thus, it is in the best interests of mankind to align their stakes under a single international order system to avoid the increased likelihood that any number of competing challenges among nations could result in open conflict.

Therefore, the emerging alternative to the international order, the axis identified in this chapter, creates a serious threat to global peace. We must either accommodate the axis countries' objections to the world order or accept the risk that inevitably dueling systems might lead to lethal conflict.

Conclusion

This chapter described the ongoing process of global realignment that might lead to world war. I began by profiling the world order created by the US and its Allies after World War II, which accelerated after the Cold War. Over the subsequent decades, a growing number of nation-states have objected to that order, and recently, those entities began coalescing around the requirement for an alternative system of global governance. Finally, the possible emergence of that alternative order may well quicken the pace to a new global war.

The second section of *Preparing for World War III* addresses the historic record of past global conflicts. What were the circumstances and indicators that led to those periods of mass instability, and what were the global consequences of those conflicts? Are there lessons from those histories for the global community in 2025? These issues are addressed in the next section of two chapters.

Section II
LESSONS FROM THE HISTORIC RECORD OF TWO WORLD WARS

We learn from history that we learn nothing from history.[193]
—George Bernard Shaw (1856–1950)
Irish playwright, critic, polemicist, and political activist

In two chapters, this section reviews the historic record of the world's two global wars. What were the circumstances, causes, and indicators that led to those periods of mass instability, and what were the consequences? Did we learn anything from those conflicts that might help us avoid World War III?

Chapter 4 takes a deep dive into the causes of the First World War and then outlines key cautions—takeaways—that ought to influence future decision-makers considering launching their nations into the next war.

Chapter 5 addresses the history of Europe between the world wars that triggered the Second World War. Historians identify numerous complexities and causes contributing to that war; interestingly, political scientists provide an alternative view using theories about war that provide insights as to the steps—the underlying and proximate causes—nation-states take along the path to war. These collective insights might also help future decision-makers avoid the pitfalls that seem so obvious upon reflection.

Chapter 4

CAUSES AND LESSONS FROM WORLD WAR I

It was not the violence of our enemies [in World War I] that would undo us, I thought, but our own spiritual weakness, the shallowness of our convictions.[194]

—Billings Learned Hand (1872–1961), American jurist

This chapter will summarize some of the most popularly recognized causes of the First World War. The problem for this author is to identify the "most" important, because, by some accounts, there are many hundreds of books and articles dedicated to identifying what "caused" the war. Therefore, forgive me if you have a differing opinion, which is quite possible, because even historians don't necessarily agree about the issue.

That said, however, there are some obvious contributors to the start of hostilities that robbed so many individuals of their lives in what came to be known as the Great War and the "war to end all wars," a label associated with the First World War because it was so devastating, especially for the primary antagonists.

This chapter begins with an overview of that war—sort of a map of the nations involved, a few details about the actual fight, and outcomes. Next, I summarize some of the sparks, both a representative sampling of the primary and tertiary reasons/causes that evidently contributed to the eventual lethal conflict, thanks to extensive work by many historians and other writers across the last century plus.

Finally, the chapter draws from those causes some lessons that ought to be considered by contemporary political leaders before they think about launching their countries into yet another devastating global war.

Overview of World War I

World War I was fought between the years 1914 and 1918, whereby the chief antagonists formed coalitions that included mostly the great powers of Europe and their colonies aligned into two alliances: the Triple Entente (France, Russia, and Britain) and the Triple Alliance (Germany, Austria-Hungary, and Italy). The conflict became the deadliest war fought in human history until that time. It included the mobilization of about seventy million military personnel and engulfed portions of three continents, claiming around thirty-seven million casualties.[195]

The First World War was horrific but failed to prevent
the Second World War only two decades later.
Photo by National Library of Scotland on Unsplash[196]

The war was also known for the first use of modern technologies such as poisonous gases, which claimed at least 91,195 lives. It garnered the loss of 6,395 ships; involved thirty-one countries; and cost a staggering $186.3 billion, which in 2024 dollars is $5,851 trillion.[197]

An often-cited primary trigger for the war was the June 28, 1914, assassination of Austro-Hungarian heir archduke Franz Ferdinand in Sarajevo, Serbia (presently the capital and largest city of Bosnia and Herzegovina), which led to the so-called July Crisis. That crisis was a series of diplomatic and military escalations by major European powers in the summer of 1914. However, as you will read in this chapter, the true underlying reasons for the conflict, which are not universally agreed upon among historians, appear to be far more complicated than the taking of the archduke's life.

It is also important to note that the First World War brought about significant changes relative to previous conflicts in terms of military traditions, tactics, and weapons. Specifically, that war saw the transition from human and animal power to machine power, accompanied by the introduction of many new weapons that changed fighting, including machine guns, poison gas, tanks, submarines, and airplanes. The conflict also evidenced the birth of the modern style of warfare, introducing the biggest changes in war-fighting tactics that redefined how large-scale combat operations came to be conducted. Finally, the tradition of war began to change with the Great War—for example, the declaration of conflict against an adversary prior to the attack; an effort to protect the lives of opposing commanders; ethical policies regarding treatment of civilians; protection of medical staffs; the view that hand-to-hand combat was more honorable than shooting the enemy from a distant and/or hidden location; and giving soldiers the opportunity to surrender.[198]

Although this chapter deals primarily with the geopolitical aspects of the reasons for the Great War, the impact for the military, as you might suspect, was quite significant. British Major General Jonathan Bailey captured that transformation in two sentences:

Between 1917 and 1918 a Revolution in Military Affairs took place which, it is contended, was more than merely that: rather it amounted to a Military Revolution which was the most significant in the history of warfare to date, and remains so. It amounted to the birth of what will be termed the Modern Style of Warfare."[199]

Analyses of the Causes of the First World War

Consider a few scholarly analyses of the causes often attributed to the war to help put the issue into perspective and assist with identifying lessons for today's leaders.

"Why Did They Fight the Great War?"

First, Aaron Gillette, associate professor of history, humanities, and languages at the University of Houston Downtown, wrote a helpful article for the journal, *The History Teacher*, "Why Did They Fight the Great War?" Dr. Gillette teaches courses on nineteenth- and twentieth-century Europe, including World War I. His article provides insights on the analysis of the causes of the First World War, which makes a useful starting point for the war-era novice.[200]

Although the article is mostly about Gillette's unique approach to teaching students to identify the war's causes, it does provide some valuable observations about the explanation for the war. Professor Gillette admits, "Although at least some of the usual 'causes' assigned to the war offer relatively straightforward threads of argument, the harmony created when these causes are assembled and prioritized is particularly complex."[201]

He puts the task of analyzing the causes of the war into perspective by explaining that "most historians from allied countries immediately after the war laid the blame for the entire debacle squarely at the feet of the German government." Then, he says, "Article 231 of the Treaty of Versailles [the so-called "war guilt clause" adopted after the conflict] famously captures this propagandistic conclusion and served merely to add fuel to the fire of post-war German resentment."[202]

"Many of the former belligerents, led by Germany," Gillette points out, "published vast quantities of documents to provide evidence for their contentions that their nations could not be reasonably blamed for causing the war." Deflection of blame for the war is to be expected, especially from those who experienced the conflict firsthand. However, a decade and more after the end of the conflict came "more tranquil reflection on the [causes of the] war." At that point, many scholars began to expose the transnational factors that contributed to the conflict, such as "secret alliances, rigid military planning, Darwinian justifications of the struggle between nations, and so on."[203]

Evidently, wrote Gillette, years after the conflict, revisionist historians focused on arguably more obscure reasons for the war, noting "poor diplomatic skills of the leaders of the period" and stating that "others turned to Marxist critiques, blaming the competitive dynamic of capitalists or...the struggle for colonies." These revisionists also deemphasized "the German contribution to the causes of the war."[204]

By the 1960s, German historian Fritz Fischer's book, *Giffnach de Weltmacht* (*Grasp for World Power*), departed from the revisionist line to allege that "the German leadership sought to quell internal dissent and the forces of democratization by embracing a program of external expansionism." Evidently, wrote Gillette, Fischer emphasized that "the 'will to war' evinced by German leaders bore a resemblance to the Nazi motives for aggression several decades later."[205]

Predictably, Fischer's writing was attacked by conservative German historians, who "rejected the notion that the political forces, which led Germany to war were somehow fundamentally different from those operating on other belligerents." The criticism of Fischer's bold declaration found considerable offense because it placed more of the blame on the Germans than on the other antagonists.[206]

Another perspective on the causes of the Great War came in the 1970s and 1980s, when historians such as Modris Eksteins, a Latvian Canadian historian with a special interest in German history, argued that "European culture in the early 20th century was permeated by a fascination with violence in intellectual discourse, in domestic politics, and in international relations." Gillette explained that some historians at the time argued that the war "was caused by the violent ferment in European culture and intellectual thought."[207]

A further metamorphosis of historian cause-finding came about at the turn of the twenty-first century, when scholars like Samuel R. Williamson, an American historian and author of *Austria-Hungary and the Origins of the First World War* (1991), considered "Austrian expansion in the Balkans as a hitherto underrated cause of the war." Another, Sir Niall Ferguson, a Scottish-American historian with the Hoover Institution, wrote in *Pity of War* that "poor diplomatic performance of British statesmen must be considered as an instigating factor of the war."[208]

Yet, other scholars who reflected on the terrorism at the time after the September 11, 2001, attacks on America, emphasized the role Serbian terrorists played in provoking World War I.[209]

Professor Gillette concludes his tour of the changing analyses of the causes attributed to the First War by stating the obvious: "The First World War is intrinsically interesting because it was so tragic." So true, as is his statement: "The war was caused by complex historical processes and the activities and decisions of multiple actors." However, it is also true that, over the past century, the many thousands of writings meant to identify the causes of the war have changed both in focus and ultimately content, and to a fault; too often they're influenced by the individual biases of the writers as well as the situation at the time of those efforts.[210]

"Thinking the Causes of World War I"

Second, even before the Great War started, the leading antagonists declared the causes of the war, wrote John Keiger, a historian of France and former research director of the Department of Politics and International Studies at the University of Cambridge. Specifically, Keiger wrote in an article entitled "Thinking the Causes of World War I" for *The Journal for International Relations and Sustainable Development* that, before Great Britain declared war on Germany, Berlin printed its "White Book," a volume filled with diplomatic documents on the causes of the war titled, "How Russia and Her Ruler Betrayed Germany's Confidence and Thereby Made the European War." Then, not to be outdone, wrote Keiger, "The day after war began, Britain responded with its Blue Book putting its case, followed by the Russians in September, the Belgian Grey Book in October, and the French Yellow Book at the end of November 1914 entitled 'How Germany Forced the War.'"[211]

Evidently, wrote Keiger, "All sides invoked the 'verdict of history' to apportion blame to the war's 'guilty authors.'" Elites from every corner defended "their nation's innocence and their enemy's guilt," he said. Further, this rally to their nation's defense was echoed by government propaganda used to shape public opinion to justify the sacrifices. In fact, these defenses soon morphed into the alleged reasons for the conflict such that, as Keiger stated, "'self-defense' implied the aggression of the other, and aggression meant responsibility." But what followed was a Pandora's box of causes, explained Keiger, "that ranged from the concept of the sovereign state, to nationalism, militarism, imperialism, honor, masculinity, and so on."[212]

The war guilt/cause (Article 231 in the Treaty of Versailles) debate was used by the emergent Soviet regime to fuel the Russian Revolution of 1917. Evidently, the Soviets wanted to discredit the outgoing state leader (Nicholas II) to bolster their communist legitimacy. So, they blamed the tsar for collaborating with the bourgeois president of France, Raymond Poincaré, whom the Soviets accused for the Franco-Russian alliance that allegedly, according to them, triggered the Great War. Of course, part of that effort to discredit tsarist Russia was also used as justification for escaping repaying France for massive pre-war loans, wrote Keiger.[213]

After the war, there was a move by all former antagonist countries to share responsibility for the conflict, which was inspired by American President Woodrow Wilson (1913–1921) who, according to Keiger, said "everyone was a victim of the international system and its secret treaties." This was echoed by David Lloyd George, the British prime minister from 1916 to 1922, who conveniently said, "The nations slithered over the brink into the boiling cauldron of war."[214]

At the time, every state reflected on the *kriegsschuldfrage*, or war guilt question. France became the primary scapegoat for blame, because it had lost the provinces of Alsace-Lorraine to Germany in 1871. After all, prior to World War I, Raymond Poincaré, France's leader, made it clear that his intention was to recover the lost provinces even by war. Further, after the conflict, Poincaré pursued "a strict application of the Versailles Treaty and the payment of reparations [by Germany]."[215]

Predictably, the Germans latched onto France as the scapegoat for their troubles, especially because of Paris' campaign that relied upon the provisions in Article 231 to justify harsh treatment. In response, the German foreign ministry created the war guilt section, which produced literature such as the journal *Die Kriegsschuldfrage* to refute the accuracy of Article 231 and encourage, as Keiger wrote, by "'sponsoring' journalists, editors, publicists, and academics in the 'cause of patriotic self-censorship.'" Evidently, the Germans' counter to Article 231 seeded the "revisionist school" that in the 1920s dominated historical writing about the origins of the war.[216]

Another explanation for the outbreak of war was the poor execution of "crisis management," wrote Keiger. He cites the 1962 Cuban missile crisis to illustrate. Evidently, as the world came to the brink of World War III, then President John F. Kennedy (1961–1963) ordered his decision-makers to read Barbara Tuchman's 1962 book, *The Guns of August*, which dealt with the frenzied international decision-making process prior to the Great War. Keiger explained that Kennedy's intention was to control the Cuban missile crisis by making certain his decision-making did not "run away with itself in the way it seemed to do in 1914, and to ensure that the lines of communication were maintained with the Soviet leadership."[217]

The point Tuchman made in her book was that the 1914 "July Crisis" that ensued after the assassination of the archduke was a case in crisis management gone wrong. Therefore, the issue for Kennedy in 1962 was to prevent war through, as Keiger wrote, better crisis management, which he defined as: "information processing, decision-making under crisis, command and control, the coordination of diplomatic and military actions, and the problems of communication with an opponent."[218]

Dr. Keiger calls out the social scientists' efforts to bifurcate the war's causes by structural explanations as well. He quotes British historian James Joll to illustrate the structural, social, and scientific aspect: "We often feel that the reasons the politicians themselves were giving [for the cause of the war] are somehow inadequate to explain what was happening and we are tempted to look for some deeper and more general cause to explain the catastrophe."[219]

To illustrate the structural aspect, Keiger cites German Chancellor Bethmann Hollweg, who, on July 30, 1914, said, "The people were peaceful 'but things are out of control,'" an obvious reference to some structural condition that had taken over the movement toward war. However, Keiger juxtaposes that decision-makers really do "sometimes" become overwhelmed by the crisis at hand. Further, as he wrote, "Human error, incompetence or losing control of events are legitimate causes in their own right." At that point, Keiger cites the work of Cambridge historian Christopher Clark, *The Sleepwalkers: How Europe Went to War in 1914* (2013), which illustrates failing human factors at the time as a cause.[220]

The most obvious structural causes by many authors of World War I analyses are nationalism, militarism, social Darwinism, public opinion, domestic political causes, imperialism, and the alliance systems. Keiger summarizes each in his article. However, for brevity's sake, I will capture only a few of those reasons below.

Nationalism "asserted nationhood through conquest," wrote Keiger. He explained that "many believed that societies and peoples behaved according to the same biological laws as animals and plants, and that they survived or died out according to strength and fitness for purpose." Of course, the result of this thinking is "social Darwinism, which "drove elites towards war as the final test of fitness."[221]

Another structuralist cause is identified as the militarization of European societies. Keiger wrote that militarization "continued apace in peacetime through compulsory military service…[coupled with] insidious propaganda [that] reinforced notions of the glory and superiority of one's own nation." This effort was instrumented by popularizing military bands, romanticizing soldiers, and fostering the proliferation of gun clubs and paramilitary organizations (such as, at the time, the Boy Scouts, who embraced the motto, "Be Prepared," which originally added the phrase "to die for your country").[222]

Accompanying the militarization of societies was the democratization of Europeans that resulted in "the extension of the suffrage, participation in state machinery from local government to the payment of taxes" and more. This meant the citizens became identified with the state, thus government filled "the vacuum left by the decline of religion and the church," wrote Keiger. Further, by extension, "war was no longer the sole prerogative of kings [as it had been from the beginning of time] or even political leaders, but was increasingly the focus of the people—and not just the middle classes."[223]

Although this new phenomenon may not have made war inevitable, it did, however, "make the mobilization of the masses easier when a crisis or a conflict came." Interestingly, Keiger asserted that, by 1914, at the precipice of war, the future antagonists "could claim that they were fighting a just war—a defensive war for the values of their nation which, after all, was superior to those of others."[224]

By extension, war became "more than ever a question of life or death, not just for individual citizens, but for states themselves." The fear, as described by Keiger, is that at the time, failing to "stand up to their opponents[,] they would disintegrate, become prey to revolution or, at best, have to live in the shadow of their rivals."[225]

The byproduct of such thinking made it easier for nations to increase military spending, engage in an arms race, and create nationwide offensive postures to be prepared to address foreign threats.[226]

Perhaps the most important structural cause is that of economic rivalry. After all, as Karl Marx wrote, "Wars are inherent in the nature of capitalism: they will only cease when the capitalist economy is abolished." No doubt, economic rivalry was intense leading up to the war, because Germany depicted the British and French as stealing their markets.[227]

"Mapping the Causes of World War I to Avoid Armageddon Today"

Another attempt to explain the causes of the Great War was provided by Martin H. Levinson, an expert in general semantics and international consulting. His article, "Mapping the Causes of World War I to Avoid Armageddon Today," categorizes several reasons for the outbreak of war in 1914.

"Orgy of Declarations"

First, Levinson identifies an "orgy of declarations" that caused much of Europe to collapse into war. He explains much of Europe went to war thanks to a series of interlocking treaties obligating nations to come to the aid of others. The initial spark starting that chain reaction was, of course, the June 28, 1914, assassination of archduke Franz Ferdinand, the heir to the Austro-Hungarian throne. The assassin was a Serbian nationalist, and the reaction by Austria-Hungary was to demand that Serbia bring the culprit to justice. Serbia rejected that ultimatum, and the Austro-Hungarian government used that response as the excuse to launch a war against Serbia.[228]

Other dominos quickly fell once Austria-Hungary declared war on Serbia. Soon the Germans honored their mutual alliance with Austria-Hungary by also declaring war. Meanwhile, Serbia, which had close ties with Russia, saw Moscow mobilize its army to prepare for conflict. Once Russia mobilized, Germany, an ally of Austria-Hungary, declared war on Russia. Soon, France, which was bound by treaty to Russia, declared war against Germany. Germany responded to those declarations by invading neighbor Belgium as a shortcut bridge to reach Paris. Soon Britain, allied to France, declared war on Germany and came to the defense of Belgium, based on an old treaty.[229]

Each of the newly warring countries launched their armed forces into the fight, and simultaneously they called upon their distant colonies and dominions to assist, which brought Australia, Canada, India, New Zealand, and the Union of South Africa into the conflict. Meanwhile, Japan honored its agreement with Britain and declared war on Germany. In response, Austria-Hungary declared war on Japan. At the time, the US declared itself neutral, which lasted until Germany's policy of unrestricted submarine warfare threatened America's commercial shipping. Coincidentally, President Wilson was partly reelected (November 7, 1916) because of his promise to keep America out of the war. Of course, that was a faux promise that Wilson quickly abandoned by April 1917.[230]

"Entangling Alliances"

A second cause identified by Levinson is "Entangling Alliances." As demonstrated above, Austria-Hungary never intended its mandate to Serbia to escalate into a global conflict. However, one reason things got out of control was the alliance system that allowed a "mindless mechanical reaction once hostilities began."[231]

The author of the alliance system is often identified as Otto von Bismarck, the minister president and foreign minister of Prussia (1862–1890) and then chancellor—the so-called Iron Chancellor (Eiserne Kanzler) of the German Republic. Bismarck built the German state using politics and war-making, wrote Levinson. In the first instance, in 1866, Bismarck launched "the Seven Weeks War," which gave Germany an undisputed victory over Austria. Soon, he sent his forces south to war with France and, once again, the Prussian army destroyed the French forces and claimed France's Alsace and Lorraine territories as war booty.[232]

Of course, Bismarck appreciated that, after the brief war with France and the acquisition of French territory, Paris would eventually seek to avenge the defeat. That suspicion persuaded Bismarck to create an insurance policy by looking to Russia to join forces with Austria-Hungary, and in 1873 the Three Emperors League (German, Russian and Austro-Hungarian empires) formed, promising to rush to the other's aid in time of war.[233]

Germany wasn't secure enough in the Three Emperors League, however, so, in 1881, it joined Italy and Austria-Hungary in the Triple Alliance. Specifically, this relationship promised that if France attacked any one of the three alliance members, the other two would join the fight against the French. Meanwhile, Italy secretly entered a treaty with France, which stipulated that it would remain neutral if Germany attacked France.[234]

Not to be outdone, in 1882, Russia formed an alliance with France, the Franco-Russian Military Convention, which promised that if either France or Russia were attacked or threatened by the Triple Alliance, the other power would provide military assistance.[235]

Meanwhile, at the turn of the century, Britain came to realize Germany had expansionist plans, evidenced by its massive shipbuilding program; that buildup shocked London's long-term policy of "splendid isolation" as insufficient for the nation's security. Therefore, in 1902, Britain formed a military alliance with Japan aimed at limiting Germany's colonial ambitions, and, in 1904, Britain signed the Entente Cordiale with France, an agreement for greater diplomatic cooperation. Soon, Russia joined with Britain, which created a "moral obligation" to aid the other in time of war.[236]

"Other Causes"

Third, Levinson lumped several other causes together that contributed to the war. Specifically, in 1905, Russia and Japan fought over mutual interests in Manchuria and Korea, which culminated in "a humiliating defeat of the Russian fleet." That defeat inspired the attempted Russian revolution of 1905 and seeded the tsar's intention to restore Russian dignity in the future. That crisis convinced Tsar Nicholas II to transform his government from an autocracy into a constitutional monarchy.[237]

By the time the Great War started (1914), Europe was already scared by numerous smaller conflicts. For example, in 1912, Italy defeated Turkish forces, after which Turkey turned over control of Libya to Rome. Meanwhile, Turkey became involved in fighting four small Balkan territories, soon bringing the powerful European powers into the mix to end the First Balkan War. The very next year, 1913, the Second Balkan War brought Bulgaria, Romania, and Turkey into conflict over land disputes. Even though these short conflicts ended, those nations continued to seethe with nationalistic fervor, providing a backdrop to damaged regional relations just prior to the Great War.[238]

On other fronts, France still sought revenge for its defeat in the Franco-Prussian War (1870–1871) and especially the loss of Alsace and Lorraine. Therefore, France devised a strategy known as Plan XVII, intended to lead to the defeat of Germany and restoration of lost territory. Meanwhile, Germany, under autocratic Kaiser Wilhelm II, wanted more colonies and prominence on the world stage. That desire prompted the drafting of the Schlieffen Plan, a two-front war strategy against France and Russia. However, Wilhelm did not expect Britain to enter the war, which was part of the German's calculation. That proved to be Berlin's miscalculation, because once the war began, Britain joined the fray.[239]

Ten Cautions from The Great War for the Future

To this point, the chapter identified many major and minor causes of the Great War. Those include a complex network of historical processes, key decisions, and many actors. Certainly, any effort to identify the most prominent causes as the real trigger(s) for that war is a difficult task, one that has eluded scholars for the past century.

However, the following effort represents my attempt to collapse the material into a set of "Ten Cautions," based on the previous discussion, that modern leaders ought to consider when wrestling with decisions about going to war.

Caution #1: Alliances are great in peacetime. However, their reliability is severely tested when the bullets start to fly. Keep in mind that, prior to World War I, Italy reneged on its obligations to the Triple Alliance by cutting a secret deal with France. The caution here is to always test the reliability of allies to assure that they're dependable once crises arise.

Caution #2: Is the political leadership's "will to war" matched by national interests and accepted by the citizenry who must pay the price in blood and treasure? The Great War demonstrated that political leaders and not a few cultural elites used the social Darwinian justification to launch their nation's sons into dying in foreign battles, even though most citizens at the time failed to anticipate the costs and national interests at risk.

Caution #3: Too often, the country's diplomatic corps and the skills of the nation's leadership aren't up to the task of avoiding conflict. Western Europe certainly knew Russia (1914) would enter the war to remove the stain of humiliation it suffered at the hands of Japan's navy (1905). Better diplomacy might have salved Moscow's feelings and prevented it from joining the fight.

Caution #4: Domestic cultural dynamics and partisan politics inevitably influence decisions to go to war. Some dynamics are hard to ignore. However, the costs/risks of fighting a war are seldom worth the domestic political gains an administration or party gains. That's probably why Wilson, when running for reelection (1916), promised to avoid war; it was a necessary political commitment. However, once he won a second term, he almost immediately launched America into the conflict. Perhaps more discerning political opponents would have identified Wilson's faux promise and exposed him for craven hypocrisy.

Caution #5: A decision to go to war is seldom simple and is too easy to blame on a single political party or country. Immediately after World War I, there was a rush to place all the responsibility for the conflict at the feet of the German government. However, in hindsight, there was plenty of guilt to go around among all the war's antagonists. Therefore, it would be wise to conduct a comprehensive cost-benefit analysis of all factors before deciding to go to war.

Caution #6: Too often a society's elites—social Darwinists—and other political-class personalities exercise great influence on key decisions, often misleading the citizenry with the justification to go to war. Remember, Germany and Russia entered World War I to divert attention from domestic problems. Carefully evaluate the messages from the ruling class against the objective facts, then make war decisions based on the national interests, not on the elite/political spin.

Caution #7: Nationalism can be dangerous when it comes to making decisions to go to war. Too often, the frenzy to rush to judgment regarding an offended national conscience is insufficient to justify the costs of war, such as Serbia's rejection of the ultimatum given by Austria-Hungary after the archduke's assassination.

Caution #8: The drums of war almost always push governments into "crisis management." Under such circumstances, cool heads must prevail—because too often, crises spawn bad decisions. Leaders must carefully consider all information processing, decision-making, command and control, coordination of diplomatic and military actions, and issues of communication with the opponent. After all, sometimes we humans become overwhelmed by the crisis; as a result, error happens, incompetence has an opportunity, and we lose control of events. Recall that Britain could have given Germany reason to rethink going to war had London announced in July 1914 that an attack on Belgium would make joining the war obligatory for them.

Caution #9: As outlined above under the heading "Orgy of Declarations," we saw how much of the world fell into the trap of war. Many of those antagonists and nation-states should have avoided joining the conflict, but they didn't have in place the necessary constraints and the will of political leaders to just say "no."

Caution #10: Don't rush into a decision, and never assume there is an easy path to victory. Leave time to investigate the situation, study the facts, test the assumptions, outline alternative courses of action, and carefully anticipate the consequences of any actions. Remember, France went to war with Germany assuming the elan of the French army would deliver a quick victory.

Conclusion

The Great War (July 28, 1914–November 11, 1918) left much carnage and a not-so-clear record as to why it was fought in the first place. The costs and confusion left in the wake of the go-to-war-decision ought to be a cautionary message to those considering such an undertaking in the future.

The next chapter considers World War II (September 1, 1939–September 2, 1945), which started a mere twenty-one years after the Great War's armistice. Some of the causes of the Second War resonate with those identified above from the First War, which means we evidently failed to learn our lessons.

Chapter 5

CAUSES AND LESSONS FROM WORLD WAR II

The world must know what happened, and never forget.[240]
—Dwight D. Eisenhower (1890–1969),
Five-star general and thirty-fourth president
of the United States (1953–1961)

A
rguably, World War II was more devastating than the First War because, in part, some of the cautions identified in the previous chapter were ignored. This chapter begins by addressing some of those unlearned First War lessons that contributed to the Second World War; it then provides a historical overview of World War II, summarizes many of the most-recognized historical causes of the Second War, and concludes with a scientific examination of the war that further exposes several motivations as well.

The Great War's Lessons Ignored

The Allies ignored some key lessons from the Great War, which helped precipitate the Second World War. After all, according to Marshal Ferdinand Foch of the French Army, the "war to end all wars" utterly failed to prevent another conflict because the Treaty of Versailles, which officially ended the First War in June 1919, gave the victors only a mere "twenty year's armistice." Soon, the Germans rebuilt their war machine and returned to the battlefield, and with a vengeance.[241]

Failing to learn from past mistakes was evidenced by the chief Allies in the First War, but wasn't lost on their wartime enemy, the Germans. Although Berlin lost World War I, it refused to accept defeat, perhaps because the Allies never occupied that country. In fact, on Armistice Day, November 11, 1918, German infantry stood on enemy soil because the fight never came inside Germany.

The Treaty of Versailles was perhaps the main cause of World War II, because the terms of the Treaty provoked the rise of Hitler and rallied the German citizenry to his populist cause. Of course, the Allies imposed the pact on the Germans without Berlin's involvement, which required a punitive peace, whereby Germany disarmed, surrendered territory, and paid reparations to defray the Allies' costs of the war. The impact of that arrangement was almost immediate and contributed to the Second War.

The Treaty's mandates brought Germany to its knees economically and fueled the population's intent to seek revenge. Specifically, the outcome of the agreement's requirements was soon compounded by global economic depression that brought Berlin to the brink of economic collapse with unemployment reaching 35 percent, mass hunger gripping much of the population, and runaway inflation destroying most every German's wealth. Politically, it was initially disastrous as well. After the war, Kaiser Wilhelm II, the German emperor and king of Prussia, fled into exile as communists challenged one another for control in the streets. Meanwhile, in a Berlin hospital, a twenty-nine-year-old Austrian corporal, partly blinded by the Great War's mustard gas, raged at his nation's defeat. Later, that Austrian, Adolf Hitler, would write in his book, *Mein Kampf* (*My Struggle*), "in vain all the sacrifices...hatred grew in me, hatred for those responsible for this deed...I decided to go into politics."[242]

In just a few years, Hitler came to power, yet the victorious First War Allies chose to ignore the rising storm in Germany. After all, the British were more consumed at the time with their crumbling colonial empire than risking another war. Meanwhile, the politically volatile French weren't any better, having changed government sixteen times just in the 1930s.

There was also the fact that, due to economic strains, Paris refused to maintain a large standing army after the Great War. Instead, it thought building a gigantic, fortified wall on the common border with Germany was sufficient to protect France from a future German invasion.

In the 1930s, as Germany rearmed, the French convinced themselves their "Maginot Line" (named after French minister of war Andre Maginot), a line of concrete fortifications, obstacles, and weapons, would deter invasion by the rising Nazi Germany. However, that line was to become a metaphor for a false sense of security, because once the Germans invaded in 1940, the Wehrmacht's forces (German armed forces) smartly skirted the

Maginot Line to the north through Belgium before entering and quickly conquering France.

Finally, the United States, which joined the First War against Germany, concluded that it gained nothing from that effort. Thus, in the 1930s, America embraced a neutral, isolationist position as Europe snowballed into yet another war. It would take the December 7, 1941, Japanese attack on Pearl Harbor and, of course, Germany's follow-on declaration of war on the US (December 11, 1941) to persuade Washington to join the Second World War.

Although the Allies failed to apply many of the most obvious lessons from World War I to prevent the Second War, they did at least one thing right. In 1939, they began to take the fight to Germany's homeland unlike in the First War. The result was that many German cities were mostly destroyed, and the Nazis were forced into an "unconditional surrender," which was made clear as Allied troops paraded through the streets of Berlin and hoisted their national flags prominently atop former Nazi government buildings.

The Road to World War II

In 1989, *Time* magazine ran a feature that spanned numerous editions dissecting the history of World War II. That effort was authored by Peggy T. Berman and Brigid O'Hara Forster, both with the *Time* staff. One of the many articles in that series, "Road to War: Every Time a Hitler Threat Ended in Compromise, Hitler Won," is the primary source of the following summary of the between-war years, a necessary overview before exploring the causes of the Second War.[243]

Germany's road to World War II was hard to miss, especially for those who watched Hitler's rise to power. Initially, Hitler, a fascist and populist, began stirring the masses with his speeches that often targeted popularly despised groups like Bolsheviks, capitalists, Jews, and the French. He even blamed some political leaders at home for the First War's disastrous outcome, and his accusations became louder particularly after his arrest in 1923 for trying to conduct an absurd "beer-hall *putsch* [a violent attempt to overthrow a government]." At trial for that offense, Hitler declared, "You may pronounce us guilty a thousand times over, but the goddess of the eternal court of history acquits us."[244]

Around the Nazis' Auschwitz I death camp were electrified fences.
Photo by Daniel Hansen on Unsplash[245]

Not surprisingly, Mr. Hitler's popularity rose as the postwar German economy doomed most citizens to poverty. Specifically, the German mark, the country's currency at the time, stalled, thanks to reparation payments mandated by the Treaty of Versailles. Then, between 1923–1925, France occupied Germany's industrial Ruhr region to incentivize Berlin's timely reparation payments. Meanwhile, as the German currency stumbled badly, hyperinflation robbed the average German of all hope because their life savings were tethered to the Weimar Republic's mark, which became known as papiermark ("paper mark"), a metaphor meaning practically worthless. At that point, Hitler found that his voice resonated among the masses, and his message was clear: He promised to return Germany to its former greatness by restoring their dignity, returning to traditional values, reestablishing male dominance, opposing communism, discarding the Versailles Treaty, and blaming the Jews.[246]

Soon Hitler rallied his so-called storm troopers, a cadre taken from the ranks of the unemployed who came to be called the *Sturmabteilung*, "assault division,"—also known as the "Brownshirts." They were infamous for violent intimidation against leftists and especially Jews. Meanwhile, Hitler rode the tide of hate that gripped the country because of their collective misery, and, as Christopher Isherwood wrote in *The Berlin Stories*, their "knives were whipped out, [and] blows were dealt with spiked rings, beer-mugs, chair-legs or leaded clubs." The widespread political fury was palpable, such that on September 14, 1930, German voters awarded Hitler's Nazi Party (officially the National Socialist German Workers' Party) 6.5 million votes, which dramatically increased its number of democratically elected Reichstag seats from 12 to 107, out of 577 total seats.[247]

Thanks to significant political divisions, the Reichstag became ungovernable. Then, after the 1932 federal elections, the Nazis earned more than a third of the total Reichstag seats, which made Hitler's growing influence hard to ignore. Meanwhile, Paul von Hindenburg, German's second president of the Weimar Republic (1925–1934), who allegedly despised Hitler, asked the "Austrian corporal" to serve as vice chancellor under Hindenburg's protégé, Franz von Papen. However, that relationship failed—in part because Hitler refused to compromise.[248]

Then, on January 30, 1933, after much political and financial manipulation, Hitler was elevated to the position of chancellor, the leader of Germany. His meteoric rise to power should have alarmed the Allies, especially when the Austrian corporal appointed Hermann Göring, a veteran fighter pilot from the Great War and early member of the Nazi Party, as a national minister without portfolio (a government minister without specific responsibility), who quickly took charge of all German state police.

Soon, Minister Göring enlisted the police as Nazi special officers, who then targeted Hitler's political opposition. Shortly thereafter (February 27, 1933), there was an arson attack on the parliamentary building, the Reichstag. Less than a month after the fire, Hitler was elevated to chancellor.

Chancellor Hitler used the arson attack as the pretext to persuade President Hindenburg to issue the Reichstag Fire Decree, which gave Hitler broad powers to make arrests, confiscate property, and impose "restrictions on personal liberty, on the right of free expression of opinion." Meanwhile, Minister Göring used the decree to declare guilt and punishment for the Nazis' communist enemies: "We will show no mercy! Every communist deputy [in the Reichstag] must be shot!"[249]

On March 5, 1933, after another election that gave Hitler 44 percent of the national Reichstag votes, he formed a governing coalition with the German National People's Party. Soon, Chancellor Hitler presented the Reichstag with an "Enabling Act," essentially empowering him and sidelining that body as a meaningless governing organization. Once Hindenburg died the following year, the Nazi leader abolished the presidency and crowned himself Führer of the Third Reich, meaning the "third realm" or "third empire," reflecting Hitler's view that Nazi Germany was the true successor to the Holy Roman Empire (800–1806) and the German Empire (1871–1918).[250]

Almost immediately, Hitler imposed what he called *Gleichschaltung*, or "coordination," standardization across the country. It was the process of Nazification that established a system of authoritarian control over all aspects of German society. That "coordination," for example, meant all political parties were banned, and the Führer ordered Joseph Goebbels, the Nazi propaganda minister, to confiscate and publicly burn the works of noted liberals and particularly Jews. Soon, Jewish citizens were barred from public office and professions like journalism. Meanwhile, some of the nation's best-known Jewish citizens like Albert Einstein left the country for good. Minister Göring soon built (March 1933) the first of many concentration camps at Dachau, a village north of Munich, to confine those who objected to Hitler's agenda.[251]

One would have thought Hitler's rapid rise to power and his radical actions would have sounded alarm bells across the rest of the world. However, they did not—perhaps because the victors from World War I forgot about the risks of tyrants, conceivably minimized the threat Germany posed prior to World War I, or were otherwise consumed with domestic issues. As William Shirer, author of *The Rise and Fall of the Third Reich*, later explained: "The Nazi terror in the early years affected the lives of relatively few Germans." Rather, he said, "On the contrary, they [the German citizens] supported it [Nazi agenda] with genuine enthusiasm. Somehow it imbued them with a new hope."[252]

There was good reason the average German might have been "imbued" with "new hope" thanks to Hitler. Soon after he took over the government, unemployment numbers dropped from six million to less than one million while national production and income doubled. The average citizen was pleased with the progress. Meanwhile, it became clear that the Third Reich's rearmament policy was behind Germany's quick economic recovery, which should have alarmed the Allies, because rearming was a clear violation of the Treaty of Versailles.[253]

Hitler's rearming campaign, which acted as an accelerant for Germany's recovery, should have shocked the Allies. However, the gravity of the situation only came to their attention when, on May 16, 1933, US President Franklin D. Roosevelt proposed the abolition of all major offensive weapons, a reflection of the peace movement in the United States at the time. Quickly, Hitler embraced Roosevelt's proposal, but with the caveat "if." The Führer said, "Germany would also be perfectly ready to disband her entire military establishment...if the neighboring countries will do the same." Predictably, while still reeling from the costly First World War, Britain and France declined Roosevelt's proposal, prompting Hitler to exercise his "if" caveat to abandon not just President Wilson's toothless League of Nations created in the wake of the First War, but also the ongoing Geneva Disarmament Talks. Then Germany's new chancellor quickly set in motion his plans to expand Germany's reach.[254]

Part of Hitler's plan included a secret order to his defense establishment to triple the size of the German army by October 1934; build two battle cruisers (warships); and start universal military service beginning in 1935. Unfortunately, and once again, these clear violations of the Versailles Treaty earned little more than a verbal protest from the Allies. The Führer's decision to bolster his armed forces was the first of many tests of the Allied powers, which Hitler won.[255]

By 1936, Hitler took the next logical step of a rising power: He tested both his growing Wehrmacht, the unified armed forces of Nazi Germany, and the Allies' increasing tolerance of violations of other Versailles-related mandates. Specifically, early morning on March 7, 1936, Hitler ordered three Wehrmacht battalions to cross the Rhine River to occupy the demilitarized Rhineland, the portion of Germany occupied by Allied forces and demilitarized under the Treaty of Versailles. At the time, Hitler boasted: "We have no territorial demands to make in Europe." Rather, he continued, "Germany will never break the peace!"[256]

Once again, the Allies failed to call Hitler's bluff; the Führer later said, "If the French had then marched into the Rhineland, we would have had to withdraw with our tails between our legs."[257]

Even though France and Britain were aware of Hitler's move into the Rhineland, they were evidently too focused at the time on domestic challenges to risk another war with Germany. Further, as it became apparent, many Allied leaders came to prefer appeasement to fighting—which, in hindsight, was a weakness that encouraged Hitler's escalating adventures.[258]

Hitler also was accustomed to lying, and the Allies tended to be gullible. For example, in 1936, the Führer signed a treaty with Austria promising not to interfere in that country's internal politics. However, he secretly desired to unite the two Germanic nations—Germany and Austria. Meanwhile, the next year, the Nazi leader ordered his generals to prepare to "overthrow Czechoslovakia and Austria." Then, in 1938, he invited the Austrian leader to the Eagle's Nest, Hitler's Alpine retreat near Berchtesgaden, at which point the Führer handed the Austrian chancellor an "agreement" and commanded, "Fulfill my demands within three days, or I will order the march into Austria!"[259]

After more back-and-forth discussion and protests from the Austrian leader, Hitler grew impatient and publicly ordered the Wehrmacht to mobilize to invade Austria. Yet another delay led to the forced resignation of Austria's leadership, then the Führer installed an Austrian Nazi stooge in his place. Soon Minister Göring directed the new leader to issue a statement that called for "the provisional Austrian government" requesting Germany to send its troops to restore order. The very next day, the interim Nazi leader announced, "Austria is a province of the German Reich."[260]

Once again, Britain and France protested the Austrian crisis, but the Allies accepted Hitler's aggression without any meaningful response. Predictably, the Führer took their lack of action as a green light to continue his intimidation campaign. Soon, he went to Vienna to carry out the Nazification of Austrian life. Most Austrians enthusiastically embraced Hitler and his Nazi endeavor. However, for those who refused, such as many leftists and Jews, he directed Heinrich Himmler, the Reich Führer of the Schutzstaffel (SS), to arrest those "unreliables." Some of those Austrians were shipped to the German concentration camp at Dachau. Meanwhile, in Germany, treatment of the Jews worsened to include the passage of new racial laws that deprived them of German citizenship; by 1938, they were barred from practicing law and medicine. Other forms of anti-Semitism came in time, like barring Jews from grocery markets and drugstores.[261]

By November 9–10, 1938, the Nazis staged a nationwide pogrom (a violent riot aimed at expelling particularly Jews) that included burning Jewish homes and synagogues, and smashing windows. The event came to be known as *Kristallnacht* (translated "crystal night" or the "night of broken glass"). Even that affront to human rights earned only Western verbal protests, but still no action, which further encouraged Hitler.[262]

By the spring of 1938, Hitler decided to attack Czechoslovakia—a country that, like Poland, was carved out of the former Habsburg Empire, which included 3.3 million Germans along with other ethnic groups. At that time, the country had a well-equipped army and a mutual defense treaty with France, which gave Hitler pause.[263]

The Führer's strategy to take Czechoslovakia began with a wave of terrorist bombings to intimidate the Czechs. Hitler paid Konrad Herlein, the leader of Czechoslovakia's Sudeten German Party, to create chaos and "demand so much from the Czechs that we can never be satisfied." Then, by May 1938, there were rumors that German troops were at the Czech frontier, prompting that government to order a partial mobilization. Meanwhile, the British and French governments assured the Czech leadership of their support. However, Allied action was curtailed after a top German commander announced there would be no German troop movements poised to invade Czechoslovakia.[264]

Soon, the Allies' unspoken appeasement policy found a mouthpiece with Britain's Neville Chamberlain, the new conservative prime minister. Unfortunately, Chamberlain had no international experience—especially in dealing with an unscrupulous character like Hitler. Soon, he arranged to meet with the German dictator at Berchtesgaden, and the Führer used that occasion to complain about the Czechs. In typical fashion, he ranted about not tolerating "any longer" that a "small, second-rate country should treat the mighty thousand-year-old German Reich as something inferior." Reportedly, the former businessman Chamberlain was shocked by the Führer's behavior and evidently threatened to leave, but not before Hitler claimed he wanted "the principle...of self-determination," addressed, specifically his claim over the ethnic Germans living inside Czechoslovakia.[265]

Subsequently, Chamberlain consulted with his British and French associates, who uniformly confirmed they had no intention of rushing to Czechoslovakia's defense against Germany. Chamberlain then persuaded the Czech leader to give into Hitler's demand, which meant surrendering the entire Sudetenland, one-fifth of the nation's territory that included the industrial heartland as well as its most defensible natural frontier.

Evidently, word that Britain and France wouldn't help defend that country persuaded the Czech leader to give into Hitler's demands.[266]

When Chamberlain rushed back to tell Hitler the Czechs had agreed to his terms, the Führer shocked the naïve British prime minister by declaring, "I am terribly sorry but that no longer suits me." Rather, the German leader said the Czechs would have to hand over the entire Sudetenland or the Wehrmacht would invade. The change in terms angered Chamberlain, who returned to London to find that the French had no stomach to face a German invasion, and the British responded by "digging trenches," anticipating another war.[267]

At that point, Chamberlain asked Italy's Benito Mussolini, a dictator and leader of Rome's National Fascist Party, to meet with Hitler and French premier Édouard Daladier. They did meet in Munich the very next day and agreed to dismantle Czechoslovakia without the consent of any Czech representative. Once Chamberlain returned to London, he stated his most famous declaration: "I believe it is peace for our time." He evidently believed the agreement with Hitler had averted another war.[268]

Unfortunately, Hitler wasn't satisfied because he wanted more than the Sudetenland. So, on March 14, 1939, he hosted the new Czech president, Emil Hacha, in Berlin. Once again, the Führer shocked his guest by declaring the Wehrmacht was prepared to invade Czechoslovakia that very morning. The choice offered to Hacha was to be "ruthlessly broken" or cooperate and enjoy "autonomy."[269]

At first, Hacha hesitated, then he reportedly fainted, like he was dead. Quickly, Hitler's personal doctor gave the Czech an injection, and before 4 o'clock the same morning, President Hacha signed away his country to the Nazis, which made the provinces of Bohemia and Moravia German "protectorates," and Slovakia was given "independence."[270]

The Berlin deal with the Czech leader drew more feckless protests from the Allies. However, that early-morning coup finally persuaded the gullible Chamberlain and his peers that appeasement would never work with Hitler. Therefore, soon, when news spread that Hitler began talking with the Poles, who were allegedly next in line for his plucking, Chamberlain offered Warsaw British military support. However, by September 1, 1939, the Wehrmacht flouted the British promise and invaded Poland.[271]

Another consequence of Western appeasement of Hitler was evidenced by Russia's Joseph Stalin, who concluded that the Allies would never challenge the Führer's aggression. Thus, the communist Stalin investigated how to align with the Germans, a relationship which Hitler quickly embraced. A week prior to the Wehrmacht's invasion of Poland, the Soviets and Germans signed the Molotov-Ribbentrop Pact, a nonaggression agreement that included a secret protocol promising to partition between them much of Eastern Europe, including the Baltic countries.[272]

Causes of Second World War: Historical and Scientific Perspective

The above historical summary of the period between the Great War and the Second World War provides plenty of rich ground to plow for both the historian and the political scientist to help identify the most important causes of World War II. What follows are two such attempts to identify those motivations from different vantage points. First, there is a purely historic perspective, and second, a summary of causes from a political scientist's view.

Causes of World War II: Historical Perspective

A historic review of the causes of the Second World War (1939–45) found distinct reasons for yet another twentieth-century war. Some are summarized below, and, not surprisingly, they template well with the go-to-war account discussed in the previous part of this chapter.[273]

Treaty of Versailles

The victors in the First World War used the Treaty of Versailles to ensure that the costs of the war were recuperated and to prevent Germany from becoming a future threat. The terms of peace forced on Berlin were set out in the treaty, and all but the Soviet Union approved the details on June 28, 1919. The particulars of the pact included the following: Germany's Rhineland was demilitarized; the coal-rich Saar area was removed from German authority; Poland was given the industrial area of upper Silesia and a corridor to the sea; France regained the Alsace and Lorraine regions; Germany was forced to pay reparations to France and Belgium; the German armed forces were never again to build tanks, aircraft, submarines, and battleships; and Berlin was forced to accept blame for starting the war.[274]

Predictably, the Germans viewed those terms as dishonorable, which became a cause royale for Hitler's populist rise and arguably a primary motivation for the Second War, because those terms became key components for the Führer's election platform.

Economic Crisis

Hitler rose to power in part because of the broken German economy. Of course, some of that crisis is correctly attributed to the provisions of the Treaty of Versailles. However, the global Great Depression (1929–1933) also exacerbated the problem as world trade and employment plummeted. At the time, Germany suffered hyperinflation that erased most savings, and the US, which previously issued loans around the world to wit the Dawes Plan,[275] stopped the practice because of Washington's isolationist strategy at the time. There was no economic relief for the Germans from any country.[276]

Those dire economic realities spurred not only the rise of the fascist Hitler, but also Berlin's efforts to become self-sufficient. Therefore, at the time, German officials realized the country required more natural resources; Hitler chose a military occupation campaign as the way to gain those means. Also, the engine he intended to use to acquire the necessary resources as well as attain financial recovery was the rearmament of the German forces, which created jobs and simultaneously grew his military. That effort wouldn't have become an issue had it not been for the Versailles Treaty. So, the economic situation became yet another sub-cause that led to World War II.

Hitler and the Nazi Party

Following the First World War was a period in which national fascist parties emerged across much of Europe. The first was in Italy under Benito Mussolini, and another was in Spain under the fascist ruler General Francisco Franco. However, as outlined in the previous part of this chapter, Adolf Hitler turned his nation of disgruntled citizens into willing partners with his Nazi Party, a fascist entity that radically transformed Deutschland.

The fascist parties throughout Europe at the time tended to share many of the same goals: absolute power and the reordering of their societies with an emphasis on "conformism, hostility to outsiders, routine violence, contempt for the weak, and extreme hatred of dissident opinions." Hitler's Nazi Party stood out as the strongest in Europe.[277]

Führer Hitler cultivated a cult-like following in Germany by reminding his fellow citizens of the humiliation of Versailles, and he promised revenge by making Germany great once again. After all, the Nazi leader could do that because he was a political outsider who easily criticized Germany's political elite—a perspective that resonated among the average citizens who, at the time, suffered from high unemployment and poverty. Hitler also promised the masses a return to a dynamic economy and called for *lebensraum* (living space) for the German people, which implied the expansion of the German homeland.[278]

Hitler also identified with the masses regarding their common enemies—Jews, Slavs, communists, and trade unionists. These were some of the presumed culprits the Führer alleged held the Germans back from a bright future. So, Hitler demonized them to his political advantage while promising that the prosperous Third Reich would last a thousand years.[279]

By 1933, thanks to German President Paul von Hindenburg's decision to invite Hitler to become chancellor, the Nazi leader used the power of the state—the Reichstag Fire Decree—to crush all opposition to establish an authoritarian regime that followed the template outlined in his jailhouse book, *Mein Kampf.* When Hindenburg died in August of 1934, Hitler merged the positions of president and chancellor to declare himself the leader, the guide, or the popular title, Führer. The rest is history as outlined in the previous section and, as argued above, Hitler's service as Germany's Führer and his Nazi party became another cause of Second World War.[280]

Germany's Rearmament

The Treaty of Versailles mandated that Germany limit the size and capability of its armed forces. However, Hitler formally repudiated that directive in March of 1935 to quickly expand his army as well as to develop the cult of Adolf Hitler by requiring all military personnel to swear their allegiance to him. Of course, the Allies didn't help their cause of keeping Germany down when, in the summer of 1935, the Anglo-German Naval Agreement, which regulated the size of the Kriegsmarine (navy of Nazi

Germany) relative to the Royal British Navy, was signed, allowing Hitler to build giant ships like the battleship Bismarck.[281]

I have already established that Hitler's program to rebuild the German armed forces was primarily responsible for the country's near-full employment by 1938, a promise the Führer made and fulfilled for the German people. That outcome was widely popular. However, a military-focused economy came at a cost: It required significant new raw materials. That thirst for new resources led to Hitler's campaign of occupying or seizing other lands—yet this was another cause that accelerated Germany and the rest of the world toward a new war.

Appeasement

Keep in mind that, at the time, the League of Nations, the prelude to the United Nations, was established after the Great War to prevent conflict and advance world peace. Germany joined that institution in 1926, but left by 1933 at Hitler's insistence, in part because the League proved to be a toothless tiger utterly impotent to stop Japan's invasion of Manchuria (1931). The League's lack of response to such crises and Germany's fielding of a robust armed forces by the mid-1930s persuaded Hitler to ignore the League and the Allies, to then expand his borders.[282]

It became clear by the late 1930s that Hitler had laid the foundation for an expansive empire. His incremental steps along the path to that point should have compelled the Allies to act:

- In March of 1936, Germany occupied the Rhineland.
- In October of 1936, Hitler signed the Rome-Berlin Axis that informally linked the two fascist countries and, by 1939, formalized the alliance, the Pact of Steel.
- In November of 1936, Germany signed with the Empire of Japan the Anti-Comintern Pact, officially the Agreement against the Communist International.
- In March 1938, Hitler unified Germany with Austria (the Anschluss).
- In September 1938, Hitler took over much of Czechoslovakia, which British Prime Minister Chamberlain celebrated by promising he had achieved "peace with honor."

- By September 1939, however, it became clear to even the appeasing elite like Chamberlain that Germany had fooled them, just in time to watch the Wehrmacht march into Poland.[283]

Why was appeasement the West's policy? Evidently, as indicated earlier, the French were weak throughout the 1930s due to a long series of do-nothing coalition governments. Meanwhile, the British were using all their resources to fight to retain London's global empire, and the popular view across Britain at the time was that another war would likely sink their hold on the colonies. Further, there was considerable doubt among the Allies that Hitler would continue his expansionist campaign beyond Germany's pre-World War I borders. That view was reinforced by a host of anti-rearmament, isolationist, and neutrality-leaning lobbies across the West, including in the US, which pursued a policy of isolation—as evidenced by a series of Neutrality Acts passed by the US Congress in 1935, 1936, 1937, and 1939. These acts were spurred by the growth in isolationism and noninterventionism at home following World War I.[284]

Invasion of Poland

The year 1939 was pivotal because of many activities, especially Germany's invasion of Poland. In March of that year, Germany absorbed the balance of Czechoslovakia and Lithuania's Memel region. Meanwhile, Nazi attacks on German Jews drew more attention, to the point that most Western leaders finally understood that appeasement was dead, and Hitler's racist worldview considered the German "Aryan" race superior, and others—especially Jews—were inferior.[285]

By the end of March, Britain and France promised Poland protection from Germany and extended the same pledge to Romania that April. Meanwhile, Turkey and Greece sought protection with Britain and France as small wars, such as the Spanish Civil War (1936–1939), spread across Europe. At the same time, Hitler reneged on the Anglo-German Naval Agreement, and by May, Berlin signed the Pact of Steel, mentioned earlier, a mutual defense agreement with Italy.[286]

By late summer 1939, Germany also signed a nonaggression pact with the Soviet Union (the Molotov-Ribbentrop Pact), primarily because the Russian leader, Joseph Stalin, was convinced the Western nations weren't willing to stop Hitler, given their appeasement policy. Also, that pact allowed Stalin to grab eastern Poland and avoid war with Germany.[287]

On September 1, 1939, the spark of war finally came with Germany's invasion of Poland. Immediately, the appeasing British Prime Minister Chamberlain warned Hitler that London would enter the war if Germany continued; it was a warning the Führer ignored. On September 3, Britain and France declared war on Germany.

Buildup to World War in 1940

The central European war didn't become a global war until 1940, after the Axis powers (Germany, Italy, and Japan) showed their true intentions. In April, Germany invaded Norway; in May, the Nazis invaded the low countries and France; in October, Italy invaded Greece.[288]

The global nature of the war became a reality with Japan's attack on the US naval fleet at Pearl Harbor, Hawaii, on December 7, 1941. At the time, Japan had already launched a full-scale war (1937) against China, then moved to occupy most of southeast Asia primarily to tap the region's natural resources to power Tokyo's war-making industry.

On December 8, 1941, President Franklin D. Roosevelt addressed a joint session of Congress. His opening line was: "Yesterday, December 7, 1941—a date which will live in infamy—the United States of America was suddenly and deliberately attacked by naval and air forces of the Empire of Japan." Moments later, he ended his short speech by stating: "I ask that the Congress declare that since the unprovoked and dastardly attack by Japan on Sunday, December 7, 1941 a state of war has existed between the United States and the Japanese Empire."[289]

So, arguably, World War II officially began when the US Congress declared war on the Japanese Empire. Then on December 11, 1941, that same body declared war on Germany, only hours after Berlin declared war on the United States. Congress approved those declarations unanimously.[290]

Perhaps not surprisingly, the "causes" of World War II outlined above from a historian's perspective are quite similar, but are packed differently by the political scientists.

Causes of World War II: Scientific Explanation

Most often, identifying the causes of war is left to historians. However, John A. Vasquez, an American political scientist at the University of Illinois, applied general theories of war to help identify the causes of World War II. His research was published in the *International Political Science Review* and is quite insightful.[291]

Dr. Vasquez explained his reasoning for this approach to ascertain the causes of the Second World War. "It has been over fifty years since the Second World War ended," Vasquez wrote, "and while historians have spent a great deal of energy explaining the origins of that war, political scientists in comparison have devoted little attention to explaining its onset in terms of more general explanations of war."

He continued, "I will attempt to develop a scientific explanation by showing how the Second World War followed a pattern of behavior roughly consistent with other wars of its type."[292]

Dr. Vasquez began his article by explaining how to apply a general theory of war scientifically. "Scientific explanation involves applying a general theory of the class of events to a specific event in history," he argued. Further, he indicates that to be a good theory, "it should be able to account for the fundamental and often underlying causes of specific cases, such as individual wars." Then, to "corroborate the best assurance," the theory in fact distinguishes "the fundamental causes," which makes two things necessary. First, the war must fit a pattern "known to bring about war"; second, it must trace "out how that pattern brought about the war." Therefore, if "properly conducted," the effort "should offer a plausible account of both why [by identifying the causes] and how the war came about."[293]

Using this analysis template not only demonstrates the scientific approach, but can provide two contributions to the effort of identifying causes of war, explained Vasquez. Specifically, "It can identify general patterns, corroborate these with replicable evidence, and weave them into falsifiable explanations." Second, "these patterns may provide us with new information about the dynamics of the war, and how it came to be a world war."[294]

Dr. Vasquez acknowledged there "are different paths to war and different types of war, each with its own set of causal processes." He presented "the typical path by which major states become embroiled in world war." However, he first defined world war as "a large-scale severe war among major states that involves the leading states at some point in the war and most other major states in a struggle to resolve the most fundamental issues on the global political agenda." Next, he identified "a series of steps that leads to interstate war," and acknowledged what historians understand, that "most interstate wars are fought between neighbors and have involved territorial issues."[295]

The typical path associated with world war begins with steps to interstate war, which are:[296]

- Rise of territorial disputes (underlying cause) handled in a power-politics fashion (proximate causes)
- Military buildups
- Alliance-making
- Repeated crises
- One crisis escalating to war when there is a physical threat to a vital issue
- An ongoing arms race
- Escalatory bargaining across crises
- Hostile spiral
- Hardliners on at least one side

He also identified three systemic factors necessary for world war:

- Multipolar distribution of capability
- Polarization into two hostile blocs
- Neither bloc preponderance

I don't intend to review the three systemic factors for world war, because, for the most part, they were addressed in previous chapters in one form or the other.

Dr. Vasquez illustrated each of the earlier noted steps, beginning with the presumed territorial dispute that sets in motion the path to regional war.

The Second World War began with "specific territorial demands made by Germany on Poland," but that followed, as previously noted, a "string of claims coming out of the Versailles settlement that sought to bring all 'Germans' under the sovereignty of the Third Reich." Those claims included "the militarization of the Rhineland, the Anschluss, and the absorption of the Sudetenland, all involving sovereign control or transfer of territory." Poland was different, however. As Vasquez wrote, the Poles "were not to be bullied [by the Nazis] and saw the territory in question as legally theirs and vitally important to their survival."[297]

This effort identifies categories of or proximate causes using the same information the historian uses to fix event-driven causes, which is for the reader perhaps just a nuance, but reinforces our understanding of the most important reasons for war.

Proximate Cause: Military Buildup

Of course, the series of territorial demands outlined above were accompanied by the six proximate causes, beginning with military buildups, "a drawn-out process that eventually resulted in multiple arms races, can be seen as beginning with German rearmament." Earlier in this chapter, we called out events that contributed to the arms race: collapse of the Geneva Disarmament Conference in 1934; announcement of German rearmament in 1935; Berlin's reintroduction of conscription in 1935; the Anglo-German Naval Accord; the militarization of the Rhineland; and more.[298]

By 1936 and the Rhineland crisis, France and later Britain promptly began to seriously consider their own military buildups. Each new dispute with Germany saw yet another spurt of arms-building activity across the Allied countries.

Those buildups had three effects, according to Dr. Vasquez. Specifically, Germany's rearmament produced "a sense of threat to the British and French sides." It also "increased British and French hostility and insecurity and led to an increase in military expenditures and preparations." Meanwhile, the Allies' response to the buildup encouraged "Hitler and Mussolini" to accelerate their own buildups "to prepare for bigger battles." Finally, because all parties came to believe "war seemed to loom on the horizon," there was a rush "to arm so that the [inevitable] war would be timed to give it [the concerned country] the best advantage it could get in the circumstances."[299]

Proximate Cause: Alliance-Making

Germany's military buildup spurred France to seek out several alliances, "convinced that it would have to fight another war with Germany and that without allies it was no match for Germany." Therefore, France sought out major states like Britain, the Soviet Union, and Italy. In 1935, for example, France signed an alliance with the Soviet Union. Other lesser nations like Czechoslovakia, Romanian, and Yugoslavia formed their own alliance, the "Little Entente." Even the Balkan states produced the Balkan Entente consisting of Greece, Turkey, Yugoslavia, Romania, and Bulgaria.[300]

Germany sought to find partners as well. On May 22, 1939, that nation and Italy signed the earlier-mentioned Pact of Steel, which suited Mussolini because of his ambitions in the Mediterranean, which were opposed by France and Britain. That arrangement seemed a natural, because Germany and Italy were both fascists who had cooperated during the Spanish Civil War (1936–1939).[301]

On a global scale, Hitler tried but initially failed to develop a tripartite pact with Italy and Japan to menace Great Britain. Eventually, Japan aligned itself with Germany in 1936 by forming the Anti-Comintern Pact, which identified the Soviet Union as the primary enemy. Then, by September of 1940, Germany, Japan, and Italy signed the Tripartite Pact, also known as the Berlin Pact, a defensive military alliance.[302]

It's noteworthy that, according to Vasquez, the statistical findings indicate that alliances among major states "are followed by war within five years."[303] Yes, this was the case for the many alliances leading up to the Second World War. Further, so-called counter-alliances tend to drag in other countries once war starts, which became an indirect cause of world war because they "increased insecurity, uncertainty and hostility" across the globe.[304]

Proximate Cause: Repeated Crises

Evidently, according to Vasquez, repeated crises reflect "a deeper set of processes that increased hostility and the perception of threat within the context of an enduring rivalry." That observation certainly appears to fit long-term Anglo-German and Franco-German relationships beginning well before the Versailles settlement.[305]

Between the world wars, those rivalries repeatedly created crises, in a large part thanks to Hitler's *lebensraum* campaign to incrementally consume land. Each time Hitler aggressively tried to acquire more territory, the Allies responded with appeasement rather than confrontation.

The result was more gains for Germany, and the rivalry intensified, as did national anxiety—and, with that, the arms race accelerated. Clearly, repeated crises are another cause for war.

Proximate Cause: Hardliners on at Least One Side

The military buildups, rush to alliance-making, and repeated crises encouraged the hardliners in all the nations. Politically, according to the steps-to-war model, the balance between the accommodationists/appeasers and the hardliners juxtaposes two competing views in the public fora: accommodationists advocated the view that losing a war or the fight is "not worth the cost," so you avoid the fight. On the other hand, the hardliners took the position that winning a war and seeing it as worth the cost is sufficient justification.[306]

In Germany, the hardliners came to power with Hitler in 1933. They drove the effort to rearm, used intimidation against their neighbors, were mostly risk-averse, silenced the accommodationists, and provided public support for Hitler's aggressive policies. Obviously, the hardliners won the day in Berlin's path to war.

On the Allied side, accommodationists/appeasers at first prevailed. However, as the German arms buildup alarmed the public and Hitler's land grabs succeeded, many citizens came to embrace a hardline view about the future and the serious threat posed by the Nazi regime. For example, although Germany's arms buildup alarmed the British military at the time, the public proved hesitant to embrace the hardline view that countering Hitler with military force was necessary. However, that view changed when Prague fell to Hitler (1938) after Chamberlain's failed appeasement approach. Soon, even the accommodationists embraced a hardline position regarding the German threat; for example, Winston Churchill warned about the rise of Hitler. He became British prime minister in 1940 after Chamberlain resigned in disgrace.

"The steps to war [in the theoretical model above] constituted the proximate causes of war," wrote Dr. Vasquez. He concluded that "the Second World War does indeed fit the hypothesized typical pattern…world wars are said to follow." After all, the Second War occurred because of territorial and economic issues that exacerbated many old rivalries among the European states. Those nations took the outlined proximate steps (causes) that led to war, such as building up their arms, making alliances, and engaging in a series of crises, as well as others not summarized here.[307]

Conclusion

Sixty million people died in World War II. The causes of and path to war outlined in this chapter are like the material outlined in the previous chapter regarding the reasons for the First World War. What is important going forward is to reflect on the cautions identified at the end of chapter 4 and the ones outlined in this chapter. Together, they provide a template that must be studied by future leaders when trying to avoid World War III.

Section III

TWENTY-FIRST CENTURY WAR-FIGHTING TECH AND THE FUTURE BATTLEFIELD

The wars of the future will be fought by computer technicians and by lawyers and high-altitude specialists, and that may mean war will be increasingly abstract, hard to think about and hard to control.[308]

—Michael G. Ignatieff (1947),
Canadian academic and former politician

The first two sections of *Preparing for World War III* addressed both the causes of the first two world wars and the current state of the globe trending toward the much-anticipated conflict. This section in three chapters provides a glimpse at the world's rush to repeat past war-making causes and the frightening weapon technologies now proliferating across the globe, and suggests how those capabilities could play out on a futuristic all-domain, global battlefield.

Chapter 6 asks the important question: Is the twenty-first-century world following the same road to war that the twentieth century twice experienced? Unfortunately, some of the earlier identified causes of those prior world wars are eerily too familiar today. If not reversed, they may well result in much the same or even worse destructive outcomes in the future.

Chapter 7 profiles weapons technologies that will define the future war. What are the new and/or improved weapon systems based on those technologies, and, as a result, what are their implications for the all-domain battlefield? Which countries are expected to possess these capabilities, what are their intended effects, and what should be the necessary global posture?

Chapter 8 describes a potential global fight. Here I will profile how that clash might begin, the conduct of that conflict across all domains, and the possible short- and long-term consequences for America and the world. Although this presentation is fictional, it is informed by war-gaming results and an appreciation for the emergent futuristic battlefield capabilities.

Chapter 6

DÉJÀ VU: ANOTHER GLOBAL RUSH TO WAR?

War is regarded as nothing but the continuation of state policy with other means.[309]

—Carl Von Clausewitz (1780–1831),
Prussian general and military theorist

This chapter examines the current global situation guided by those past world war motivations to inquire whether the twenty-first century world is following the same disastrous path to war seen in the twentieth century. Are the causes associated with the past global wars predictive of a future global conflict? Perhaps. However, it is helpful in any case to consider them in terms of contemporary geopolitics and then let you, the reader, decide whether repeat reasons for the Second World War might be prescriptive of a World War III.

In chapter 5, I summarized two distinct approaches to identify the "causes" of World War II based on historical and political science analyses. Both approaches share some common reasons for that conflict, which provide the outline for this chapter: 1) military buildups; 2) frequent crises; 3) ideologically opposing hardliners; 4) international agreements/ institutions that disfavor certain parties; 5) polarizing alliances; and 6) appeasement policies by opposite adversaries.

Past Causes That Might Indicate Future Conflict

I begin summarizing each of the six "causes" with a brief reminder of how each of those motivations contributed to the outbreak of World War II. Then, using contemporary sources, I elaborate on whether those causes are evident today.

The global rush to arm up with sophisticated weapons is indeed frightening.
Photo by Vony Razom on Unsplash[310]

Cause #1: Military Buildups

You will recall that Hitler's rearmament campaign served two purposes: energize Germany's economy and provide the Nazi regime a strong armed forces that would help deliver Hitler's promised *lebensraum*. No doubt, the military's role became evident once Hitler began his series of territorial demands. The Wehrmacht was the Führer's hammer used to intimidate each of his political targets.

An unintended byproduct of Hitler's military buildup was to encourage other nations to join the arms race. Eventually, that ongoing competition convinced much of the world in the late 1930s that "war seemed to loom on the horizon." Similarly, today, there is yet another rush to arm up, and many nations across the globe believe conflict is yet again inevitable.[311]

The primary indicator of the current global arms race is the growing expenditure for arms, which reached $2.443 trillion in 2023, an increase of 6.8 percent in real terms from 2022. This was the steepest year-on-year increase since 2009, according to the Stockholm International Peace Research Institute (SIPRI). Of course, that record spending was led by the United States, China, and Russia. However, for the first time since 2009, military spending went up across all five of the world's geographical regions, with particularly large increases in Europe, Asia, and Oceania, as well as the Middle East.[312]

"The unprecedented rise in military spending is a direct response to the global deterioration in peace and security," said Nan Tian, a senior researcher with SIPRI's Military Expenditure and Arms Production Programme. He continued, "States are prioritizing military strength, but they risk an action-reaction spiral in the increasingly volatile geopolitical and security landscape."[313]

Evidence of the contemporary military buildup and action-reaction abounds. Russia keeps spending more on its military, up 24 percent in 2023 alone, which was16 percent of total government spending, or 5.9 percent of that country's GDP. Predictably, Moscow's enemy of choice, Ukraine, was a large military investor in 2023 as well, which accounted for 58 percent of that government's total spending.[314]

Russia has paid a heavy price for Putin's imperial dream of reconstituting the old Russian empire vis-à-vis conquering Ukraine, however. Specifically, by October 2024, Moscow suffered more than six hundred thousand killed and wounded, spent over $211 billion fighting, and lost at least twenty medium or large ships damaged or sunk in the Black Sea. Yet, according to Pentagon officials, the Kremlin has quickly recovered its force to continue that fight.[315]

In 2024, US Secretary of Defense Lloyd Austin said, "Russia has ramped up its production. All their defense industry really answers directly to the state, so it is easier for them to do that a bit quicker." General CQ Brown, the US Chairman of the Joint Chiefs of Staff, echoed that view: "Russia has aggressively reconstituted its military force."[316]

Those two antagonists, Russia and Ukraine, had a direct impact on defense spending across the NATO membership. In 2023, NATO spent $1.341 trillion, or about 55 percent, of the world's total military expenditure for the year. But the investment in national militaries stretched far beyond Europe and NATO.[317]

The People's Republic of China (PRC), the world's second-largest military spender, allocated an estimated $296 billion in 2023, according to SIPRI, an increase of 6 percent over the previous year. Further, this was the twenty-ninth consecutive year-on-year increase of Beijing's military spending, and that record wasn't lost on its neighbors, who sense a growing threat from the communist regime.[318]

It is worth mentioning at this point that estimates regarding China's investment in its national defense vary widely across multiple sources. In 2023, the Department of Defense' report on China states that in 2022, the PRC's annual military budget increased by 7.1 percent to $229 billion, "continuing more than 20 years of annual defense spending increases."[319] However, the 2024 US Commission on National Defense Strategy (CNDS) pegs China's defense investment at $711 billion in 2023. Why such a gross disparity?[320]

The CNDS report acknowledges that actual Chinese defense spending is "unknown." However, a January 2024 assessment of "comparative buying power of China's total defense budget in 2022 was $711 billion," states the report. Further, the same report indicates that Admiral Samuel Paparo, commander of the US Indo-Pacific Command, agrees with the higher figure. "According to Paparo, China's military budget is likely three times what Beijing publicly claims, which would put it at about $700 billion annually," according to the CNDS report.[321]

Xiao Liang, a SIPRI researcher, said, "China is directing much of its growing military budget to boost the combat readiness of the People's Liberation Army [PLA]…[which] prompted the governments in Japan, Taiwan and others to significantly build up their military capabilities." Specifically, in 2023, Japan allocated $50 billion, an 11 percent increase over the previous year, and Taiwan's military also grew by 11 percent, reaching $16.6 billion in 2023.[322]

The PLA's military expansion goes far beyond growing the world's largest ground army, the world's largest missile force, an air force equipped with fifth-generation fighters, and the world's largest naval force. It is making frightening advances with strategic assets as well. Specifically, "The PLA has rapidly advanced in space in a way that few people can really appreciate," said Major General Gregory Gagnon, deputy chief of space operations for intelligence for the US Space Command. Since 2015, General Gagnon said the Chinese Communist Party has increased its on-orbit capability by 550 percent.[323]

Further, in 2024, China's rapidly growing nuclear arsenal shocked much of the world. The number of operational nuclear warheads in Beijing's inventory increases every year—so much that SIPRI predicts that, by 2030, China's nuclear arsenal mounted on active intercontinental missiles will grow to match the American and Russian capabilities.[324]

China's global ambitions are also evidenced by its investment in foreign ports capable of sustaining its large fleet of warships. Specifically, in May of 2024, China brought online its second permanent overseas military base at Cambodia's Ream naval base. Media reports indicate that a secret deal granted China's PLA exclusive access to that base. Beijing's first overseas base is located at Djibouti, the Horn of Africa, which came online in 2015.[325]

China has ambitions to create facilities for its military, especially its navy, across the world. In particular, Chinese firms have invested heavily in port facilities all over the globe, raising concern that Beijing seeks access to "dual-use installations" capable of military operations, such as the port being built with Chinese funds at Gwadar, Pakistan, on the Arabian Sea. In fact, a 2020 Pentagon study names eighteen countries as possible future bases for Chinese military facilities. Meanwhile, China's expanding overseas footprint includes satellite-tracking stations and intelligence-gathering facilities in several countries, including in the Western Hemisphere.[326]

China's military buildup has garnered significant attention among our allies like the Japanese. For the first time since their defeat in World War II, the Japanese are transforming their Self-Defense Forces into a tool of national power that can help it address the rising threats posed by China and North Korea. Of course, that accumulation requires the will to invest in a larger and more capable defense force as well as to adjust the constitutional limitations imposed by the US on Tokyo at the end of the Second War. There is reason to believe that is happening.[327]

Tokyo's emergent defense role in the Indo-Pacific region, according to Japanese Foreign Minister Yoshimasa Hayashi, is to "foster even closer defense cooperation with the United States and our mutual partners." At the time, Japanese Prime Minister Fumio Kishida cited Russia's invasion of Ukraine as a warning of the threat facing Japan from an increasingly militarized China. Yet, there remains some doubt among the Japanese people about the financial and human capital commitment required to build up that force.[328]

Japan's historic military investment is no longer in doubt, however. Tokyo's defense budget has increased each year for the past nine years, and it is buying the latest technologies. For example, it has purchased a couple of versions of the F-35A Lightning II Joint Strike Fighters and Tomahawk cruise missiles, and has ramped up domestic production of missiles, including a hypersonic model.[329]

What's clear to the Japanese is that their security environment has become more dangerous, thanks to China antagonizing Taiwan, North Korea testing missiles and nuclear devices, and Russia waging war in Ukraine. Those threats to Northeast Asia's stability have created concerns among the Japanese citizenry so that they appear more willing than in the past "to go along with a more muscular defense," according to Phillip Lipscy, director of the Center for the Study of Global Japan at the University of Toronto.[330]

Smaller countries like the nearby Philippines are ramping up their military modernization efforts as well. In June 2024, President Ferdinand Marcos Jr. approved "Re-Horizon 3," a multistage modernization initiative, in response to Chinese aggression in the South China Sea. That effort includes acquiring modern weapons and equipment to bolster its defenses—especially the country's domain awareness technologies—to improve surveillance, reconnaissance, and intelligence-gathering capabilities.[331]

Warfare fever has impacted the Middle East as well. In 2023, Mideast countries increased their military investments by 9 percent to $200 billion, the highest in more than a decade. Israel's military spending soared to $27.5 billion in 2023, mainly driven by Israel's response to the brutal Hamas attack into southern Israel in October 2023.[332]

Countries elsewhere across the globe followed the lead of those identified above to increase their military investment in 2023, all due to perceived threats. The Dominican Republic saw a 14 percent increase in 2023 in response to the worsening gang violence in neighboring Haiti. Mexico grew its arms spending 55 percent from 2014 due to escalating criminal activity.[333]

Other nations representing the balance of the globe—India, South Sudan, Brazil, Algeria, Iran, and many more—saw significant increases in military spending in 2023 because of the heightened perception of threat to their national security as well.

In conclusion, the world hasn't seen such a military buildup since just before World War II. The heavy investment in arms and military manpower around the world today could well make a future conflict more inevitable. After all, as pointed out earlier, the accumulation of arms and the alignment among major states "are followed by war within five years."[334]

Cause #2: Frequent Crises

Hitler rose to power in part because of the broken German economy. Of course, some of that crisis is rightly attributed to the stark, draconian provisions imposed on that country by the Treaty of Versailles. However, the global Great Depression at the time also exacerbated Germany's problem, as it did world trade; consequently, employment plummeted across much of the globe. At the time, Berlin suffered hyperinflation that erased most personal savings accounts, and the US, which previously issued loans around the world—including to the Germans due to the Dawes Plan,[335]—stopped that practice because of Washington's isolationist strategy at the time.[336]

Therefore, the dire economic realities that savaged much of the world by the late 1920s and early 1930s spurred not only the rise of the fascist Hitler, but also Berlin's efforts to focus on becoming self-sufficient despite the Treaty's mandates such as steep reparation payments.[337]

At the time, German officials realized the country required more natural resources to fuel an economic recovery, so Hitler, once he became Führer in 1933, chose military intimidation as the mechanism to acquire those means. Soon he began to ramp up rearmament, which created jobs and quickly improved the economy—and, all the while, it rapidly grew the Wehrmacht. Therefore, with the German economy on track to recover and a stronger military at hand, the Nazi leader began a campaign to swallow up his neighbors primarily for their natural resources, which no doubt contributed to the eventual World War II.

Contemporary crises don't necessarily have to replicate the path chosen by Hitler. However, a variety of them occurring throughout the world today can have much the same effect, and might compel humanity to fall into yet another global war. Consider a litany of troubles that threaten our contemporary lives in terms of economic and security hardships.

In 2024, the World Economic Forum surveyed 1,500 global experts from academia, business, government, the international community, and civil society to identify the most pressing risks. Most (54 percent) said they expect a significant degree of instability and a moderate risk of worldwide catastrophes. "Another 30% see things getting even worse, envisioning looming global catastrophes and with a 'stormy' or 'turbulent' period ahead in the next two years."[338]

Worse, that group of experts is pessimistic about the coming decade. Nearly two-thirds (63 percent) said that, by 2034, they believe the world will be rather turbulent, faced by a host of crises.[339]

They identified the top ten risks (potential crises), which are a combination of manmade and natural events. Those risks anticipated over the coming decade include extreme natural events (earthquakes, hurricanes, droughts, and more); resource shortages that contribute to starvation and encourage even perhaps armed conflict (energy, food); misinformation and disinformation circulated by maligned parties to manipulate entire populations; adverse outcomes of artificial-intelligence technologies only now coming to maturity; involuntary migration that impacts entire regions of the world; and massive cyber insecurity, which jeopardizes every modern economy.[340]

Consider some of the top risks that could spin out of control and result in global calamities that might contribute to armed conflict.

A worldwide depression like the Great Depression in the 1920s and early 1930s isn't completely out of the realm of possibility. After all, financial instability today is more dependent on fiscal and monetary support from governments, and, at this point, most nations are severely stretched thanks to debt, interest rates, and outsized central-bank balance sheets. Therefore, the next financial crisis that affects the entire world could put us all at risk because our authorities are ill-equipped to respond. If that happens, then those same governments might take actions that threaten the interests of their neighbors and, more generally, the entire world. That is fodder for another war.

There are also a host of security hotspots across our world, potential crises that could easily ignite. The war between Russia and Ukraine could expand to engulf much of Europe. The ages-old, on-again, off-again conflicts between Israel and a variety of Islamist regimes keep that region on edge, especially with Iran spewing its hatred through a host of proxies. Certainly, the "great power competition" between the US and China keeps the Asia-Pacific region a hotbed of activity as the PRC constantly threatens to take Taiwan and the Korean Peninsula anticipates the next move by Pyongyang, which could involve the use of a nuclear weapon. Instability defines much of the African continent, thanks to coups and the consequence of major powers competing for resources. Finally, much of Latin America is politically volatile, marked by numerous internal and otherwise regional disputes.

It seems clear that an assortment of crises, both natural and manmade, will inevitably disrupt life for much of the future world. Those problems do appear to be increasing in frequency and intensity, and could spawn even larger situations that could contribute to global war.

Cause #3: Ideologically Opposing Hardliners

The world has never lacked ideologically charged hardliners, those unwilling to tolerate others who fail to embrace their views. Certainly, fascists enjoyed a boom after the First World War, which contributed to the Second War.

Arguably, the first fascist regime to emerge after the First War was in Italy under Benito Mussolini, but, as demonstrated in the previous chapter, the most dangerous fascist movement came to Germany in the early 1930s under Adolf Hitler's rise to power. Hitler, Mussolini, and other fascists at the time tended to share similar goals for their regimes: absolute power and the reordering of society with an emphasis on "conformism, hostility to outsiders, routine violence, contempt for the weak, and extreme hatred of dissident opinions."[341]

Our contemporary world is populated with many ideological differences and not a few fascists, even those who insist on having their way. We have an assortment of religious hardliners, especially across the Islamic world in places such as in Iran and Saudi Arabia. The communists in China, North Korea, and Belarus promote their Marxist ideas and use their grip on power to keep their populations in check while promoting their agenda across a growing swath of the world.

Of course, conflict occurs when these ideologically charged leaders run into opposition within their own countries, in their geographical region, and globally. Symptomatic of those clashes is evidenced by the US-China contest over the island nation of Taiwan, officially the Republic of China.

Today, that confrontation is reminiscent of the Cold War (1948–1991), and we see many lessons learned from the Berlin crisis (1961), which pitted Soviet communists against the West, especially the United States.

Let's briefly review the history of the Berlin Wall and consider similarities today with the Taiwan situation, because the lessons from the Cold War's Berlin crisis are instructive as we confront the hot rivalry with the rulers of communist China today.

Although the Berlin crisis (1958–1961) isn't necessarily ideal as a straightforward comparison with Taiwan, it does illustrate how to deal with communist hardliners. The key difference is that today's Taiwan is strategically important to China because Beijing considers the island nation a province of the mainland. However, at the time of the Berlin crisis, the city was never that significant for the former Soviet Union. Further, the long-term US policy toward Taiwan is strategic ambiguity, whereas during the Cold War, then President John F. Kennedy was committed to defending West Berlin.

There are similarities between Berlin and the Taiwan situations that make the comparison worthy of further study, however. Dmitri Alperovitch outlines some of those parallels in his 2024 *Foreign Affairs* article, "Taiwan Is the New Berlin." Specifically, Alperovitch calls out similarities including: "a race for diplomatic and economic influence, a conventional and nuclear arms race, a space race, a scramble to establish military bases in Africa and East Asia, an ideological struggle between authoritarianism and democracy, a tech and economic war, and an espionage war."[342]

Mr. Alperovitch, chairman of Silverado Policy Accelerator, a geopolitical think tank in Washington, DC, set the context to understand the comparison. He explained, "Between the end of World War II and the early 1960s, the question of who would control Berlin—the Americans and their allies or the Soviets—had been the Cold War's most dangerous flash point, threatening to escalate the two countries' rivalry into a hot or even nuclear war."[343]

Today, Taiwan, like West Berlin in the Cold War, is a small country, but it's at the center of tension between two superpowers, the US and China, and both nations appear ready to go to war over the island nation. Of course, there are reasons the US cares about the fate of the Taiwanese, including the fact that it's a democratic nation—but, more strategically, it is the world's leading semiconductor-manufacturing powerhouse, a critical technological resource for every modern society. Another key issue is the fact that whoever controls Taiwan manages the South China Sea. After all, two-thirds of world trade transits that region, which is claimed by the communist regime.[344]

The Cold War's tension over Berlin led to what Alperovitch claims was the "midwifing the United States' 1970s détente with the Soviet Union," which arguably failed to prevent the 1962 Cuban missile crisis. Leading up to that agreement, the sides tried but failed to improve relations. "Only when Washington was able to convince Moscow that it was serious about defending the city," wrote Alperovitch, "did the Soviets blink and pull back from confrontation." At that point, the Soviets then built the Berlin Wall, which held a hot conflict at bay until 1991 and the fall of the former Soviet Union.[345]

By comparison, the Taiwan crisis has escalated in recent years in terms of rhetoric and, especially, military demonstrations by both sides. More than likely, going forward, muscular deterrence like that demonstrated by the US over Berlin in 1961 regarding the West's airlift campaign will be necessary "to convince China that an invasion of Taiwan would trigger catastrophic consequences is the United States' best chance to achieve a similar détente with China," Alperovitch wrote.[346]

Today, there are many hardliners with opposing ideological worldviews that could easily seed future conflict. Certainly, that is why a Berlin-like détente is needed not just regarding the status of Taiwan, but also half a world away in Europe. Russian President Putin boasts a similar agenda for Ukraine, and that situation requires a Berlin-like agreement as well. After all, the tyrant in the Kremlin expects Kyiv to bow to Moscow's sovereign claim to keep it from becoming an integral part of NATO and the European Union.

Both the Taiwan and Ukraine situations alarm the world, and the repercussions are significant. For example, "War is no longer a concept from the past," warned Poland's Prime Minister Donald Tusk. "It is real, and it started over two years ago. The most worrying thing now is that literally any scenario is possible. We have not seen a situation like this since 1945."[347]

Yes, the threat from contemporary hardliners like Xi and Putin is real, and their rhetoric and actions must not be ignored. Unfortunately, upon reflection on the period leading up to World War II, we should recall that Hitler's intentions in his book, *Mein Kamp*, were disregarded, as were his actions to abandon Versailles' mandates…and then he turned on his neighbors. Those words and actions were mostly overlooked by the Allies until it was too late. Today, we're seeing similar hardliners—not just in China and Russia—who are spouting harsh words and taking actions that should remind us not to be complacent before events get out of hand and the world becomes engulfed in yet another tragic war.

Cause #4: International Agreements/Institutions That Disfavor Certain Parties

The victors in the First World War used the Treaty of Versailles to ensure that the costs of the war were recuperated from Berlin and to prevent Germany from becoming a future threat. Those terms of peace forced on Berlin were set out in the treaty, and all Allies but the Soviet Union approved the details of that accord on June 28, 1919. The particulars of the pact were outlined in chapter 5 of this book, and included details such as the demilitarization of Germany's Rhineland.[348]

Arguably, Germany's response to the particulars of the Treaty of Versailles significantly contributed to the Second World War. Therefore, if there is a parallel today to that treaty, then it ought to be reconsidered by all nations before events get out of hand.

Unfortunately, there is a strong correlation today, which was the topic addressed in chapter 3 of this book, in the section entitled "Objections to West's Unipolar International Order." Specifically, a growing and significant number of countries—the authoritarian regimes led by China and Russia—have serious objections to the US-favoring world order, which Harvard professor John Ruggie labels "American hegemony." Those objections, if not addressed, could thrust the world into a multipolar order, which appears to be happening, and could lead to reactions not that dissimilar to what we saw from Hitler's Germany that led to the Second World War.

Cause #5: Polarizing Alliances

Germany's military buildup spurred France to seek out several alliances, "convinced that it would have to fight another war with Germany and that without allies it was no match for Germany." Therefore, France sought out major states like Britain, the Soviet Union, and Italy with which to align. For example, in 1935, Paris signed an alliance, the Franco-Soviet Treaty of Mutual Assistance, with the Soviet Union. Other, lesser European nations like Czechoslovakia, Romania, and Yugoslavia formed their own alliance, the "Little Entente." Even the Balkan states produced the "Balkan Entente," consisting of Greece, Turkey, Yugoslavia, Romania, and Bulgaria.[349]

Germany sought out alliance partners as well. On May 22, 1939, Germany and Italy signed the earlier-mentioned "Pact of Steel" that suited Mussolini because of his ambitions in the Mediterranean region, which were opposed by France and Britain. That arrangement seemed to be a natural, because they were both fascist governments that had cooperated with Madrid during the Spanish Civil War (1936–1939).[350]

On a global scale, Hitler tried but initially failed to develop a tripartite pact with Italy and Japan to menace Britain. Eventually, Japan aligned itself with Germany in 1936 in an agreement known as the "Anti-Comintern Pact," which identified the communist Soviet Union as the primary enemy. Then, by September 1940, they (Germany, Japan, and Italy) finally consummated the "Tripartite Pact," also known as the "Berlin Pact," a defensive military alliance.[351]

Something like alignment seen prior to World War II is happening today as well. Chapter 3 of this book addressed the emergent international reordering of the world's countries and the evolving polarized alliance system. Specifically, in 2022, President Biden described the global struggle over international order and alignment as one "between democracy and autocracy, between liberty and repression, between a rules-based order and one governed by brute force."[352]

Of course, the post-World War II US alliance network is part of the current international order, which serves a specific purpose for all the players. In particular, "the US alliance system is built on hierarchy, dependency, and the stubborn persistence of American power," wrote Robert E. Kelly and Paul Poast for *Foreign Affairs*. They explained that America's network of alliances helps it achieve and maintain global influence. In exchange, America's allies can dramatically reduce their defense costs by depending on the US's security umbrella, and the added benefit for the allies is their increased trade gains with the United States.[353]

Why do our allies put up with the US, especially its geopolitical bullying ways? That is simple, wrote Kelly and Poast:

They [the US allies and partners] face military threats on their borders, and they want access to US markets. The United States is economically and militarily strong enough to act as an importer of last resort for smaller economies and to project power to defend weaker countries.[354]

Opposing the US-based, pro-West international order and its numerous alliances like NATO is a growing alternative; call it the Sino-Russian axis. That emergent, alliance-like relationship led by authoritarian regimes was profiled in chapter 3. However, as mentioned earlier, the autocratic presidents of China and Russia, Xi and Putin, insist that every nation can choose its own form of government and methods of implementing "democracy," albeit based on its own history as well as social and political systems. They don't want the West dictating to them. Then again, both regimes are ideological enemies of the West. After all, China is led by a communist regime, and Russia, which Putin boasts is a federal democratic state, is in practice a dictatorship and personality cult.

Both of those states are drawing "dividing lines based on the grounds of ideology" by establishing "blocs" and "alliances" among like-minded partners using associations such as BRICS, EAEU, SCO, and others. They might not yet have treaty-based relationships like NATO, but time will tell whether many of those same anti-West nations formally align with China and Russia—the new axis—and, when they inevitably do formally link, that will be yet another indicator that we're drawing close to World War III.

Cause #6: Appeasement Policies by Opposites

Arguably, appeasement to Hitler's aggression was a key Allied weakness that contributed to the start of World War II. Time and again, the 1930s Allies granted concessions to Berlin to avoid war. The problem was the impression they left with Hitler, which was that the Allies had a very high tolerance for German aggression.[355]

Why was appeasement the West's policy, especially in the 1930s, relative to Germany? As pointed out earlier, in the 1930s, the French were weak due to a long series of do-nothing coalition governments. The British were using all their attention to retain their global empire, and the popular view at the time was that another war with Germany would likely sink London's hold on those colonies. Meanwhile, there was also considerable doubt that Hitler would continue his expansionist campaign beyond Germany's Pre-World War I borders.[356] Then there were a host of anti-rearmament, isolationist, and neutrality-leaning domestic lobbies across the West, including the United States. Specifically, the US pursued a policy of isolation, as evidenced by a series of Neutrality Acts passed by the US Congress in 1935, 1936, 1937, and 1939. These acts were spurred by the growth in isolationism and noninterventionism views at home following World War I.[357]

Unfortunately, today, appeasement is once again at play across the world. Certainly, for more than two decades, the US and its European allies have made clumsy attempts to appease both Putin and his Chinese counterpart, most recently President Xi. At this point, especially with Russia, we have evidently failed—and virtually the same is true with China, despite a host of appeasing moves from multiple US administrations starting with the Richard Nixon's in 1972, and more so in recent decades to include the Biden administration.

As a result, we're hearing echoes of the 1930s and the rise of new tyrants in our fevered diplomatic chaos, with the world's leading nuclear states now at loggerheads because we've failed once again to learn lessons from history about appeasement.

Remember, according to Winston Churchill's March 24, 1938, address to the House of Commons, appeasement is a "stairway which leads to a dark gulf." He continued, "It is a fine broad stairway at the beginning, but after a bit the carpet ends." Today, we have the same problem Britain's Chamberlain faced in the 1930s; at the time, he failed to get into Hitler's head.[358]

"We are all members of the human race," argued Chamberlain in 1938, in reference to the Führer. "There must be something in common between us, if only we can find it." But there wasn't anything in common, and as a result, he couldn't get into the German's head, much less to persuade Hitler through appeasement, and the rest is history.[359]

Today, our leadership wants to get into the heads of authoritarian regime leaders like Putin and Xi. How should the West respond to these rogue leaders? After all, as Chamberlain found out with Hitler, there is no sure way to avert conflict if one side, like the Nazi leader, is set on war; it is clear from Hitler's public statements and his own book, *Mein Kampf*, that war was the inevitable outcome.

We can always make the outcome worse either by clear military weakness or by vacillating and appeasing. Evidently, that is part of Putin's calculation in Ukraine that persuaded him to attack in February 2022. Now, Xi is making a similar assessment about Taiwan, and, as Churchill said, the stairway of appeasement "leads to a dark gulf."[360]

Democracies tend to favor appeasement or its synonym, "engagement." However, in April 2023, the British foreign secretary, James Cleverly, appears to understand that appeasement is sometimes wrongheaded. Cleverly reflected on China's huge arms buildup to surmise that "prudence dictates that we must assume the worst. And yet of course we could be wrong."[361]

Chamberlain and the other leaders in the 1930s were wrong about Hitler. They ignored the Führer's own words, especially in *Mein Kampf*, as well as the dictator's many bold actions. Evidently, we're making the same mistake today by discounting what the Chinese leader, Xi, has written and said that is quite sobering.

Prior to the Second War, according to the Nazi leader, the Allies didn't understand Hitler, and disaster ensued. After all, the Führer said to his generals in 1939: "The enemy did not reckon with my great strength of purpose. Our enemies are little worms (*kleine Wurmchen*); I came to know them in Munich."[362]

We risk much the same conclusion today with rogue leaders like Putin and Xi. Appeasing dictators like those in Beijing, Moscow, Tehran, and Pyongyang is a dangerous game that can lead them to determine, as did Hitler, that today's Western leaders are also "little worms."[363]

Conclusion

The six causes of the Second World War outlined above are all present today, and they join others that advance the sobering possibility that yet another global war cannot be too far in the future.

The next chapter in this section addresses the frightening weapons technologies available for a future conflict. They are transforming warfare and radically increase the price all combatants and their countries might pay for miscalculation.

Chapter 7

TECHNOLOGY RESHAPES THE FUTURE BATTLEFIELD

The great growling engine of change—technology.[364]

—Alvin Toffler (1928–2016),
American author, businessman, and futurologist

The previous chapter identified the evident ongoing worldwide repetition of key Second World War causes that might be predictive of a future war. Therefore, as we lean forward to prepare for that potential conflict, we must consider the impact emergent technologies had for past wars, then answer the pregnant question: What happens if we fail to maintain a technical edge over our likely adversaries, should we soon stumble into World War III?

This chapter answers that "So what?" question and then considers the critical path ahead. Specifically, how are emergent technologies reshaping the future battlefield? What are the broader implications of those innovations for the next global war?

As an aside, I've avoided providing in this book a deep dive into all current weapons systems and their capabilities, because technology develops so quickly that anything presently in our arsenals could soon be outdated. After all, profiling the abilities that could likely define the future battlefield is critical for those planning for that war. Also, whether the next conflict happens in a couple of years or in another decade-plus, it's important that our national security planners consider how emergent technologies employed on that future all-domain battlefield might play out.

Finally, let me state a caveat to the rationale for my approach to the technological implications for the modern battlefield. I am, frankly, quite familiar with the current inventory of US weapons and platforms because I am a defense contractor working with that issue. Therefore, it would be a simple cut-and-paste exercise for me to list each major air, land, space, sea, and cyber system with their capabilities as well as how they would be doctrinally employed. However, the reader needs to think beyond our current arsenal and employment scenarios into the complex fighting environment of the future, especially the interoperability of emergent technologies across the military services and among our allies, as well as the implications they will inevitably have for the all-domain battlefield.

As an aside, appendix A, "Modern Weapons and Their Capabilities," provides a selective sneak peek at near-term and longer-term emergent weapons and other frightening possibilities. Also, for context, appendix B compares the current military competencies of the three major antagonists: the US, China, and Russia.

Technology Has Shaped Warfare Throughout History

Military technology has put its stamp on the history of warfare, and it continues to do so even today. A contemporary revolution in technology is reshaping warfare in frightening ways that impact the future fight in all domains—land, sea, air, space, and cyber.

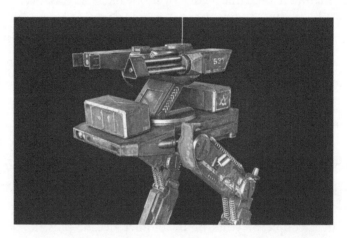

Technology is reshaping the battlefield in ways beyond
even the sci-fi thinking of a few years ago.

Photo by Sergey Koznov on Unsplash[365]

Entire books have been written about the evolution of military technology. This is not one of those books. However, and quite briefly, I will provide a glimpse of military technology's impact on warfare across time, beginning with ancient civilizations and continuing to the present, to suggest it has always—especially today—continued to play a significant role in shaping our armed forces' capabilities and the ever-changing nature of the battlefield.

The fact that technology shapes warfare is important to appreciate, but it isn't deterministic. Rather, it provides opportunity for the warfighter to remold warfare over time, as illustrated below with some examples.

The history of military technology dates to ancient times when primitive weapons such as swords, bows and arrows, and catapults were the only implements of war. Then, along came armor to protect knights, and in the ninth century, the Chinese invented gunpowder, which opened the door to firearms in the fourteenth century. Those handheld weapons eventually gave way to new arms such as rifles and machine guns. Knowledge then advanced to give us steam power for ironclad battleships and locomotives to move supplies and transport troops to the battlefields.

The First World War underwent perhaps the most significant revolution in military technology. After all, it was our first modern, mechanized industrial war, one that tapped the manufacturing might of nations to provide their combatants with resources unlike any before: heavy artillery, machine guns, tanks, motorized transport vehicles, high-level explosives, chemical weapons, airplanes, field radios, aerial reconnaissance cameras, advanced medical know-how, and much more.

The Second World War evidenced a further revolution in technology that altered warfare as well. Many of the developments that emerged from World War I underwent vast improvements by the Second War, such as superior vehicles, medicines, and various weapons. Further, innovations from World War II gave us the atomic bomb, ballistic missiles, radar, the jet engine, synthetic rubber, the mass production of infection defeating penicillin, electronic computers, and many more.

Today, our heads spin with all the new technology, changing not only the efficacy of our weapons but how battlefield effects are delivered via unmanned aerial vehicles, precision-guided munitions, and cyber platforms. Competition to harness those applications is fierce, which begs the importance of understanding the phenomenon in a different way.

Melvin Kranzberg, cofounder of the Society for the History of Technology, offers that "technology is neither good nor bad, nor is it neutral."

Rather, it is a process "of manipulating the material world for human purposes." How it is used ultimately dictates whether it ends up being classified as good or bad.[366]

Alex Roland, a professor emeritus of history at Duke University, wrote for the Foreign Policy Research Institute an article on the topic, "War and Technology." In it, he offered propositions about military technology that help us understand its role in warfare.[367]

Professor Roland indicates that technology "shapes warfare," and "war (not warfare) [that] shapes technology." He explained that military technology is "not deterministic," it "opens doors," and actually "is not different in kind, but in degree."

Below is what the professor meant by these propositions.

"Technology shapes warfare, not war," wrote Roland. He explained, "Warfare is the conduct of war. It is the clash of arms or the maneuver of armed forces in the field." Further, he wrote, "War is a [political] condition in which a state might find itself; warfare is a physical activity conducted by armed forces in the context of war."[368]

Roland continued, "Technology defines, governs, or circumscribes warfare. It sets the stage for warfare. It is the instrumentality of warfare." In fact, the words that best describe the impact of technology are that "it changes warfare" and it is the "primary source of military innovation throughout history." For example, he said, "naval warfare does not occur without ships." It's also true that air warfare doesn't exist without planes, which facilitate multifaceted actions with strategic bombing, close air support, and dog fights among fighters. Today, pilotless drones carry out reconnaissance and can serve as a weapons platform. Thus, the "vehicle defines the warfare."[369]

Another aspect of this line of understanding technology's role in warfare is the "distribution of the weaponry." Professor Roland illustrated the importance of "distribution" by citing the First Gulf War (1990) and how Iraqi dictator Saddam Hussein tried to defeat the US Army, but failed, because "the quality and quantity of the American technology prevailed."[370]

Next, Professor Roland said that "technology does not determine warfare," rather, it "presides in warfare, but it does not rule." He explained that when innovations appear, they "determine the nature and even the result of warfare." For example, he noted, "Chariots were perhaps the most dominant instrument of warfare before nuclear weapons." Canadian historian William H. McNeil stated that the chariot became the "superweapon" in the eighteenth century BCE, which meant states either adopted that platform or "ceased to compete in interstate war," because the "chariot defined, drove, governed, [and] circumscribed ground warfare."[371]

The "superweapon" chariot lost its significance with the introduction of iron weapons, which gave the infantry "new power to stand up to chariots." At that point, the "determinism of the chariot evaporated." Similarly, throughout history, new technologies routinely replaced formerly dominant capabilities—gunpowder, strategic bombing, ballistic missiles, and more.[372]

Finally, Professor Roland asserted that the technology of war is "the open door." He cited medieval historian Lynn T. White Jr. to illustrate the view.

Dr. White wrote in *Medieval Technology and Social Change* that the introduction of the "stirrup" for mounted warriors at the Battle of Tours, also called the Battle of Poitiers, fought on October 10, 732, allowed the "heavily armed and armored mounted knight to lean into his lance and overwhelm mounted and unmounted warriors alike with irresistible force." In this instance, White argued, the stirrup was a "catalyst," and did not "create feudalism"; rather, it "opened doors." That is, the "availability of the stirrup in Europe," if adopted, would "make the heavily armed and armored mounted knight the mainstay of an emergent military system," albeit until the fourteenth-century invention of the English longbow.[373]

In this context, wrote Professor Roland, White's "open door" becomes a conceptual tool for thinking about military technology. Therefore, "humans must decide if they are going to, or can, take up a given military innovation [and thus] technology is a possibility, not an imperative." He illustrated the more modern version of the "open door" concept. Specifically, between the two world wars, both Britain and the US developed strategic bombers to project military power. Meanwhile, the European powers focused on fielding fighter aircraft to gain air superiority over future regional battlefields.[374]

Thus, even though "people invent and innovate" and "open the door," decisions to "open the door" for a particular technology depends on a military decision to include it. But that doesn't make the technology "deterministic." Rather, the decision to incorporate the technology is a personal, political, and economic choice—a catalyst with warfare consequences.[375]

Finally, Professor Roland indicated that "modern military technology is not different in kind, but in degree." Then, he explained, "World War II was the first war in history in which the weapons in use at the end of the war differed significantly from those employed at the outset." The list of emergent technologies by 1945 is significant: the atomic bomb, jet aircraft, guided missiles, microwave radar, proximity fuses, and others.[376]

What happened to contribute to such rapid military innovation that impacted warfare? President Dwight Eisenhower (1890–1969) later called that ingredient the "military-industrial complex," which created a perpetual arms race that not only contributed to the Allies winning the Second World War, but became a military innovation employed to win the next war.[377]

The birth of the "military-industrial complex" means the "introduction of systematic, institutionalized innovation [that] makes modern military technology seem radically different from all that went before," wrote Roland. That difference is simultaneously real and illusory. He continued, "The reality stems from the accelerated pace of technological change in the modern world and an unprecedented mastery of energy and materials ranging across a dimensional scale from nanotechnology to floating cities like the modern aircraft carrier."[378]

Professor Roland concluded:

> The tools of war have been evolving slowly throughout the course of human history, but only in the modern world has there been an institutionalized and rationalized mechanism for continuously and systematically innovating military technology.[379]

So What? Necessity of Maintaining a Technological Edge

Former Defense Secretary Mark Esper (2019–2020) once said, "History informs us that those who are first to harness once-in-a-generation technologies often have a decisive advantage on the battlefield for years to come." Our survival may depend on that "decisive advantage," because our numerous enemies seek our demise and are aggressively arming their militaries with the latest technologies.[380]

There will always be debates about how best to invest the taxpayers' money, especially on national defense. What former Secretary of Defense Esper said is especially true for today; that's why we must continue to effectively invest tax dollars to maintain a technological edge over our adversaries. Our way of life and freedom are ultimately at stake.

Colin Demarest, a reporter at *C4ISRNET* who covers military networks and cyber and information technology issues, wrote for *Axios* that "conflicts abroad and defense-contract competitions at home illuminate in real time the future of America's war machine." He suggested that the answer to the question: "So what?" is, "Governments and militaries that grasp these challenges and master the changes will dominate the future." Dominating the future is linked to the preservation of our way of life.[381]

The challenge to dominate the future battlefield in part is to stay ahead of our adversaries in terms of technology. Specifically, Demarest illustrated the accelerating pace of battlefield innovation by citing troubling developments, such as "cheap, abundant drones," that "are devastating far more expensive systems in eastern Europe [Ukraine]." We saw much the same problem off Yemen's coast in 2024, where the Houthi rebels employed Iranian-provided rockets, ballistic missiles, and drones to disrupt global maritime trade in the strategic Red Sea. Our response to those attacks was to use incredibly expensive missile systems like the $30,000 Martlet missile to take down inexpensive armed drones, rockets, and missiles.[382]

A variety of bad actors—nation-states and non-state actors like the Houthis—are employing the latest technologies, even though they're cheap versions, to advance their interests; to protect our equities, we must stay a couple steps ahead of those enemies.

Consider the proliferation of tech-related challenges affecting our way of life today, which must be addressed on a variety of emergent modern battlefields. Examples of these hi-tech systems are outlined in appendix A, "Modern Weapons and Their Capabilities."

- **Information battlefield**: Nation-states like Russia and China and their proxies are using disinformation campaigns to shape international perceptions across the world. Why? They want to influence elections to favor their radical agenda, using a modern version of psychological warfare.
- **Directed-energy battlefield**: Science fiction is now a reality, thanks to emergent, directed-energy weapons that can literally fry electronic platforms from many miles away. These are

becoming cheaper, they're proliferating across the world, and they are already in use under limited situations.

- **Cyber battlefield**: Cyber warfare is here to stay. Cyber "bullets" are modern ammunition and, once harnessed by artificial intelligence and controlled by maleficent agents, all data systems become vulnerable to hacking and loss, even sophisticated military systems used across all domains—including space.
- **Intelligence battlefield**: Even rogue regimes like North Korea now have access to overhead satellite imagery that provides them with real-time information about their adversaries, and distance is no longer a factor, thanks to space-based and publicly available data platforms.
- **Nuclear battlefield**: Nuclear arsenals are growing rapidly, such as in communist regimes like China and North Korea. Although assured destruction kept détente with the Soviets in the Cold War, there are fewer guarantees today that these weapons of mass destruction will not be used in the future by a variety of states or perhaps by non-state actors.

General Mark Milley, former chairman of the US Joint Chiefs of Staff, weighed in on the "So what?" question in 2023 with his article in the *Joint Forces Journal*, "Strategic Inflection Point." He wrote, "Geostrategic competition and rapidly advancing technology are driving fundamental changes to the character of war." Then, he cautioned, "Our opportunity to ensure that we maintain an enduring competitive advantage is fleeting."[383]

General Milley explained that we're adjusting our forces "to deter our adversaries." However, he said, "We must make fundamental changes now to win the next war." He illustrated his point by citing D-day 1944, because today's world isn't that different from that dark day, which at the time was "clouded in fog and mist." Further, at that moment in history, America and its Allies had to adapt "to address an uncertain future."[384]

After all, as outlined in previous sections, there is significant and growing opposition to the rules-based international order enforced by a network of US allies and backed up by a Western military alliance network. Unfortunately, as General Milley rightly warned, "We now see tears in the fabric of the rules-based international order as adversarial global powers [read "China and its authoritarian partners"] continuously challenge the system. The time to act is now."[385] President Ronald Reagan warned us about what's really at stake:

> Freedom is a fragile thing and it is never more than one generation away from extinction. It is not ours by way of inheritance; it must be fought for and defended constantly by each generation.[386]

Technologies Change the Character of Modern War

The modern battlefield is unlike any other in history. Current all-domain operations combine "space, cyber, deterrent, transportation, electromagnetic spectrum operations, missile defense—all of these global capabilities together...to compete with a global competitor and at all levels of conflict," said General John Hyten, the former vice chairman of the US Joint Chiefs of Staff.[387]

General Hyten explained our daunting all-domain challenge: We must seek the "ability to integrate and effectively command and control all domains in a conflict or in a crisis seamlessly—and we do not know how to do that. Nobody knows how to do that."[388]

Certainly, the US is trying to crack that nut. Former Chairman of the Joint Chiefs of Staff General Joe Dunford advanced the idea of global force management, an effort to look across traditional jurisdictional lines to control global fires—weapons both physical and nonphysical (like cyber). General Milley added to Dunford's effort with four new elements: global plans, global operations short of fires, global integration of messaging, and global integration of deterrence.[389]

An important part of that effort is the fielding of the Joint All-Domain Command and Control (JADC2), which brings together information from many sensors, communications systems, and data fusion engines. Together, these tools make it possible to simultaneously present targeting data to any weapon platform, thanks to the fusion of input from sensors such as submarines, a Marine Corps infantry squad, an F-35 jet fighter, an Apache gunship, an orbiting satellite, and many more.[390]

So, how do we equip our force with the necessary tools to effectively and efficiently perform in the all-domain future battlefield as technologies advance?

The Director of National Intelligence (DNI) tasked the National Intelligence Council's Strategic Futures Group to tackle that question. That group produced a paper, "The Future of the Battlefield," which considered a range of potentially revolutionary technologies and how they might change the character of how war is waged.[391]

The DNI paper investigated their "crystal ball" to suggest potential changes across "three distinct aspects of warfare": hardware, software, and users. By "hardware," the group means weapons systems and new technologies. "Software" is a range of issues that includes doctrine, training, and ways new technologies might be used. Finally, the "users" are states or non-state actors that might employ these technologies, weapons, and doctrines.[392]

Each of those aspects of future warfare are detailed below with some elaboration for further context.

Hardware: New Weapons Technologies

No doubt, emerging technologies are likely to change battlefield weapons in four broad areas—connectivity, lethality, autonomy, and sustainability.[393]

Connectivity, according to the DNI report, means "ways in which combatants detect and locate their adversaries, communicate with each other, and direct operations." We gain an advantage when we can collect vital information accurately and quickly so we can then analyze and rapidly and securely send instructions to our combat forces.[394]

This is made possible thanks to many sensors and big data analytics that are key to real-time detection and information processing. The world's leading militaries are aggressively seeking this outcome by harnessing emerging technologies—such as artificial intelligence—that will provide persistent surveillance and improve our decision-making.[395]

The sought-after end state for future connectivity is our ability to disrupt, degrade, and disable our enemy's highly connected, information-dependent systems.

Lethality is "the damage that new weapons and weapon systems can inflict on battlefields." Our ability to use various surveillance technologies increases the effectiveness of our weapons. Specifically, we anticipate that future accuracy for our weapon systems will be enhanced by the integration of satellite-provided imagery, positioning, timing, and navigation information.[396]

Our tactical weapons such as guided rockets and artillery will be joined in the fight by an assortment of ballistic and cruise missile systems, as well as long-range precision strike weapons to include hypersonic systems, which are yet to be proven in combat, as well as directed-energy weapons (lasers and high-power microwaves).

Strategic weapons of mass destruction may well increase with technological advances as well. We've seen Syria's repeated use of chemical weapons in the past decades and the alleged use of toxic agents by both North Korea and Russia for assassinations. However, what's likely in the future is that all nuclear states will sustain and modernize their nuclear arsenals. For example, Russia is modernizing its strategic nuclear forces to include a new road-mobile intercontinental ballistic missile, new missiles for submarines, upgraded heavy bombers, and the fielding of a bomber capable of launching hypersonic weapons.[397]

Also, China's People's Liberation Army (PLA), according to the Pentagon's annual report to Congress, is quickly modernizing its nuclear triad forces—sea, ground, and air-launched weapons. Evidently, the PLA will soon have a second-strike capability; that is the ability after suffering an initial attack to respond once again.

Autonomy includes the "ways in which robotics and AI can change who (or what) fights and makes decisions." No doubt, autonomous systems will play key roles in future warfare, which will provide enabling technologies to new and existing platforms to decrease human interaction in deadly environments.[398]

Unmanned vehicles are already in use on many battlefields. Expect them to mature across most domains in the future, especially by assuming repetitive activities such as resupplying ammunition and food, as well as scouting enemy positions, laying and recovering mine fields, and searching for enemy submarines. Expect a proliferation of killing drones, from miniature to large scale, to soon be available to join all-domain forces.

Lethal autonomous weapons will also become common, and may not include humans in the firing-decision loop. Although there are clear ethical and legal issues with these platforms, we should anticipate a future in which truly autonomous, lethal platforms will roam the multi-domain battlefield and make independent targeting and engagement decisions; a true brave new world is coming to the battlefield.

Swarming unmanned systems have already been observed across ground and sea domains. This capability is becoming cheaper and more frequent and, in the future, they will be able to communicate with each other, adjust their tactics, and change targets as necessary thanks to robust artificial intelligence.

Of course, the evolution of autonomous systems and their operational deployments are closely linked to advances in AI in terms of enhanced target recognition and in support of humans in human-machine teaming, including decision-making. At present, the Chinese are aggressively pursuing the use of AI applications such as in data analysis, simulations, and command decision-making. Russia's President Vladimir Putin claims his nation leads the world in the development of AI, a frightening proposition.

Sustainability involves "the ways that militaries supply and support their deployed forces." This category is a catch-all for new technologies that address robotics, additive manufacturing, biotechnology, and energy technology that affect military logistics and sustainment.[399]

Some obvious technology-driven capabilities under the sustainment rubric include unmanned vehicles for logistical support, the likelihood that 3-D printing will be used to produce combat-related items with new materials including metals and ceramics, and logistics advancements such as on-demand spare parts and less expensive equipment. Further, the critical field of biotechnologies addresses the soldier's improved ability to fight and survive, which is empowered by new medical devices, diagnostic systems, and their enhanced capacity to address injuries while in combat. Also, innovative energy technologies might include small, easily transportable nuclear reactors and high-density electrical power storage to support logistics and weapon systems.

Software: Developing New Concepts[400]

"Software" doesn't necessarily mean computer code (language), but rather technologies that contribute to the advancement of the military art, such as new doctrinal concepts for how to employ the tools of war. The DNI report identified four discrete but not necessarily mutually exclusive visions for how future combatants might use new capabilities and their associated tactics: fast offense, zone defense, distributed warfare, and hybrid or non-kinetic warfare.

1. **Fast offense** is the release of a devastating opening salvo of weaponry that strikes the enemy's military and/or critical infrastructure before he can respond. Under this scenario, offensive capabilities would have to be prepositioned without giving the enemy any early warning.[401]

2. **Zone defense** is the use of new technologies that are defensive-oriented. This approach taps innovations that enhance the mostly stationary defender's situational awareness to closely protect his airspace, maritime area, and ground location. Certainly, a phalanx of sensors with an assortment of unmanned ground and aerial systems would perhaps be sufficient to execute this tactical concept.

3. **Distributed warfare** employs numerous high-speed and highly accurate, lethal platforms that target the enemy's expensive, high-value, and difficult-to-replace platforms and weapon systems. The DNI indicates that a mitigation strategy against distributed warfare is the "further development and implementation of [counter] distributed forces and operations."[402]

   Cyber operations fit the distributed warfare concept. They can degrade or deny the use of military hardware and, as a result, render those platforms and associated units temporarily unable to perform their mission. We should expect that in the future, cyberattacks will be integrated into a combined arms approach—all-domain operations—to achieve information superiority. We know China and Russia view military cyber operations during a conflict as part of an integrated information warfare campaign. The intent of those actions is to disrupt the enemy's weapons and operations by hacking surveillance and weapons-guidance systems.[403]

4. **Hybrid and non-kinetic warfare** describe operations in the "gray zone," such as the use of deniable proxies including private military companies (PMC). We've seen Russia and Iran use proxies or PMC like the former Russian Wagner Group in a variety of armed conflicts, and they might also prove useful for non-kinetic actions such as severing undersea fiber-optic cables and information operations.

The Users: Employing New Weapons and Military Art[404]

The ultimate weapon is the unpredictability of the individual actors, nation-states, or non-state actors that select technologies based on their unique threat perceptions and the perceived vulnerabilities of their targets. The DNI report states, "The extent to which these actors encourage initiative and innovation or are otherwise open to change is likely to determine their success mastering the full potential of new technologies and doctrines."[405]

The use of a range of emergent technologies depends upon the attacking entity. Great powers like China enjoy access to a wide range of capabilities like hypersonic missiles, cyber, and nuclear arms. However, less wealthy states and non-state actors can still enjoy strategic-level effects using relatively low-cost autonomous weapon systems and cyber tools. For example, in 2019, Iran demonstrated creativity when it combined a variety of techniques and weapon platforms to conduct a long-range strike on Saudi Arabia's oil production facilities. That attack used both armed unmanned aerial vehicles and cruise missiles to shut down more than 5 percent of global oil production in Saudi Arabia. Similarly, Tehran used another combination of low-end platforms in its April 13 and October 2, 2024, attacks on Israel, which were meant mostly to deliver a strategic message without resulting in significant ground effects. Why? Because Iran knew a devastating attack would earn a similarly destructive response from the Israelis.

Other entities, like PMCs, acting secretly at the behest of their great power sponsor, might have access to the latest technologies for their operations. Also, a PMC might identify a new approach using advanced technologies to accomplish a mission a nation-state might never conduct. Further, insurgents and or terrorist groups will likely have access to less expensive, albeit easy-to-acquire, technologies like unmanned aerial vehicles, which are outfitted with explosives to destroy a variety of targets.

Technological Implications for Future Battlefield

The DNI's study of the future battlefield also considered the implications of the ongoing technological revolution. However, that report highlights a key reservation about the impact of war-fighting innovations. Specifically, some tech used in past fights had limited effects, while others quickly demonstrated profound outcomes. Thus, the DNI cautions, "Identifying precisely which and to what extent new technologies and techniques will have the most impact on the future character of warfare is notoriously difficult."[406]

The report develops four technology-related trends likely to demonstrate a major effect on the future battlefield, however. They are: "increasingly available advanced technologies, perceived sanctuaries less safe, heightened risk of miscalculation and escalation and more deadly, though not necessarily decisive." Each of those is summarized below.

Increasingly Available Advanced Technologies[407]

Unfortunately, military-relevant technologies are proliferating and becoming less expensive. As a result, we should anticipate that new tech to be available for both state and non-state actors. Consider some of those innovations and their strategic impact for future conflicts.

Space technology and services are now becoming widely available to the public, thanks to commercial entities such as Elon Musk's SpaceX. Likely, purveyors of space-related, dual-use services mean high-resolution imagery, for example, will be available for various militaries but also for commercial customers.

The cyber industry is harnessing ever-cheaper technologies that result in more players on the dark web.[408] The use of cyberspace enables small countries and a host of non-state actors to achieve strategic effect without significant expense. This proliferating capability is a serious threat against tech-dependent states and commercial enterprises.

There is also the possibility of new PMCs that harness cutting-edge military capabilities for a fee. The DNI points out that PMCs that use autonomous weapons might "enable lesser military powers to avoid the cost of developing a modern military and training skilled personnel."[409]

Perceived Sanctuaries Less Safe[410]

Modern technology destroys the perception that there are sanctuaries out of the enemy's reach. After all, long-range, precision-strike capabilities tethered to AI means that "areas once thought to be relatively safe from conventional attack because of distance will be increasingly vulnerable." Similarly, the cyber attacker is unbound by geography, and virtually any critical infrastructure is vulnerable if the enemy can access the concerned network.

Heightened Risk of Miscalculation and Escalation[411]

The human factor plays a key role in the environment dominated by advanced weapons systems and the employment of hybrid and non-kinetic warfare. These technologies in the hands of both friend and foe run the real risk of unintended escalation resulting in direct interstate conflict.

The DNI report highlights some possible scenarios for miscalculation and escalation. In the situation where both sides possess first-strike precision weapons, and as geopolitical tensions rise, the leadership in both entities "might feel pressured to strike first out of fear of losing their advanced arsenals of hypersonic and other weapons to an opponent's first strike." After all, it is a longstanding common doctrine to use your opening strike to blind the enemy's sensor systems and deadliest offensive platforms.

There is also the scenario wherein a nation hires a PMC to conduct "gray zone" activities, which include the use of certain sophisticated technologies. Even though the hiring nation avoids public acknowledgment of their PMC's actions, such as using cyberattacks to disable critical infrastructure or disrupt an election, the targeted entity might decide to respond directly to the PMC's sponsor.

More Deadly, Though Not Necessarily Decisive[412]

No doubt, a future war could begin with unbelievable violence. However, as the DNI report indicates, that first strike might be followed by a "protracted and inconclusive" war. After all, history is replete with the starter entity of hostilities believing it had the advantage, which at the time might be true. However, that edge might be turned on its head because the advanced war-fighting technologies and concepts that prompted the offensive ultimately failed.

The Japanese attack on Pearl Harbor in 1941 demonstrates this view. Initially, that attack on the US Navy's Pacific Ocean battleship fleet anchored around Ford Island (Pearl Harbor) was significant. However, it "galvanized" the United States and ended poorly for Japan. Therefore, in the future, it is possible that advanced and increasingly lethal weapons might deliver a similarly substantial result with significant casualties in the opening moments of a conflict, expecting the targeted nation to concede or otherwise withdraw from combat. However, like the US' response to the Japanese attack, in time, the fortunes of the parties could be reversed.

Conclusion

The future battlefield will be radically different than in the past. Technology has played a critical role in the past wars, and will likely contribute to victory in the future. Therefore, the nation's survival is at stake unless we maintain a technological advantage over our enemies. After all, the emergent developments outlined in this chapter could well redefine future military conflicts and defense strategies; as a result, we end up with a shift in the very nature of warfare.

The US and our allies must adapt to and harness these revolutionary changes in military technology. Further, although we can only guess how World War III might begin, what is clear is it will be like no prior global conflict—and perhaps more deadly for all humanity.

The next chapter provides a fictitious description of World War III scenarios. How might it begin? What role will emergent technologies play in that war? What are the potential long-term consequences of that fight? Yes, it might be a fictitious presentation, but it is informed by those who know warfare and apply their knowledge in simulations to realize the effects of frightening capabilities associated with developing technologies.

Chapter 8

A FOOL'S ERRAND: PREDICTING WORLD WAR III

The understanding that a third world war could be the end of civilization should restrain us from taking extreme steps on the international arena that are highly dangerous for modern civilization.[413]

—Vladimir Putin, President, Russian Federation (2018)

Admittedly, any effort to accurately predict the potential trigger(s) and underlying causes of World War III, much less how that conflict will be executed and the consequences, is nothing short of a fool's errand. However, many respected people from across the spectrum of humanity have in the past speculated about such a future war. Therefore, I will join those "fools" to make an educated stab at wandering down the same prophetic path, and, like those others, I will risk history proving me totally wrong...or not.

This chapter begins by addressing some of the possible triggers that might trip the world into another global war. After all, there is widespread concern that, once again, worldwide conflict is at our doorstep. Previously in this book, I surveyed some of the causes historians say led to the past two world wars. Here, I will summarize what some of my contemporaries speculate about potential events that might be the last straw(s)—the triggers that could spark such a situation in the twenty-first century. Then I will add my perspective to that mix.

Just how might a third world war play out? I've already outlined in the previous chapter the likely impact of emergent technologies for the future battlefield. That fight will certainly be very different than prior global conflicts. My portrayal of that war is based on several assumptions, many of which are likely flawed. However, I identify them below and then describe that potential conflict in rather specific, though frightening, terms.

Finally, although the trigger(s) that might launch the future war and the details about the execution of that conflict are truly conjecture on my part, the consequences of that conflagration are far more certain; at least some of them are relatively easy to anticipate, given the history of wars and the effects of modern technologies. Here, I will identify and then detail some of the most egregious combat outcomes for humanity and especially modern civilization. This sobering account explains why every person, no matter their position or country, ought to fight hard to preserve the peace.

Is Another World War Inevitable?

Although there is widespread belief that another world war is inevitable, predicting the timing and particulars of execution for such an event is incredibly difficult, for a variety of reasons. Then again, expert opinions about the likely causes of a twenty-first-century global conflict vary, making it hard for the average person to know whom to believe. Despite the risk of being found wrong, I will add my own perspective to that of others, which arguably further clutters the marketplace of ideas about the next war.

Modern war must be the last resort because of the potential devastation.
Photo by Unsplash in collaboration with Alex Shuper[414]

Let me begin by quoting Juan Bautista Alberdi, the father of the Argentine constitution, who wisely wrote: "There can be no just war [an issue he has with fourth-century Saint Augustine's view known as the "just war" theory], because there is no judicious war. War is the temporary loss of judgment." Mr. Alberdi also wrote in his 1870 book, *The Crime of War*, that "wars will be rarer as responsibility for their effects is felt by all who promote and invite them." Perhaps we're vulnerable to starting another war today because too few people carry the memory of past wars, much less the burden for launching those conflicts—which, if more of us carried those memories, the likelihood of another conflict would be significantly diminished.[415]

Even though many of us would agree with Mr. Alberdi that "war is the temporary loss of judgment," the threat of a future world war doesn't seem to be abating. Evidently, as stated earlier, the possibility of conflict is a serious concern among much of humanity. For example, a 2022 study by the American Psychological Associated found that 81 percent of 1,500 participants considered global uncertainly to be a leading stressor. Further, Google Trends demonstrates that the level of interest by searchers of the Internet regarding the topic "World War III" continues to rise, and, if that's not enough, a 2023 survey by US News & World Report found that three-quarters of seventeen thousand people from across the world agreed with the statement, "I fear we are moving closer to World War III."[416]

Why is there so much angst about another global war? Well, most of us are subjected to a constant barrage of media reports about conflict: the war in Ukraine, Chinese saber-rattling against Taiwan, civil wars and coups across Africa, criminal gang violence in the Americas, the latest flare-up in the Mideast, and much more. That drumbeat of war-related media reports is almost deafening as sounds and pictures of new threats, the cries of humanity, and bomb blasts echo off our living-room ceilings virtually every night from televised news reports about the latest crises.[417]

There also seems to be no shortage of experts promising they can predict the war. The reader should be quite skeptical about any such claims, primarily because forecasting the future, much less another war, is seriously problematic—or, as this chapter's title suggests, it's a fool's errand.

Robert A. Johnson, a former British army officer, and at the time director of the Oxford Changing Character of War Research Program, wrote a compelling article, "Predicting Future War," for the US Army War College journal, *Parameters*. In that piece, Dr. Johnson provided considerable sage advice about the popular process of predicting war.

He cautions that the character of war is evolutionary; therefore, the possibility of war is difficult to discern, especially during long periods of peace. He acknowledges, however, that "while there may be trends and enduring principles of strategy and international relations, it is the variability of conditions, changes in the application of technology, adaptation, and the dynamics of conflict that make prediction, and consequently planning, very challenging."[418]

Dr. Johnson admits: "The problem of prediction [about war] has not prevented bold assertions, and some dystopian visions of the future have been propagated through sensationalist tracts and even, apparently, in serious scholarship." He then identifies some people he labels as "modern prophets of doom who foresee a Hobbesian anarchy." Some, Johnson points out, such as the United Kingdom's war-making doctrine, anticipate a coming "hybrid" (mix of political, conventional, and irregular warfare) battlefield that will be "contested, congested, cluttered, connected and constrained." He also calls out this "hybrid" battlefield because it is complicated by strategic trends that anticipate a violent future, thanks to diminishing natural resources, climate changes, and explosive populations.[419]

Why are predictions about war so diverse? Dr. Johnson explains, "It is tempting to make projections in the present based on the types of wars that seem the most prevalent today and to assume that for the foreseeable future, all wars will fall into this pattern." He goes on to say military analysts try to accurately identify the characteristics of future war, primarily because of the investment governments make in their armed forces to prepare for the next war. However, "the difficulty is that success is contingent on context."[420]

That is the rub, according to Johnson: "The dynamics of war frequently change the conditions under which the conflict was entered." After all, "aims…evolve just as rapidly and comprehensively as the conflict itself." He argues that a tenuous situation is why history is so important to the strategist, because it encourages critical reflection "to ask questions, and to challenge the positivist assumptions that crowd our field of view." He admits, "We cannot entirely escape our present, but we should seek to break free of unreasoned supposition about the future through critical thinking."[421]

I began this section of *Preparing for World War III* with a chapter summarizing the most prominent causes of the Second World War and then demonstrated that those causes are very much in force today. Whether they will contribute to a future war is yet to be determined. However, given Dr. Johnson's sage advice, we must conduct a bit of critical reflection, which once again takes us back to the lessons one would hope we learned from World War II.

Therefore, that begs the question: What might be the final straw, the trigger that launches the world into another war? After all, many causes related to both previous world wars were identified in the previous section of this book. Although the series of underlying reasons may be long, no one can with certainty declare the final crisis that pushes the world over the top into conflict. However, many historians agree the actual trigger event for the First War was the assassination of Archduke Franz Ferdinand, and the trigger for the Second War was Germany's September 1, 1939, invasion of Poland.

Consider some potential triggers for the Third World War, the actual last straw(s) perhaps in a long series of crises leading to the commencement of hostilities.

Trigger: The Last in a Series of Seemingly Unrelated Crises

In section II of *Preparing for World War III*, I summarized the history of the Second World War. What should have been obvious is that conflict was caused by a series of events, not one single crisis. Specifically, recall that the final crisis—the trigger—was Hitler's invasion of Poland after the signing of the Molotov-Ribbentrop Pact. However, many significant events led up to that climax: Japan's invasion of Manchuria in 1931; Italy's invasion of Abyssinia in 1935; the demilitarization of the Rhineland; the Anschluss with Austria; and the Sudeten crisis of 1938, among others.[422]

After all, as most historians will agree, and as stated earlier, World War II did not arise from a single event but from a series of activities, "like water rising until it breaches a dam," a view shared by Bret Stephens in his *New York Times* article, "This Is How World War III Begins."[423]

Mr. Stephens, an opinion columnist with the *Times*, used the rising-water metaphor to illustrate the theory that there tends to be multiple adversities that lead to war. He cites the situation that led to Russia's 2022 invasion of Ukraine to illustrate the theory. Specifically, he argues that a series of events began in 2008 with Moscow's assault into the Republic of

Georgia, then Russian troops took Crimea (2014) and much of eastern Ukraine in 2022. Another Russian-caused crisis, which preceded Ukraine, was its carpet bombing of Aleppo, Syria, and the use of exotic radioactive and chemical agents against Russian dissidents on British soil (2019). Other Russian spawn crises joined this series, such as Moscow's interference in US elections (2016 and 2020) as well as a variety of Russian proxy hacks of American computer networks. We can add to the mix the murder of Russian Boris Nemtsov (2015), a liberal political figure, and the evident poisoning of Putin's political enemy, Alexei Navalny (2024).[424]

What is important is how the West responds to these crises. Mostly, the US-led West published condemning press releases after each event mentioned above, and Western leaders complained at the United Nations…but nothing more. Therefore, as Stephens observed, Putin got the message. The West wouldn't do much of anything other than complain if, in 2022, the Russian army invaded Ukraine. Of course, upon reflection, the West's response to Putin's actions wasn't any different from the appeasement shown to Hitler throughout the 1930s as he created one crisis after another. After each event, the West issued a condemning statement, but never took any meaningful action against the Nazis—that is, until it was too late and World War II began with the Wehrmacht's invasion of Poland.

Eventually, in the case of Ukraine, the West came to Kyiv's aid with arms and humanitarian aid. We sanctioned Russia, but not before Putin gobbled up four Ukrainian provinces. Of course, Putin acted because Biden and our NATO allies mostly appeased the Russian leader before the invasion. Why? Evidently, Biden and most of our allies either really believed or were just cowered by Putin's threats about causing World War III and/or the use of nuclear arms.

Today, a similar set of crises, though perhaps unrelated and more widespread, could push us into a global war. However, there is generally one last crisis that will prove to be too much, thus will trigger that war. Below are some of those potential last straws.

Trigger: Provocative Military Action

Scott Anderson wrote for the *New York Times* an article, "Provocative Military Action," that considers "modern-day superpower conflict through the lens of the past." Specifically, he references two books in his article: *The Return of Great Powers* by Jim Sciutto and *Up in Arms* by Adam E. Casey.[425]

Arguably, Anderson's article was meant to be a hit piece against the 2024 candidacy of Donald J. Trump for president. However, it illustrates a potential trip wire to war, no matter the political orientation of the president at the time.

Evidently, President Trump had been in office only a few months when Iran made another show of its ballistic missiles, which typically garnered interest inside the Washington Beltway. In that instance, Tehran's test missile flew across that country's airspace and landed harmlessly inside Iranian territory.

At the time, retired Marine General John Kelly served as President Trump's chief of staff and later as secretary of Homeland Security (2017–2019). Evidently, General Kelly, according to Sciutto, recalled the occasion after there was a report of yet another impending Iranian missile launch that Mr. Trump said he "wanted to shoot…down." Kelly told the president, "Well sir, that's an act of war. You really need to go over to congress and get at least an authorization." Trump responded, "They'll never go along with it," to which Kelly said, "Well, I know. But that's our system."[426]

Mr. Anderson took that anecdote from Mr. Sciutto's book, which illustrates numerous other accounts of twenty-first-century brinkmanship. Evidently, according to Sciutto, Kelly "managed to talk his old boss [Trump] out of some of his worst ideas only by suggesting they would hurt his standing in public opinion." He also recalls telling Mr. Trump that "Americans, generally speaking by polling, think that we should be involved in the world," a reference at the time used to help cool the president's heels regarding his threat to pull the US out of the North Atlantic Treaty Organization.

Leaders unfamiliar with the international security arena need wise counselors like General Kelly to help guard against actions that could trigger a war. The fact is that most political leaders come to office with little or no meaningful international and security experience. Therefore, unless they have sage advisors like General Kelly, they may order provocative military action without understanding the consequences.

Trigger: Lack of Guardrails to Prevent Catastrophe

The Cold War (1948–1991) created a host of guardrails to keep the US/ West and the Soviets from falling into a global war. However, after the former Soviet Union collapsed, many of those old necessary guardrails, such as arms control and lines of communications, were abandoned. For example, recall that in the winter of 2023, a mysterious Chinese balloon drifted across the United States. At the time, the Pentagon tried to contact the Chinese military about the balloon, but the PLA command "refused to pick up the phone."[427]

The lack of guardrails to quickly mitigate or restrain one or more parties could become a trigger for war under a variety of crises scenarios.

Trigger: Overzealous Actions by Proxy Mischief-Makers

Sometimes people down the chain of command, or even outside players like other governments, create chaotic situations that could provoke superpower showdowns. It's easy to imagine white-knuckle encounters over contested areas between great powers that get out of hand. For example, there is the possibility that proxies like North Korea could foment a showdown, which might quickly get out of hand, igniting a series of events that mushroom into a very serious problem or outright war that could draw in the superpowers.

There are a host of possible examples of proxies creating scenarios that incite superpower showdowns. Consider confrontations in the South China Sea between Western allies like the Philippines with the aggressive communist Chinese, or provocative actions by North Korea against Japan, such as launching missiles that strike that nation. These actions could spark a US-China confrontation. Then there are past examples of yet-to-be resolved incidents like the mystery over who blew up the Nord Stream II pipeline in 2022. The *Wall Street Journal* reported in 2024 that Ukrainian authorities were responsible for the incident, yet, in response to that report, Polish Prime Minister Donald Tusk said those responsible should "apologize and keep quiet." Why? So not to create yet another crisis that could trigger a great power confrontation.[428]

Trigger: Proxies Come to Blows and Bring in Their Sponsors

The world is once again morphing into a multipolar environment, whereby the key superpowers are building their benches with ties to partner countries or proxies. Many of the countries aligned with China, and a few with Russia, are tinderboxes with problems that could quickly become inflamed internally and with their neighbors. It wouldn't take too many of these proxy states to implode or launch conflicts with their neighbors before the great powers are drawn into the conflict(s) and then the circumstances of these operations trip over one another into a broader, global war.

A potential example of this trigger might be a war that pits Iran, Russia's proxy, against Israel, a strong US ally. Other countries where the superpowers could be drawn into the fight might be Ukraine in Eastern Europe, South America (Colombia), and African countries (Nigeria, Somalia, Ethiopia) where different groups are aligned with either Russia, China, or the United States.

Trigger: Unacceptable, Catastrophic Attack on Space or Cyberspace Infrastructure

Historically, America has enjoyed the security provided by broad oceans on either flank. However, technology is overcoming the security of those protective barriers, especially across the space and cyber domains. Clearly, China and other powers, like Russia, are rapidly closing the gap on those fronts. For example, China's space program is incredibly aggressive and includes antisatellite systems, its own network of communication satellites, intentions to station humans on the moon to exploit resources, and much more. Todd Harrison, a senior fellow at the American Enterprise Institute, said, "I would say China is well ahead of us there [in weaponizing space]. The United States has a lot at stake in space."[429]

Competition in the space and cyber domains is heating up, and our advantage is seriously waning. Benjamin Jensen, a senior fellow at the Center for Strategic and International Studies, opined, "War has used the space domain and the cyber domain for decades. It's a question of the way they're [China and others] used runs contrary to our vision of what warfare is as a society."[430]

Perhaps a non-kinetic, albeit crippling, attack on our space or cyber assets that shutters critical infrastructure could become a trigger for war.

Trigger: Rise of One Superpower (China) and the Fear
This Instills in the Other (US)

Harvard Professor Graham Allison, best known for his 1971 book on the Cuban missile crisis, *Essence of Decision*, doesn't consider a US-China war inevitable. However, he does set up the possibility of war in his 2017 book, *Destined for War: Can America and China Escape Thucydides' Trap?* In that book, Allison, a political scientist, proposes that a modern war might happen much like the war between the fifth-century BC ascendant Athens and ruling Sparta became "inevitable." Why? "When a rising power [like Athens] threatens to displace a ruling power [like Sparta], the resulting structural stress makes a violent clash the rule, not the exception," wrote Allison. Further, in his book he reviews sixteen other similar accounts, such as Portugal and Spain resorting to war over trade and empire, to illustrate his "inevitable" theory.[431]

Regarding the US-China front, Allison argues, "China continues amassing economic and political clout and an American-led global order appears less sustainable." Therefore, it becomes "frighteningly easy to develop scenarios in which American and Chinese soldiers are killing each other." He also notes that especially when mistrust and worldviews are so irreconcilable, it will not take much to push them into conflict. He asks:

> Could a collision between American and Chinese warships in the South China Sea, a drive toward national independence in Taiwan, jockeying between China and Japan over islands on which no one wants to live, instability in North Korea or even a spiraling economic dispute provide the spark to a war between China and the US that neither wants?[432]

Another perspective regarding this trigger is offered by Kevin Rudd, a former prime minister of Australia and a China scholar. Rudd outlined ten distinct plotlines—possible Taiwan war triggers—in his book, *The Avoidable War: The Dangers of a Catastrophic Conflict between the US and Xi Jinping's China.*

One of Rudd's ten plotlines that leads to war over Taiwan is what he labels as America's "Munich Moment," a flashback to 1938 when the Allies agreed with Nazi Germany and fascist Italy to allow German annexation of Czechoslovakia, which was discussed in chapter 5. In this scenario, Rudd argues the communist regime takes Taiwan by force and Washington fails to respond. Another is the US rushes its forces to the aid of Taiwan and loses the fight, which Rudd writes would "signal the end of the American century."[433]

Any of these events could become a trigger out of which war emerges.

In conclusion, the causes outlined in chapter 6 for a future world war and the triggers identified above may completely miss the mark regarding a possible World War III. However, like the analysts studying the geopolitical situations in the springs of 1914 and 1939, who failed to anticipate the triggers that finally brought the world to blows, similar situations perplex us today. We could be wrong, but there is no denying the possibility, given the panoply of causes and triggers, that war could quickly engulf the world stage once again.

What Kind of War Could It Be?

Some experts argue that the world's next global war will be very much like a full-blown civil conflict, even though it will encompass mostly cities. Others believe it will be a series of interconnected hotspots across the globe, like a near-boiling series of proxy clashes. Yet others see a full-scope, Armageddon-like battle, with all technologies playing out across the world's landscape and all domains engulfed in the fight to the death.

Consider a brief overview of those three kinds of war albeit fictional.

Mostly a Western, Urban Civil War

One view about the possible Third World War is that much of the West will implode into civil war, which results in the destruction of mostly global cities—especially across North America and Western Europe. David Betz, a professor with the Department of War Studies at King's College in London, argues there are "indicators showing that our current societal arrangements are failing at an accelerating rate," and that civil war appears to be our future.[434]

Professor Betz begins his essay, "The Future of War Is Civil War," by pointing out how wrong H. G. Wells (1866–1946), the world's greatest futurist, described the world of the year 2000. Specifically, Wells "got a few things right, a few things wrong," wrote Betz. Wells, according to

Betz, ran awry regarding technology, but his social predictions were pretty accurate, which feeds the thesis of Betz's essay about the coming widespread civil war.[435]

Wells' technological predictions "were so off the mark as to be a little humorous," wrote Betz. For example, "On the matter of aerial warfare he [Wells] opined that it would be dominated by balloons attacking each other with aerial rams and suggested it was quite possible that heavier-than-air flight could be perfected long before 2000 and possibly 'as early as 1950.'" Therefore, Betz puts the technological aside to "focus on what seem to me to be the more potent forces driving us toward a future of war which is civil war centred upon the destruction of 'global' cities through exploitation of their intrinsic instability."[436]

The "shape or character of the wars to come" is described by Betz as "a distinctive rural versus urban dimension; jarring societal splits along the fracture lines of multiculturalism; a 'hi-lo' mix of weapons featuring extensive innovative reuse of civil tech for military purpose, particularly attacks on infrastructure; and a 'shock of the old' reversion-mutation to savage tactics, notably the use of famine and destruction of shelter as tools of coercion."[437]

Unfortunately, according to Betz, the "reality is that society has already passed the tipping point after which prevention of the eruption of violent civil conflict is impossible." He explains that the coming civil war is "political war par excellence," and "all of what the armed forces are doing to prepare for 'war' is going to be irrelevant except as assets to be divided, violently, and flung at each other until all are destroyed or worn out by use as sophisticated maintenance regimes and integrated logistical systems fracture and fail."[438]

However, the problem with Betz's proposal is that civil war that includes only great cities isn't necessarily world war. Certainly, those conflicts will have a profound impact around the world, but they wouldn't necessarily rise to the level of the fighting seen in the twentieth century's two global wars.

A Series of Proxy Wars across the World

Another view about World War III is that it has already begun. Leo Glasgow wrote in his article, "World War III Has Already Begun": "The coming years will change the face of the earth: we need to wake up to the changes and mentally prepare for a time that puts to question our place in the world."[439]

However, according to Mr. Glasgow, a student at Cornell University, "It does not have to feel like there is a global conflict for there to be one." He argues that there are plenty of markers of war today. "The difference between this war and the previous ones is a shift to proxy wars fought by the global hegemony, like what we're seeing in Ukraine," he wrote. He states that, in lieu of traditional interstate war, most of the current conflict "is thrown onto the shoulders of the third-world" in the form of proxy wars—"echoes of the Cold War."[440]

The 2024 wars between Israel and Hamas and Ukraine and Russia illustrate this view. "Iran sends hundreds of ballistic missiles to Russia," writes Glasgow. "Many missiles fired at Ukraine come from North Korea. North Korea, earning billions from these missile sales, also works with Pakistan and Hamas." He then asks: "How can someone look at a full circle like that and deny the existence of a global conflict?"[441]

There are also the threats bouncing off the ionosphere. North Korean dictator Kim Jong Un threatens to "deal a deadly blow to thoroughly annihilate" his enemies (read "South Korea," "Japan," and "the US"). Russia's Putin is fond of threatening nuclear war, such as the time he reminded the world of his country's nuclear capabilities by shouting "Don't they get that?" Then there is China, America's primary enemy, which often employs subtle threats like stating that US-China relations impact the "destiny of mankind."[442]

An aspect of the proxy fight is the "hybrid" conflict as well. It is noteworthy that, in early 2024, a leaked German Ministry of Defense document stated: "The country's armed forces are gearing up for a 'hybrid' Russian attack in eastern Europe," a reminder of Putin's use of mercenaries and "hybrid" tactics—"little green men"—to take over Ukraine's Crimea in 2014.[443]

The leaked German material identified several alarming hybrid scenarios. One, according to the document titled "Alliance Defense 2025," anticipates the mobilization of two hundred thousand Russian troops used for a "spring offensive" in Ukraine, which coincides with "severe cyberattacks" against the Baltic states to seed discontent among Russian nationals in Estonia, Latvia, and Lithuania.[444]

Those events are followed by a large-scale military exercise inside Belarus and the simultaneous movement of mid-range missiles to Kaliningrad, the Russian enclave between Lithuania and Poland. Meanwhile, Russia launches a propaganda campaign warning NATO about Moscow's intention to take over the Suwalki Gap, a Polish-Lithuanian corridor between Belarus and Kaliningrad. Then Moscow's misinformation crusade announces alleged "border conflicts" or "riots with numerous deaths" to sow unrest in the Suwalki Gap area, all part of Putin's takeover plot.[445]

This scenario seems quite possible, given Putin's past actions in the Republic of Georgia and Ukraine. However, even though the German Defense Ministry did not deny the authenticity of the leaked document, a spokesman said, "I can tell you that considering different scenarios, even if they are extremely unlikely, are part of everyday military business, especially in training."[446]

Arguably, the frequency of "small" wars throughout history makes this hypothesis—global war by proxy conflicts—not really a new phenomenon. After all, events of the past demonstrate that small, proxy conflicts mark virtually every era of human life, ancient to present. Perhaps the issue is so poignant that we sense our present time is different because we are constantly bombarded by around-the-clock news reports about the latest crises.

A Full-Scope, All-Domain Fight to the Death or Surrender

Years ago, I served with the US Army in Europe during the Cold War. My job was both that of an operations officer (war planner) and infantry combat company commander, focusing on preparing to fight the Warsaw Pact (Soviets and their East European allies), should their forces attack across the international border separating what was then East and West Germany. Our plans were very detailed, and I knew every inch of my area of responsibility, the so-called General Defense Plan. Fortunately, the Soviets never attacked, and we were all spared the tragic consequences of war.

Today, we're preparing for another major war, perhaps this time simultaneously in Eastern Europe and the Western Pacific. The planning for those campaigns is maturing as we exercise our readiness, restock our arsenals, and assemble our all-domain, joint war plans. Unlike the fight we anticipated with the Warsaw Pact during the Cold War era, I believe a war in Europe and/or one in the Western Pacific will be very different than any we prepared to fight along the Iron Curtain.

Perhaps one of the best renditions of that anticipated conflict during the Cold War era came from the hand of British author Sir John Hackett in his bestselling 1978 novel, *The Third World War*. At the time, that novel satisfied the global itch for information over growing anxieties about the possibility of real conflict. Although Hackett's book was fiction, it realistically portrayed the expected fight, which began with overwhelming numbers of Soviet tanks pouring across the West German Fulda Gap in a race to the Rhine River and a quick victory.[447]

Hackett's novel was influential at the time because it gave a plausible vision of future war and provided the means for thinking through the problems of superpower conflict, according to Adam R. Seipp, a professor of history at Texas A&M. Further, wrote Dr. Seipp, the novel addressed the technical aspects of future armed conflict as well and provided the reader "the opportunity to consider and debate a wide range of issues related to superpower conflict."[448]

My goal with *Preparing for World War III* is much the same as outlined by Professor Seipp. To this point in the chapter, we have reviewed possible war causes, identified some possible conflict triggers, explained the necessity of conducting critical reflection on prior wars, and identified two alternative types of the future battle. Certainly, civil and hybrid fights, proxy wars fought across the world, are alternatives to a full-blown world struggle. However, the scenario of most interest to readers is likely the broader, all-encompassing superpower-on-superpower combat using the latest technologies and happening over much of the globe in all domains. That fight is sketched below.

I begin by making several assumptions about that future contest. First, the Third World War will involve operations across all domains. Second, it will involve the total resources of the involved nation-states and be fought with a clear victory that leads to one of the parties tendering their surrender. Third, the conflict happens after a series of crises, and by the year 2030. Finally, the world at the time of this struggle will be polarized: On one side is much of the West aligned with the United States, and the balance is aligned with communist China. Any changes to these assumptions will obviously alter the conduct of the war as well as the possible outcomes and consequences for all parties.

Each of the triggers outlined earlier in this chapter could spark the future global war, including massed military forces near the enemy's borders, much like seen by Russia on Ukraine's border in 2021–2022; unacceptable demands by adversaries; renewed insurgencies; destruction of satellites; cyberattacks on critical infrastructure; assassination of key leaders; and others. Likely, one or more of these sparks will light up the skies, and fear will rapidly spread around the world, which will drive tough political decisions to be made in most national capitals. Then, of course, as caution is thrown to the wind, hostilities quickly get out of control.

Certainly, as tensions build, foreign-policy ties are quickly severed, and incidents previously managed diplomatically may become full-blown catastrophes. Meanwhile, allies on both sides use their diplomatic and military might to prepare for the possibility of hostile action. In the case of alliances, key leaders will huddle in emergency executive sessions and even order their multinational forces into positions poised for attack and/or defense.

Economies start to reflect the growing anxiety associated with imminent hostile action. At the first hint of conflict, world markets dive into chaos, and investors panic by resorting to sell-off actions or moving assets to more secure locations. As a result, market value and currencies trend sharply downward.

The prospect of war seriously disrupts international commerce. Existing trade agreements collapse, and sanctions against the threatening countries are quickly assembled. Global supply chains dry up as countries and alliances look inward to sustain themselves during troubled times. Meanwhile, as commerce dries up, nations face critical supply disruptions that hinder providing essential goods and services to sustain anxious populations.

The intricately connected global economy faces a true catastrophe. Quickly, almost all consumers—from governments to individual citizens— begin to realize just how far-reaching war can be for a global economy. Unrest settles on every community as the masses gather around their televisions for updates about the brewing crisis.

It is unlikely that China will allow the US and its allies to fully mobilize to then launch a first strike, no matter the trigger that might bring our nations to blows. However, it's also improbable that Beijing will launch a preemptive strike like Japan's Pearl Harbor attack in 1941. Rather, like the triggers above, a series of crises will occur, then a last straw provokes the sides to come to blows. That trigger could be any of those identified earlier, or even the US' surging of aircraft carrier groups in the Western Pacific, moving fighter squadrons to Japan and South Korea, or relocating batteries of hypersonic missiles to the Philippines. Then, the communist Chinese must decide whether to push forward or back down.

Let's assume Beijing's decision is to go to war. Quickly, both kinetic and non-kinetic actions are put into motion, and soon the effects are felt, and follow-on responses aren't easily contained; global conflict becomes a reality.

Modern technologies define that conflict from the beginning moment of hostile action. The first "shots" in a very fast-paced environment will take place primarily in the information domain. Both the US/West and our alleged enemy, the communist Chinese regime, will target the United States' use of data for military advantage.

Therefore, the first hostile action will be massive cyber and/or electromagnetic pulse (EMP) attacks. The objective is to quickly "blind" the other side by knocking out communications equipment, the computers required to operate modern warplanes, and each country's electrical network, as well as by destroying satellites and undersea cables that carry data.

Not just military-related infrastructure will be attacked, however. Expect China to turn on its offensive cyber capabilities and electronic warfare to jam all communications, which means commercial entities such as cellphone networks, banks, gasoline stations, hospitals, and food distributors are all immediately impacted.

These activities throw societies into chaos, forcing nation-states to address domestic crises just as their enemies move to the next step of warfare.

The biggest military danger is unplanned escalation, which is tethered to secret government rules of engagement. Once command centers are totally or partially blinded, thanks to compromised cyber networks and disabled satellites, then the risk of unintended consequences becomes a serious problem. Political and military leaders manning underground command bunkers recalibrate their next move. Will they apply minimalist or maximalist responses? What is the guidance from their national command authorities? Shortly, they turn to AI aids for informed decision-making, and then pressure grows for them to act to stay ahead of the adversary.

Of course, those AI aids help offset enemy advantages and the limited available communications by pairing human beings and portable machines to buy back a qualitative balance. But the consequence of that mix puts much of the important decision-making into the grasp of machines, thus the outcomes become less predictable.

It's always possible that if either or both sides retain the ability to control their nuclear forces, then the first kinetic strike could be with nuclear weapons, which would dramatically escalate the conflict's magnitude and devastation. Such an unprovoked nuclear attack against the United States would likely be countered with a massive launch resulting in destruction on a significant scale. However, because of the immense devastation associated with a nuclear war, most nation-state actors may not launch such a phalanx, at least initially.

Rather, the first kinetic strikes will likely be from hypersonic missiles—supercharged projectiles that fly worldwide many times the speed of sound and carry either conventional or nuclear warheads. Some are low-flying and maneuverable, making them unpredictable and hard to intercept. They will target command-and-control centers, critical infrastructure, and strategic platforms.

The consequences of this series of kinetic events can be globally destructive. If not careful, we're quickly thrown back into the Stone Age, with no electronic communication, limited electricity, a water shortage, and limited medical aid. Generally, chaos reigns—even inside governments and their military commands.

Those initial attacks, both kinetic and non-kinetic, could be over in a matter of minutes. Then both sides will pause, albeit briefly, to reevaluate their next steps. Meanwhile, forces across the world will be alerted—ideally before most satellites are disabled or by established, condition-based protocols—to move to planned locations and await orders. Aircraft will be airborne, missiles put on the ready, warships deployed, ground forces assembled with uploaded munitions, and the US Joint Chiefs are relocated to secret bunkers around the National Capitol Region.

What follows will depend on orders issued from the national command authorities. No doubt, movements of forces could draw responses from our enemies, and we will respond accordingly. Whether the initial attacks are followed by others could take some time. However, a variety of factors will be considered, and the US president will have to decide the nature and timing of our response.

You get the thrust of what might follow the initial exchange of kinetic and non-kinetic fires. I don't intend to explore how each of our eleven unified combatant commands might respond, with their many units and combat platforms. However, each command has a host of operational/contingency joint plans and a wide variety of joint forces, and they will begin to ready them for execution and, as necessary, respond to possible damage from the initial strike(s).

What is certain in such an environment is that our guard is at the maximum level across all domains—everyone is figuratively leaning forward in their "foxholes." However, time is not on our side, thus we will move to the ready as soon as possible and strike upon receipt of orders.

How long might such a war last, and when will it end? It's highly unlikely we will see another scene like the one that ended World War II in the Pacific with the USS Eisenhower dropping anchor in Hong Kong's harbor and top Chinese generals and admirals surrendering their swords to American generals. Rather, it will end with one of the sides being beaten and still preparing for the next battle.

Of course, the best outcome is for America to be victorious, with the Chinese government and its allies capitulating like the imperial German government surrendered ending World War I. Evidence of that win would be the destruction of a significant portion of the PLA, severe economic hardships across China, the Chinese communist party losing its grip on that government, and chaos mounting across that country.

Alternatively, China could win and force the US to accommodate in a variety of ways that leave our armed forces severely damaged and our economy in ruins. It is anyone's guess how our federal and state governments would respond, and whether the Chinese communists would seek to occupy Washington.

Whether the above scenario matriculates into World War III is hard to predict. Certainly, we know from the past that a trigger event like the Japanese attack on Pearl Harbor pushed America into the Second World War. One of the many triggers outlined above could well result in a global clash, and then, Katie bar the door, all hell breaks loose and total war begins. Meanwhile, either as war continues or as it comes to a quick end, the consequences for our nations and the balance of civilization must be tallied.

Consequences of Modern Warfare

The consequences of a modern world war that harnesses the high-tech capabilities identified in the previous chapter could be devastating. Below we will consider some of the most egregious consequences that might result from a conflict like the one described above.

A global war under modern conditions has the potential to unleash an unparalleled level of suffering, death, and destruction. Certainly, the displacement of many millions, if not billions, of people who are then subjected to severe food threats, lack of shelter, and little medicine creates an unprecedented set of challenges. The flow of war refugees impacts bordering countries, not that different from what Eastern Europe experienced in the wake of the 2022 Ukraine war, but potentially on a far more massive scale.

As millions cross international borders and potentially seas in search of safety, welcoming countries are quickly overwhelmed. Inevitably, resources are severely strained as basic services fail to meet native citizens overwhelmed by refugee populations.

Lands upon which wars are fought soon lose agricultural production, which quickly leads to local and regional food shortages. In turn, hungry people seek nourishment, which results in riots or violence as desperation grows.

War generally means many—both combatants and innocent civilians—are killed and wounded on a massive scale. This surge in death and injuries quickly overwhelms healthcare services; hospitals are overflowing with the influx of patients requiring acute treatment. Meanwhile, as public services such as clean water and electricity diminish or stop, there is an increase in the spread of disease, exacerbating the humanitarian crisis.

A global war's humanitarian toll can be truly horrific, with untold millions left homeless, starving, and sick. That is a terrible price, but the devastation a modern war would bring to economies, diplomacy, technology, and agriculture would also alter our world in ways never seen before on a global scale.

Another effect of war is the tangible cost. For example, looking back at the past two world wars, the United States paid dearly in both treasure and blood. World War I cost the US $334 billion (14.1 percent of its GDP at the time), which was spent just fighting the enemy in Europe, albeit for only six months in the conflict.[449] The bill for World War II rose to $4.1 trillion (37.5 percent of the US' GDP). The difference between the wars was mostly because America spent just six months in the first war compared to four years in the second.[450]

The price paid in American blood was tremendous as well. World War I, although brief for the US, claimed 116,516 American service member lives and wounded another 204,002. World War II was more costly; 405,399 were killed and another 670,846 were wounded.[451]

Fortunately for America, the previous two world wars were fought on other lands. If the next conflict touches our homeland, the expense in civilian lives and destroyed infrastructure could be astronomical. After all, consider the costs to rebuild after the Second War, then extrapolate that to America today. What might that price be?

Sixty million people, mostly civilians, died in the Second World War. At the conclusion of the conflict, many millions did not have a home or a country. Those displaced persons became refugees, often unwelcome in other countries.

Many of the world's wealthiest cities were reduced to rubble in the war. Most European industrial countries came out of the conflict with their resources, agriculture, and manufacturing largely destroyed. Then came the abnormally frigid winter of 1945–1946 to Europe, which exacted yet another toll on those populations.

The price of helping Europe recover from that war is difficult to calculate. However, America helped with its Marshall Plan, officially known as the European Recovery Program, an aid program aimed at revitalizing the economies of European nations. Yet, the $13 billion in economic aid to sixteen European nations was a drop in the bucket of the overall costs and needs for recovery. Those funds went to helping rebuild infrastructure, modernize industry, and support agricultural development. It took numerous decades to recover.

How much of our treasure and blood will be spent on a Third World War, especially if all or a portion of it is fought here on the American homeland? That's why we need to decide if that investment is worth the risk and, if not, then we must sue for peace: Prevent the war in the first instance. Of course, much depends on whether we're given the option, because the next war could be provoked with a first strike on our homeland, and, like the Japanese attack on Pearl Harbor, we must respond to remain a free nation.

Conclusion

This chapter identifies some triggers that might trip the world into the next global conflict. Here, I proposed three scenarios that might characterize the next war, including the worst, a truly global conflagration across all domains pitting nearly equal superpower belligerents backed by a host of allies. I provide assumptions about that massive battle and offer insights into how it might be executed. We end that description with a review of the possible costs/consequences, citing the potential toll for humanity and our future—assuming there is anything left to salvage.

The next section of *Preparing for World War III* addresses how we might prepare for such a fight and, if possible, deter such a tragic situation that would likely transform all our lives.

Section IV

PREPARING FOR AND, IF POSSIBLE, DETERRING WORLD WAR III

It is an unfortunate fact that we can secure peace only by preparing for war.[452]

John F. Kennedy (1917–1963),
Thirty-fifth president of the United States

Section IV in two chapters considers how the US/West must prepare for the possibility of World War III. Alternatively, and to coincide with those preparations, much like during the Cold War era, we need significant efforts to deter that potential conflict from ever happening.

Chapter 9 addresses how the US and its allies must invest to prepare for the worst, a World War III. It requires a national commitment not just to finance an upgraded military, but to harden our infrastructure, maintain a robust economy, and steel the public for the possibility of real sacrifice, which comes if we stumble into a conflict.

Chapter 10 addresses a parallel effort to our war preparations. Specifically, we must invest just as much energy in deterring a future war as we expend preparing for conflict. That comes in many shapes and sizes. Certainly, having many allies that collaborate with our military demonstrates readiness—a significant aspect of meaningful deterrence. We must also create a military posture—via placement of our forces throughout various regions of the world—that deters any enemy from triggering a conflict in the first place. Fortunately, we can draw from the experiences and tools that successfully kept the US and the Soviets from stumbling into an intractable war from the midst of the Cold War and reconsider our deterrence failures prior to the Second War.

Chapter 9

NECESSARY STEPS TO PREPARE FOR WORLD WAR III

To be prepared for war is one of the most effective means of preserving peace.[453]

George Washington (1732–1797),
First president of the United States

This chapter addresses how the US and its allies must invest to prepare for global geopolitical failure, World War III. Those efforts
require a total commitment by government and the whole citizenry on all fronts because the risk is so great.

In three parts, this chapter identifies the actions necessary to prepare America for World War III. First, we must define and prioritize the
threats. Second, we must identify our military-readiness gaps and vulnerabilities thanks to those potential perils. Finally, we must chart a plan to
address those shortfalls so America is prepared should our deterrence fail
and global war happens.

What Security Threats Does America Face?

"The threats the United States faces are the most serious and most challenging the nation has encountered since 1945 and include the potential
for near-term major war," states the congressionally created 2024 Commission on the National Defense Strategy (CNDS). Therefore, our president
must constantly review those threats, weigh their risks for conflict, and
prioritize America's preparation efforts accordingly.[454]

The Government Accountability Office (GAO) provided some assistance on the matter when it polled four government agencies to identify
the top national security threats facing America. The agencies included
in the GAO's survey were the Department of Defense, Department of

State, Department of Homeland Security, and Office of the Director of National Intelligence.[455]

The top four threats facing America, according to the GAO report, are nation-state members of the authoritarian axis identified earlier in this book: China, Russia, Iran, and North Korea. Other than those four countries, the balance of the twenty-six threats facing America are generic antagonists and/or situations such as unstable governments, terrorism, new adversaries, information operations, and artificial intelligence that potentially risk our security, in part contributing to a future global war.[456]

The US president addresses the threats facing America beginning with the issuance of a National Security Strategy (NSS). That document prioritizes the federal government's efforts to mitigate those risks and uses it to justify the administration's security-related budget submitted to Congress.

The various federal agencies carefully study the president's NSS, especially the prioritization of effort, then translate assigned areas of responsibility into a department strategy that becomes the basis for their execution plans. For example, the Department of Defense reviews the president's guidance and then writes its National Defense Strategy (NDS), which echoes the president's guidance with more specificity, particularly for each military service by threat. Subsequently, that strategy is operationalized into execution plans by the Joint Staff and the various combatant commands and military services, which are then used to create a budget submitted to the Congress seeking funding to resource (man and equip) the delineated capabilities needed to address our many challenges.

Typically, Congress determines whether there is sufficient budget to appropriately address all requests from the agencies. Therefore, the president makes hard decisions to prioritize efforts, which means we accept risk by not fully funding some required efforts associated with certain vulnerabilities.

How much risk have we accepted? After studying the GAO's threat list and knowing some of our strategies and level of resourcing, I've concluded that we're accepting substantial risks, which exposes us to significant harm because some of the perils potentially endanger our existence and could contribute to a future global war. However, for illustration purposes, I will briefly summarize only the extent of the challenges posed by the four countries at the top of the GAO's list: China, Russia, North Korea, and Iran. Further, although the other twenty-two threats identified by the GAO pose significant dangers for the US, I'll spare you that analysis except to state that capabilities such as cyber, artificial intelligence, weapons of mass destruction, and counter-space systems are already part of the arsenals deployed by the four authoritarian regimes.

What is the nature of the overall peril posed by these threatening nation-states, from most to least threatening?

China: The People's Republic of China poses the most serious existential threat for the United States. In fact, the NDS declares China to be our "pacing challenge," and the CNDS goes even further by declaring that China is "outpacing the United States and has largely negated the U.S. military advantage in the Western Pacific through two decades of focused military investment."[457]

The GAO report comes to a similar conclusion, stating: "China is marshalling its diplomatic, economic, and military resources to facilitate its rise as a regional and global power." It continues, "This may challenge U.S. access to air, space, cyberspace, and maritime domains. China's use of cyberspace and electronic warfare could impact various U.S. systems and operations."[458]

Beijing is heavily investing in its national defense establishment. The CNDS report indicates that China almost matches total annual US defense spending, with $711 billion in 2023 alone, and that doesn't include a March 2024 increase in annual defense spending of 7.2 percent.[459]

Another report on China's military threat is the annual analysis published by the Pentagon, which is just as alarming. The 2023 edition of that account sent to the US Congress outlines the nature of the growing Chinese challenge. Specifically, the Pentagon report states the PRC is amassing national power to achieve "the great rejuvenation of the Chinese nation" by 2049, which is essentially the revision of the international order to favor China, an issue addressed earlier in this book. Some of the particulars of that "revision" are outlined below.[460]

China's industrial base is on a wartime footing. Specifically, it has caught up with the US in its ability to produce weapons at mass and scale. Today, it is the world's largest shipbuilder, "with a capacity roughly 240 times as large as the United States." Just in the three-year period ending in 2024, Beijing's defense industry "produced more than 400 modern fighter aircraft and 20 large warships, doubled the country's nuclear warhead inventory and more than doubled its inventory of ballistic and cruise missiles, and developed a new stealth bomber." In fact, Beijing now acquires weapons systems "at a pace five to six times as fast as the United States," which led Admiral John Aquilino, the former commander of the US Indo-Pacific Command, to describe Beijing's military expansion as "the most extensive and rapid buildup since World War II."[461]

China's armed forces, the People's Liberation Army, has become quite aggressive, especially in the Indo-Pacific region. For example, between 2021 and 2023, the US documented more than 180 instances of "PLA coercive and risky air intercepts against U.S. aircraft in the region. Over the same period, the PLA also conducted around 100 instances of coercive and risky operational behavior in the air domain against U.S. allies and partners."[462]

China also employs its maritime capabilities to harass its neighbors and foreign vessels like those of the US transiting the South China Sea, over which Beijing has laid a sovereign claim. Specifically, Beijing uses China's Maritime Militia (CMM), an armed reserve force of civilians that assists the People's Liberation Army Navy (PLAN) and the China Coast Guard (CCG) to "safeguard" maritime claims to include the conduct of surveillance, reconnaissance, and more. It is noteworthy that CMM vessels are often mixed in with Chinese commercial fishing vessels, suggesting ambitions to expand operations into new areas.[463]

China uses these same maritime assets to enforce its sovereign claims. For decades, China's offshore island campaigns have been quite aggressive and, beginning in the 1950s, included the 1974 seizure of the Paracel Islands from South Vietnam, the 1994 occupation of Mischief Reef in the Spratly Islands, and incidents near Iroquois Reef, which lies in the Philippines' exclusive economic zone (EEZ). More recently, Chinese naval vessels have endangered allied nations' ships across the vast South China Sea. For example, in February 2023, a Chinese Coast Guard vessel engaged in dangerous maneuvers against a Philippine coast guard vessel operating inside Manila's EEZ. During that encounter, the Chinese used a military-grade laser to bind Filipino crew members. Again, in August 2023, another Chinese Coast Guard ship employed a water cannon against a Philippine boat carrying supplies to troops aboard a warship Manila intentionally grounded on a shoal in the South China Sea.[464]

The Vietnamese have suffered at the hands of Chinese Coast Guard personnel as well. On September 29, 2024, Chinese vessels operating near the Paracel Islands boarded a Vietnamese fishing vessel with up to forty officers to attack the fishermen. "The beatings resulted in broken limbs, and even knocked the captain of the vessel, Nguyen Thanh Bien, unconscious," according to *VnExpress International*. Further, according to press reports, the Chinese boarders "ransacked the vessel."[465]

Duan Dang, a maritime security analyst, told *USNI News* that such incidents "and other actions by Beijing within the Vietnamese exclusive economic zone are not new, saying that 'China's aggressive tactics extend to regularly deploying survey vessels into Vietnamese waters, exerting undue pressure on Vietnam to halt its legitimate oil and gas projects within its own exclusive economic zone and continental shelf. Moreover, China often threatens and attacks Vietnamese fisherman.'"[466]

Of course, China labels any pushback for such incidents by the Philippine or Vietnamese governments as destabilizing to the region. For example, in September 2024, American and Filipino officials agreed to keep a US midrange missile system in northern Philippines indefinitely to boost deterrence against China. Predictably, the Chinese conveyed their alarm to the Manila government, "warning that the deployment of the missile system could destabilize the region."[467]

Philippine Defense Secretary Gilberto Teodoro Jr. rejected China's demands regarding the American missile system, indicating that Beijing was interfering in Manila's internal affairs. Then Teodoro complained, "Before they start talking, why don't they lead by example? Destroy their nuclear arsenal, remove all their ballistic missile capabilities, get out of the West Philippines Sea and get out of Mischief Reef." Teodoro continued, "I mean, don't throw stones when you live in a glass house."[468]

China's protests against any threat and its own provocations are a reflection not just of the communist giant's policy of intimidation across the region, but also of the fact that the PLA has the capabilities of an emergent world power, thanks to its significant investment in other capabilities, such as its nuclear, space, and counterspace forces. Specifically, the PLA is strengthening its "strategic deterrent" by a concerted effort "to accelerate its modernization, diversification and expansion of its nuclear forces, as well as the development of its cyberspace, space, and counterspace capabilities."[469]

China's capabilities in space are especially worrisome. Beijing is our most powerful adversary in that domain, with almost five hundred intelligence, surveillance, and reconnaissance satellites, and many are dual-purpose. Half were added in 2023 alone. By comparison, the US has around three hundred dedicated military or intelligence satellites.[470]

The PLA has a rapidly expanding offensive space weapon capability that began in 2007 with a demonstration of its anti-satellite system. Today, China can destroy, capture, or move off-orbit our satellites using ground-based weapons—likely lasers—meant to decommission US satellites out to twenty-two thousand miles above Earth, which is something the PLA could use to seriously degrade any future US military operation. Further, China has a military space plane. Specifically, the PLA launched its first Shenlong reusable space plane in late 2023, which is used for top-secret military missions such as preparing to capture, move, or disable adversary satellites. Then, as introduced earlier in this book, China tested its Fractional Orbital Bombardment System, which could deliver a nuclear warhead from space.[471,472]

Perhaps most worrisome is the PRC's deepening relationship with Russia. After all, the PRC views its "no limits" partnership with Russia, a product of public statements by both Putin and Xi, "as integral to advancing the PRC's development and emergence as a great power." This relationship is evidenced by the quid pro quo situation associated with Russia's ongoing war with Ukraine. China buys cheap Russian energy, and in turn sells Moscow sophisticated weapons components like microchips that help Russia's war effort in Ukraine.[473]

China and Russia, along with their growing cadre of allies and foreign partners, also hone their combat skills by conducting joint military exercises such as "Ocean-24," a September 2024 maritime exercise that spanned the Pacific and Arctic Oceans and the Mediterranean, Caspian, and Baltic Seas, and involved more than four hundred warships, submarines, and support vessels; ninety thousand troops; and more than 120 aircraft. President Putin said that war game was the largest of its kind in more than three decades; it involved fifteen countries.[474]

Also, quite distressing is the Chinese Communist Party's geopolitical calls to prepare for "an increasingly turbulent international climate." The context for that statement is an enlarged global role for Beijing, which is backed up by the PLA's policy of counter-intervention that targets US presence in especially the Indo-Pacific region. A key aspect of that effort is the PLA's 2027 commitment to modernize its capacity to credibly bring about the forced unification of Taiwan.[475]

The Chinese have the tools to exploit many of the situations outlined in the GAO's threat list and beyond. Specifically, the PRC is investing heavily in the development of capabilities like artificial intelligence to ensure the PLA can "fight and win wars" against a "strong enemy [read "the US"]." Of course, that includes the rapid growth of its operational nuclear arsenal to more than one thousand warheads by 2030; the development of conventionally armed intercontinental ballistic missiles to threaten our homeland; and their explosive military space and cyberspace programs.[476]

The threat from the PLA is serious. Consider that in February 2024, US Strategic Command Commander General Anthony Cotton elaborated on that threat when he testified before Congress that China "has approximately 1,000 medium and intermediate-range dual-capable conventional or nuclear ballistic missiles capable of inflicting significant damage to U.S., Allied, or partner forces and homelands in the Indo-Pacific."[477]

China's growing arsenal is what Jeffrey Lewis, a missile expert at the Middlebury Institute of International Studies in California, explained is creating a new era. "We're entering an age where the United States and China are engulfed in what feels like an arms race."[478]

It is undeniable that the PRC's investments in the PLA mean it intends to become a global threat to US forces and American interests, especially in the Indo-Pacific region. Also, we should not doubt its intentions, much less Beijing's will to use its emergent and sophisticated phalanx of all-domain military capabilities to perhaps start a global war.

Russia: The GAO report states that "Russia is increasing its capability to challenge the United States across multiple warfare domains, including attempting to launch computer-based directed energy attacks against U.S. military assets. Russia is also increasing its military and political presence in key locations across the world."[479]

Of course, Russia's war of choice against neighbor Ukraine has drawn the most attention since attacking that country in February 2022. That war has become a wake-up call for NATO, which provides Ukraine the arms and aid needed for Kyiv to defend itself from incessant Russian attacks. That war has put all NATO member states on notice that, should Moscow succeed in Ukraine, it might follow up with efforts to further attack other European countries to reclaim areas such as the three Baltic states (Latvia, Estonia, and Lithuania), which were previously part of the former Soviet Union.

Perhaps the most alarming Russian threat against the US was President Putin's declaration that he is ready for nuclear war. He warned the West of that fact just ahead of his March 15–17, 2024, reelection victory that gave him another six-year term. Putin, in making that threat in a Russian state television interview, said, "From a military-technical point of view, we are, of course, ready." He then said Russia boasts a "more modern" nuclear arsenal than the balance of the world. However, he provided a caveat to that statement by cautioning that he does not mean the world is heading for nuclear war.[480]

Of course, Putin's preelection boasting wasn't the only time he threatened the West with his nuclear saber. In February 2024, he cautioned the West not to send its troops to Ukraine because such a move would risk starting a nuclear war. That warning came after French President Emmanuel Macron suggested NATO troops might be sent to aid Kyiv.[481]

Also in early 2024, a US lawmaker publicly said that US intelligence warned of a grave, albeit unspecified, security threat from Russia. A couple of days later, President Biden clarified the issue by stating Moscow was developing an anti-satellite space weapon. "What we found out," Biden said, "was there was a capacity to launch a system into space that could theoretically do something that was damaging. Hadn't happened yet." He continued, "And my expectation—my hope—was it will not."[482]

What became clear at the time was that the US, Russia, and China are all developing counterattack capabilities for the space domain, fueling fears of potential future space wars. Unfortunately, other countries like France are developing space-based counter-attack capabilities as well.[483] One particular concern is that either adversary, Russia or China, might set off a nuclear blast in space to cause satellite blackouts in specific regions, the EMP effect mentioned in the previous chapter of this book.

It is also noteworthy that the team of Russia and China is aggressively building capabilities to exploit the Arctic. The region's melting sea ice presents great opportunity for Russia's Arctic coastline because of its commercialization as a shipping route, which provides short travel between Asia and Europe. Of course, the region also offers a host of raw materials such as minerals and energy, which is not lost on either Russia or China.[484]

Although China is not an Arctic nation, it has teamed with Russia by providing a host of polar satellites, unmanned underwater vehicles for mapping the sea bed, and three icebreakers to maintain shipping lanes. These capabilities grant Beijing the tools to help exploit the Arctic. Meanwhile, Russia and China are cooperating on building infrastructure and ice-class contained vessels for year-round Arctic operations.[485]

Meanwhile, Russia is growing its military's Arctic capabilities on the Barents Sea to protect access to the north Atlantic. On its east coast across from Alaska, Moscow maintains a strategic submarine force near Vladivostok. Together, Russia and China's growing footprint in the Arctic threatens the US' sparse communications and data infrastructure, which makes the US/West especially vulnerable to Russia's nuclear threat.[486]

On the conventional front, Moscow has turned a significant portion of its industrial base back into the business of manufacturing weapons and munitions to fuel the war in Ukraine. Further, the threatening rhetoric coming from the Kremlin has many NATO members convinced that if Putin ultimately defeats the Ukrainians, he will in a few years continue his march first into the Baltic states and then deeper into Western Europe. If that happens, then it becomes a US issue, because we are party to NATO; any member that is the victim of an armed attack, such as by Russia, can invoke NATO's Article Five, which obligates all alliance members, including the US, to assist the ally attacked. Arguably, that would perhaps become the beginning of World War III.

Of course, Russia has other capabilities that have threatened or can threaten US interests at home or elsewhere, including information operations, artificial intelligence, biotechnology, hypersonic weapons, missiles, aircraft, a sophisticated navy equipped with numerous undersea weapons, a mature cyber capacity, and more.

We also know Moscow is serious about further developing these capabilities, because it heavily invests in its security sector. For example, in 2024, Russia devoted 29 percent of its federal budget to national defense to reconstitute its military and economy after its failed initial invasion of Ukraine in 2022. By comparison, in 2024, the US spent 3 percent of its

GDP on defense. Meanwhile, the Kremlin is known to possess considerable capabilities, which are being stockpiled to eventually satisfy President Putin's ambition to return his nation to the global leadership role it held during the Cold War.[487]

Even though Russia today is a shadow of its former self, it maintains many of the residual competencies outlined above and, as a result, can threaten the US homeland and our interests around the world on many fronts. Some could provoke a global war, especially if Moscow partners with the Chinese communist regime.

Iran: "Iran is expanding the size and capabilities of its military and intelligence forces, as well as developing technology that could be used to build ICBMs [intercontinental ballistic missiles] and cyberwarfare," according to the GAO report. Of course, another threat was recognized in 1984 when the Islamic Republic of Iran was designated by the US Department of State as the world's "foremost state sponsor of terrorism." Specifically, Tehran sponsors through military aid and training the Palestinian group Hamas, an acronym for its official name, *Harakat al-Muqawama al-Islamiya*, which attacked into southern Israel on October 7, 2023, triggering Israel's Gaza campaign to destroy the group.[488]

More broadly, Iran's armed forces is the largest in the Middle East, with 580,000 active-duty personnel and another 200,000 trained reservists including the Islamic Revolutionary Guard Corps (IRGC), according to the International Institute for Strategic Studies. The IRGC operates the Quds Force, an elite unit that trains and equips Tehran's proxies such as Hamas, Hezbollah in Lebanon, the Houthis in Yemen, and the Palestinian Islamic Jihad also in Gaza. The IRGC also controls all of Iran's ballistic missiles and naval forces that threaten Persian Gulf shipping.[489]

Iran's military strategy focuses on deterrence, with an emphasis on developing precision and long-range missiles, drones, and air defenses. In fact, Tehran has the largest arsenal of ballistic missiles and drones in the region. For example, it possesses cruise missiles, anti-ship missiles, and ballistic missiles that can range more than 1,200 miles—reaching all of the Middle East, including Israel, as demonstrated on April 13 and October 2, 2024, when missiles launched from Iranian territory landed inside Israel.[490]

Iran also produces drones that can travel up to 1,550 miles while evading radar to deliver kinetic weapons effects. Some of Tehran's large inventory of drones as well as ballistic missiles have been effectively employed by Russia against Ukraine and elsewhere.[491]

Iran also has a nuclear program that has advanced since the US withdrawal from the Joint Comprehensive Plan of Action (JCOPA) in 2018. It is widely believed the regime has a covert nuclear weapons operation. Because of that suspected program, JCPOA, Tehran is under United Nation's sanctions and is being monitored by the International Atomic Energy Agency (IAEA), the UN's watchdog that keeps track of nuclear enrichment facilities around the world. The IAEA reports on changes that might suggest Tehran is moving closer to having sufficient enriched uranium for a nuclear weapon. Other entities, especially the state of Israel, report that Iran does in fact have a secret nuclear weapons program. In 2018, Israeli Prime Minister Benjamin Netanyahu unveiled what he claimed was a "half ton" of Iranian nuclear documents taken from a Tehran facility, proof the Islamic nation has a nuclear weapons program.[492]

Given the above facts and suspicions, Iran poses a multifaceted threat for the entire region based on the high probability it could eventually modify any number of its ballistic missiles to deliver a nuclear warhead. Further, some of the regime's sponsored terrorist groups have frequently targeted US military personnel throughout the Mideast places in such as Iraq, Syria, and Jordan. Also, part of Iran's terrorist efforts includes launching cyberattacks against US entities and interests around the world.

More generally, Iran poses an economic threat against US interests. Multiple times over the past half century, Tehran has nearly closed or threatened to close the Strait of Hormuz, the waterway between the Persian Gulf and the Gulf of Oman, using its fleet of IRGC-operated speedboats and small submarines. Stopping energy-carrying tanker ships from transiting the strait becomes a global economic issue, because annually one-third of the world's liquefied natural gas and almost 25 percent of total global oil consumption pass through that waterway.

North Korea: North Korea has been a problem for the US and its neighbors, South Korea and Japan, since 1950, beginning with the Korean War (1950–1953). On June 25, 1950, North Korean troops attacked across the 38th parallel into South Korea. At that time, the United Nations Security Council denounced the attack and recommended that member countries repel the North Koreans. Twenty-one countries, including the US, which provided 90 percent of the military personnel for that effort, rushed their militaries to aid South Korea and eventually pushed the North and its Chinese ally back across the 38th parallel.

Active combat ended on July 27, 1953, with the signing of the Korean Armistice Agreement and the creation of the Korean demilitarization zone (DMZ) along the 38th parallel. However, the armistice only froze the conflict, and today the North Korean government occasionally violates the peace using provocative actions and words against South Korea, our treaty ally. The threat remains serious, because the communist regime maintains its 1.2-million-man armed force arrayed mostly along the DMZ. However, a large standing military isn't the only significant problem posed by the communist state.

For decades, the North Koreans have kept up the threat to South Korea and its allies by perfecting its ballistic missile program and nascent nuclear weapons arsenal, which includes an estimated thirty or more nuclear warheads.[493] Meanwhile, the possibility that Pyongyang might take action on its aggressive rhetoric and launch a nuclear-tipped ballistic missile at the US has influenced Washington to build its Ground Based Midcourse Defense system armed with thirty interceptors at Fort Greely, Alaska, and fourteen interceptors at Vandenberg Air Force Base in California.

North Korea is a menace—especially for the US and the nations in Northeast Asia, South Korea, and Japan. Specifically, Pyongyang fields the fourth-largest armed forces in the world; hosts a nuclear-tipped ballistic missile program; has a variety of clandestine capabilities; and has a robust cyber enterprise that has in the past attacked US interests.

Finally, the July 2024 Commission on National Defense Strategy report indicates North Korean dictator Kim Jong Un has "raised military tensions with South Korea to an unprecedentedly high level and, in at least some analysts' view, has made a strategic decision to go to war."[494]

What Gaps and Vulnerabilities Must Be Addressed?

Americans deserve candid assessments of the costs of going to war. Our political leaders should measure the potential prices of the worst-case outcome of geopolitical failure, which is waging and losing a future war.

The West's relations have seriously deteriorated, particularly with China and Russia in recent years, ushering in yet another Cold War-like situation. Unfortunately, and unlike the West's Cold War (1948–1991) with the former Soviet Union, the new cold war is not guaranteed to remain cold. Further, during the original Cold War, virtually no one on either side knew that survival was even possible if events got out of hand. That is certainly true today, and perhaps is even worse.

In the first Cold War, both sides restrained themselves out of a healthy respect for the other's nuclear capabilities. That is not so clear today, however. It isn't certain that we've learned the lessons from the old Cold War and at the same time are appropriately preparing ourselves for the worst outcomes today, albeit while doing what's necessary to prevent our nation from crumbling peace into conflict.

In fact, I believe we're failing on both fronts. That is why we must assess our preparations for the worst outcome—a future global war that, in part, is fought on American soil, and one we could lose—as well as doing our level best to keep the peace.

Consider the current readiness of our armed forces to fight such a war and of our population and homeland to experience the effects of at least some of a future fight that takes place on American soil.

Are Our Armed Forces Prepared?

One of the chief purposes of the US government, according to our Constitution, is to protect this country from foreign threats, to wit, to declare war (Article I, Section 8, Clause 11). What isn't in doubt, as demonstrated in the first part of this chapter, is that America faces an array of significant threats, and some could quickly plunge us into another global war.

Unfortunately, years ago, because of the end of the Cold War (1991) and thanks to many competing domestic demands at the time for more budget authority, the US government—gradually at first and now for decades—cut back on defense investments. Yes, we continue to spend a lot of money for our national defense, but that isn't the criteria to consider here. Rather, put aside our overall defense spending as the measuring stick, which is often flawed and inefficient, to recognize that our security establishment remains ill-equipped and manned to address the number and level of significant threats facing us today.[495]

In 2023, the US military spent approximately $820.3 billion, or roughly 13.3 percent of the entire federal budget for that fiscal year. In March 2023, the Department of Defense (DoD) requested $842 billion for 2024—a 2.6 percent increase, which failed to keep up with the 3.4 percent inflation rate.

In April 2024, the Biden-Harris administration requested a DoD budget of $926.76 billion, which once again failed to keep up with inflation.[496] Secretary of Defense Lloyd Austin said that request will address three key priorities: defending the US, "taking care of our people, and succeeding through teamwork." However, that budget misses the mark by a wide margin if we are serious about preparing the US for a possible global war.[497]

Parenthetically, although I don't have space here to delve into all the reasons we spend so much on defense,[498] the problem is we don't have what we need to properly defend our country and our overseas interests. Why? Our pork-filled legislative process wastes billions of annual defense dollars; our all-volunteer force is incredibly expensive (even though our active-duty force end-strength has fallen 37 percent since 1980),[499] especially when compared to a conscripted-based force like in China and Russia; our weapons production systems are run by profit hungry capitalist companies, not by state-controlled entities; and our defense bureaucracy is often wasteful and generally inefficient.

Most telling about our current military shortfall across our national security establishment is our strategy that calls for fielding an armed forces only capable of fighting one regional war at a time, much less another global conflict. After all, years ago, especially during the Cold War, the US military was manned and equipped to fight two regional conflicts. Today, a one-regional-war-at-a-time strategy is totally naive and inadequate given the numerous and sophisticated threats on our plate, especially if we assume the real likelihood that three simultaneous regional engagements—Europe, Asia, and Mideast—will continue to grow over the next decade. Simply said, we don't have sufficient forces and equipment considering all the threats, which means we risk defeat on multiple fronts.

Therefore, to be sufficiently prepared to maintain our superpower status in a complex world that faces many threats, we must ready both our armed forces and the nation for World War III. That herculean effort involves filling the gaps in our military capabilities to realistically address many challenges, as well as to prepare all Americans mentally for conflict, and harden our infrastructure such as the electric grid, should that fight find its way to our homeland.

Filling the Gaps

America's primary global competitor is communist China. Should Beijing attack Taiwan, the situation could quickly escalate into a three-front global war and would involve the US on each front. Our armed forces would promptly be stretched and must accept substantial risk in many threat areas.

One of those fronts will be in Europe. Since Russia's 2022 invasion of Ukraine, the US has enjoyed the luxury of imposing significant costs on Moscow by supporting Kyiv. Our working assumption has been that we (the US/NATO) can sequence our deterrence of Russia through our proxy, Ukraine, while gradually turning our attention and posturing more forces to oppose the growing threat in the Indo-Pacific, i.e., China.

Unfortunately, the leadership among Russia's allies in China and Iran have a contrary plan. While Moscow is preparing for a long war in Ukraine that could come to involve the US directly, Tehran is dead set on keeping the Mideast in turmoil, and Beijing is ramping up its pressure in East Asia, especially against Taiwan. Thus, America could face serious challenges in three diverse geopolitical areas and will do so for the foreseeable future.

That reality brings into focus a major American shortfall: Our current armed forces are not designed, manned, and equipped to fight wars against two, much less three, major rivals simultaneously. Yet, the worst-case scenario today has the US and its allies fighting on three far-flung fronts, each in our enemies' own backyards, where they have numerous strategic advantages.

Years ago, the US had the capacity to fight on multiple fronts, and in World War II, we were blessed with the ability to outproduce our opponents, while those battles never touched our homeland. However, that's no longer the case. Today, we find that communist China has a much larger military than ours, and our homeland is at risk from a host of strategic weapons. Further, it isn't certain that we can avoid a war with Russia in Eastern Europe, and our forces in the Mideast are clearly in harm's way.

I call your attention to a comparison of military capabilities in appendix B. That contrast shows the inventory of military personnel, units, and hardware for the US, China, and Russia. It should be evident that the US has significant gaps, especially compared with the aggregate of China and Russia capabilities, which are likely to align against the US in a future conflict and get much worse as we fail to grow our budget as both our adversaries grow their investment.

Where Are Our Military Gaps?

In early 2024, the conservative Heritage Foundation published a comprehensive assessment of the US military's readiness. Specifically, that report states:

> The active component of the U.S. military is two-thirds the size it should be, operates equipment that is older than it should be, and is burdened by readiness levels that are more problematic than they should be. To the extent that progress has been made, it has been at the expense of both capacity and modernization.[500]

That assessment by military service and select capability areas is summarized below. Also, I strongly commend to the reader the part of Heritage's report that reviews the history and processes used by the Pentagon to build our force structure to address threats such as the Quadrennial Defense Reviews (QDRs) conducted in 1997, 2010, and 2014. As an aside, I participated in the 2010 and 2014 QDRs while serving as a Pentagon staff officer and agree with Heritage's statement that those reports were used "as justifications for executive branch policy preferences," rather than building the armed forces to address the growing host of contemporary threats.[501]

Below is Heritage's analysis of the capability of each of our military services.

The US must field an all-domain, sophisticated,
and properly postured armed forces to prepare for future war.
Pictured here is a Royal Australian Air Force F-35A joint strike fighter.

Photo by John Torcasio Unsplash[502]

- **US Army**: Heritage rates the US Army as "marginal," based on the fact that it has less "than two-thirds of the forces in its active component that it would need to handle more than one major regional conflict (MRC)." Although the Army is committed to modernizing its forces, "it will be a few years before they are ready for acquisition and fielding." Further, what's obvious is that "the Army is aging faster than it is modernizing." Heritage concludes that "the Army has a better sense of what it needs for war against a peer, but funding uncertainties could threaten the ability of the service to realize its goals."[503]

- **US Navy**: Heritage scores the US Navy as "weak" based on two criteria: technology and replacement. Specifically, our Navy is losing the technology war to our competitors, China and Russia, and we are failing to replace our aging fleet to keep up with our adversaries. Evidently, our naval fleet is too small for our global demands, and our shipyards are inadequate to support required, timely repairs. Our fleet is projected to man 280 ships by 2037, which is much lower than the four hundred required to meet operational demands. Therefore, our Navy is not able "to arrest and reverse the decline of its fleet as adversary forces grow in number and capability."[504]

- **US Air Force**: Our Air Force is "very weak," according to Heritage. Evidently, it can deploy only six hundred air-worthy fighter aircraft today, which is enough for one major conflict, but twice that number would be required for more than a single-theater war. Another factor to consider is the geographic disposition of our aircraft, especially regarding the ability to quickly relocate to a crisis area and replace combat losses. Further, our modernization program for F-35s, fifth-generation fighters, and KC-46 advanced refueling aircraft falls significantly short to offset other aircraft retirements. Also, to save dollars, our pilots currently earn too few flying hours to maintain their combat effectiveness. Finally, "there is not a fighter squadron in the Air Force that holds the readiness levels, competence, and confidence levels required to square off against a peer competitor, and readiness continues to spiral downward," states the Heritage report.[505]

- **US Marine Corps:** Unlike the other services, according to the Heritage report, our Marine Corps is "strong." It remains so for two reasons: "because the Corps' capacity is measured against a one-war requirement rather than the two-war requirement to which the other services are held and because the Corps has made extraordinary, sustained efforts to modernize, which improves capability, and enhance its readiness during the assessed year." However, funding appears to reduce the number of deployable Marine battalions, which is currently at 73 percent of the required level. The Corps is also "hampered by old equipment in some areas" but is making good progress with its aviation component and amphibious combat vehicle fleet.[506]

- **US Space Force:** Heritage rates the USSF as "marginal," because its "current visible capacity is not sufficient to support, fight, or weather a war with a peer competitor." However, it is making progress with the addition of the Ascent and Tetra-1 satellites, both offensive systems. Likely, although veiled by secrecy, it is developing other systems as well, but they may not become deployable before the next war. Further, the numbers and types of intelligence, surveillance, and reconnaissance (ISR) assets and global positioning, navigation, and timing (PNT) requirements for strategic-level activities are insufficient for current peace-time operations, much less for a three-theater global war. Finally, many of our ISR and PNT assets "have exceeded their designed life spans," and the Defense Department keeps deferring replacement systems.[507]

- **Nuclear Forces:** America's nuclear capability is rated "marginal." The Heritage report explains: "The status of U.S. nuclear weapons must be considered in the context of a threat environment that is significantly more dangerous than it was in previous years." Our nuclear forces now face multiple nuclear-armed enemy states. Further, that threat is made more challenging because the Biden administration cancelled or delayed various programs to upgrade our nuclear portfolio, which compromises those systems' reliability. "In fact," Heritage states, "nearly all components of the nuclear enterprise are at a tipping point with respect to replacement or modernization and have no margin left for delays in schedule—delays that appear to be occurring despite the best efforts of the enterprise."[508]

Overall, the Heritage report declares America's military readiness as "weak" for the reasons outlined above. That means our "force is at significant risk of being unable to meet the demands of a single major regional conflict while also attending to various presence and engagement activities [elsewhere]." Therefore, the evidence indicates our ill-equipped armed forces are unable to handle two, much less three, simultaneous MRCs such as in Europe, East Asia, and the Middle East.[509]

The Heritage report is mostly focused on our primary potential adversaries and the requirement to fight multiple geographically dispersed conflicts. It doesn't necessarily address some of the other threats identified by the GAO report, such as terrorism, pandemics, mass migration, and new adversaries. Evidently, in those areas we must be prepared to accept more risk.

Americans and Our Infrastructure Not Fit for War

World Wars I and II were fought overseas and not here on American soil, except for Japan's invasion of the Aleutian islands of Attu and Kiska.[510] Unfortunately, given modern technology, especially capabilities such as space and cyber weapons, it's highly likely our population and homeland will be directly affected by the next war. Therefore, we must prepare ourselves for that possibility.

The fact is America isn't ready for that possible conflict. Our population will require national unity, the mobilization of all our resources, and a willingness to sacrifice not seen in multiple generations. There is no evidence the will and resources are in place to address such a challenge.

Briefly consider a picture of our lack of preparedness.

We have already established that our armed forces are ill-prepared for a multi-regional, global war. Part of the problem is that, for decades, our defense-industrial base has underperformed. In recent years, thanks to the Russia-Ukraine war, our defense production has increased 10 percent to address the high consumption of military ammunition in a major conflict. However, even that elevated production rate is far less than might be required to sustain simultaneous combat operations across multiple regions in a future war. Further, it might take years to replenish our stocks and those of dependent allies to the pre-Ukraine levels.

In fact, waiting until shots are fired in anger is much too late to bring our defense-industrial base into the brewing crises. After all, emergency and draconian steps will become necessary to reroute key materials from our consumer-based economy, repurpose production facilities, revise prohibitive environmental regulations to address a national mobilization effort, and, not the least, shift the workforce to arms-related manufacturing.

Another challenge is finding the financial resources to fund the war. After all, in the previous world wars, the US outspent our adversaries. For example, in World War II, our national debt-to-GDP ratio almost doubled, from 61 percent of GDP to 113 percent. However, today, our debt far exceeds our GDP. Therefore, if we saw today a similar rate of expansion as realized in World War II, then we might expect the debt to swell to 200 percent of the GDP or higher. Evidently, according to the Congressional Budget Office, that debt load would risk catastrophic consequences for our economy and financial system, primarily because we wouldn't have the resources to simultaneously service the war and the national debt.[511]

Other war-related perils to our economy could in part be triggered by two adversaries, Iran and Russia. Likely, as explained earlier in this chapter, Tehran would seek to shutter the Hormuz Strait, pushing global oil and natural gas prices up while increasing inflationary pressures, thus accelerating our debt. Meanwhile, foreign countries like China that hold US debt could sell off those equities to drive up yields for US bonds, further straining our economic stability and spiking inflation. That combination of economic actions will almost immediately result in shortages across all sectors of our economy as supply lines dry up.[512]

I've already established that if we fall into a multi-region conflict, our armed forces are ill-prepared. One of the consequences of that fight, based on tabletop war gaming, could result in significant human costs, beginning with our combat losses. Then again, if our adversaries bring the fight to our homeland, either with conventional or nuclear capabilities, civilians would be included in the death toll and our infrastructure not already destroyed by cyber and EMP attacks might be even more gravely impacted, thus spreading the pain across the entire country.

Of course, most Americans cannot envision what such a world war would mean for them because they have never faced such hardship, much less the simultaneous loss of life and wealth, which is much too common for populations caught in armed conflicts, as demonstrated in section II of this book, "Lessons from the Historic Record of Two World Wars." It is true that a few of our older citizens may share some fleeting memories of past wars and the associated sacrifice. For example, even though we were victors in World War II, that outcome came at a great price in treasure and blood, which affected most citizens at the time. That situation was also true for the Cold War with the Soviets, which left its scars as well. After all, those of us who were alive during the Cold War might recall warnings from leaders like President Harry Truman, who spoke about the possible consequences of nuclear war with the Soviets. "We can look forward to destruction here," he said, "just as the other countries in the Second World War." Evidently, that frightening prospect kept both the US and the Soviets from allowing tensions to escalate to a nuclear holocaust.[513]

Unfortunately, we're at the same place once again. Recent war games held by American think tanks help us imagine the consequences of a Third World War. Most identify China as our primary adversary in that conflict, and the initial kinetic engagements in that war are bloody, especially in East Asia. For example, war games pitting the US and China, triggered by the Taiwan crisis, hosted by the Center for Strategic and International Studies, resulted in the swift loss of two US aircraft carriers, each carrying at least five thousand personnel. Those staggering losses in the early stages of that conflict might prompt calls for the Selective Service to require young Americans to be drafted into military service, which would create considerable domestic social unrest.[514]

In one war-game scenario hosted by the Center for a New American Security, the tabletop exercise ended with China detonating a nuclear weapon near Hawaii. Then, "before they knew it," Beijing escalated attacks to target critical American infrastructure, which shut off power in major American cities, obstructed most emergency services, and shuttered most communication systems.[515]

Thus, domestic chaos would ensue as power and water stopped flowing. Food would become scarce, and hospitals would cease to operate. The impact for our society would be almost immediate on a scale we have never realized in our history.

Therefore, our best hope, given these frightening scenarios, is to prepare for the worst while working overtime to prevent and deter such a war. However, as history demonstrates, the best efforts of humankind often fail, and war happens.

Preparing Our Military and Nation for the Unthinkable

On May 30, 1940, J. C. McManaway, a West Virginia lawyer who formerly served in World War I, delivered a Memorial Day speech entitled "America Must Prepare." He reflected on "our last two great wars," the Civil War (1861–1865) and the First World War (1914–1918). Specifically, he focused on our nation's failure to appropriately prepare for those earlier wars and called for America to ready itself to join World War II.

"In re-reading the history of the United States from 1850 to 1861," said McManaway, "it is almost incomprehensible that the people of the North refused to see the coming of this storm [the Civil War] and failed utterly to prepare for it." He continued, "Even after South Carolina had seceded [from the Union] in December 1860, and the Confederate Government was formed in February 1861 [in Richmond, Virginia], no steps were taken, and the Northern Press still treated the threats of secession—not as though they were a fact—but as thought they were an argument."[516]

America was also grossly unprepared to fight in World War I. "We used the inferior Enfield rifle [in the First War]," said McManaway, "because we had no factories to make [the more modern and capable] Springfield rifles, to equip our army. No American gun was fired in France. No American plane flew in France before the armistice. Our young men were not trained; our regular army had learned their profession only out of books. They had never seen a modern army. Their efficiency could only be tested by written examinations."[517]

That sobering history about our not being prepared for conflict was fortunately reversed by the time we joined the Second World War. However, as our history demonstrates, war doesn't necessarily give us a lot of advanced notice before the unthinkable happens. Therefore, we must take extra precautions to put in place sufficient deterrence, which is the topic of the next chapter. However, for now, consider some necessary steps to rebuild our armed forces and prepare our nation for the unthinkable.

Preparing Our Military

The previous part of this chapter outlined the Heritage Foundation's assessment of each of our armed services. The full report provides far more detail about each service's capabilities, especially given the anticipated threats. Addressing the evident gaps and vulnerabilities in our armed forces is a good place to begin here.

Our preparation to rebuild our forces begins with a strategy that recognizes the threats and puts in place the necessary requirements. Therefore, our new national security strategy (NSS) must, as a minimum, call for the ability to simultaneously conduct at least two major regional conflicts with additional resources to address an emergent third conflict. Further, that strategy must in some fashion address each of the threats identified by the GAO report. Those challenges must be clearly defined and assigned to our various federal departments.

Fortunately, on May 29, 2024, Senator Roger F. Wicker (R-MS), the ranking member of the Senate Armed Services Committee, released a plan, "21st Century Peace Through Strength: A Generational Investment in the U.S. Military," that calls for generational investment in our defense establishment. That plan argues that the US military requires a "generational" investment as well as reform. Senator Wicker's plan could be the blueprint to prepare the US armed forces for World War III, which must follow the publication of a new NSS that realistically calls for an appropriately sized modern armed force to address our numerous threats.[518]

Senator Wicker admits his plan is expensive. Therefore, he calls for an immediate increase in the defense budget, followed by growing our defense spending to 5 percent of our GDP in the coming years. By comparison, the US spent 3 percent of our GDP in fiscal year 2023 for defense.[519]

No doubt 5 percent of our GDP dedicated to defense spending is very expensive; it's about $1.25 trillion in 2024 funds before considering inflation. However, our alternative is either to spend what is necessary now, such as investing in a much more capable military and a right-sized defense industry to prepare for war, or accept the risk. Our hope is that those investments will help deter our adversaries, or, alternatively, we can defer the investments now to accept more risk and then fight a future war, albeit underprepared. Of course, the result of that conflict could become a strategic loss, which will inevitably end up being more expensive in terms of our treasure, blood, and future freedoms.

Part of rebuilding our military requires investment in our industrial base, which the Commission on National Defense Strategy report states "is unable to meet the equipment, technology, and munitions needs of the United States.... A protracted conflict, especially in multiple theaters, would require much greater capacity to produce, maintain, and replenish weapons and munitions."[520]

Senator Wicker's plan addresses those shortfalls with what he labels "Rebuilding the Arsenal of Democracy." Our industrial policies must change to keep pace with twenty-first century technological development. Presently, military development programs take much too long, and they're not very predictable. As Senator Wicker indicates, we need a healthy industrial base that rewards success.[521]

A critical part of modernizing our military is investing in effective research and development. We need fresh ideas and the application of the latest science and technology to improve combat performance. Further, given sufficient funds and substantive reforms, America will once again lead the world in this vital area.

We must also prepare our population and critical infrastructure for the coming war. Specifically, we must invest to harden our infrastructure against cyber and EMP attacks, the likely targets of our adversaries early in the conflict. Unless we prepare for the worst, our country could quickly fall into chaos when the electricity, water, and the Internet stop functioning.

A coming war will also seriously hinder our ability to feed our population, in part because almost all vehicles have electronics that will certainly be fried by EMP attacks and therefore won't be able to deliver food to local stores, even if somehow, they can acquire fuel. Besides, our form of exchange—mostly debit and charge card transactions—is likely to be jeopardized by the severing of satellite links between stores and banks. Therefore, the risks of social unrest—especially when the population lacks key services—and reduced access to food thanks to the lack of transportation will probably increase domestic tensions.

There is also the real possibility of kinetic attacks that could leave many American civilians dead and wounded. That will seed even further chaos, in part because we have become soft and are not accustomed to sacrifice—much less to suffering.

Preparing for battle is hard, expensive, and unpopular. Only the most disciplined societies take steps to prepare for the worst cases. Societies that refuse to prepare inevitably collapse and surrender to their foe.

Conclusion

Preparing for war, as George Washington said, is "the most effective means of preserving the peace." Unfortunately, as I have indicated above, America hasn't always prepared for war and, as a result, we've paid a high price.[522]

In this chapter, I outlined some of the most serious threats facing America today. Standing against those threats is our weakened, under-armed, and marginally manned military—plus a national population unaccustomed to sacrifice and a critical infrastructure that is especially vulnerable to cyber and EMP attacks. I concluded this chapter with a call to revamp our armed forces using the plan outlined by Senator Wicker and to harden both our national infrastructure as well as steel our collective backbones to withstand the sacrifices that could very well be required should we fall into a global war that brings the fight to the American homeland.

The next chapter outlines the importance of deterrence, which is closely related to preparation for war. Good deterrence often preserves peace.

Chapter 10

DETERRING
WORLD WAR III

The most fundamental paradox is that if we're never to use force, we must be prepared to use it and to use it successfully. We Americans don't want war and we don't start fights. We don't maintain a strong military force to conquer or coerce others. The purpose of our military is simple and straightforward: we want to prevent war.[523]

Ronald Reagan (1911–2004),
Thirtieth president of the United States

Earlier chapters identified the causes and triggers that ushered in the First and Second World Wars. However, what we haven't considered in any detail to this point are the actions taken by various nations to prevent crises from spinning out of control and resulting in armed conflict. That topic warrants attention, because deterring war deserves at least as much effort as preparing for one.

Our adversaries are equipping themselves with
the most sophisticated capabilities known to man.
Photo by Hermeus on Unsplash[524]

Deterrence comes in many shapes and sizes, and is easy to define: "the action or the fact of deterring people from doing something."[525] More specifically, the effort prevents an adversary from taking an unwanted action. Deterrence can be practiced, according to a RAND Corporation study on the concept, "by denying a potential aggressor pathways to conduct an attack successfully, through defensive measures that credibly deny a potential aggressor its objectives, or by threatening severe punishments if it does engage in aggression."[526]

Let me put the term into context. The Latin phrase, *Si vis pacem, para bellum*, which means, "If you want peace, prepare for war," is a concept attributed to the second-century Roman emperor Hadrian and used by modern American leaders like former President Ronald Reagan (quoted above), who at the time was referring to holding back the former Soviet Union. From that phrase comes the aphorism, "Peace through strength—or, failing that, peace through threat." That is the very essence of deterrence throughout history.

Numerous American leaders have expressed that view. On December 13, 1793, President George Washington called for deterrence when he made his fifth annual address to Congress: "If we desire to secure peace, one of the most powerful instruments of our rising prosperity, it must be known, that we are at all times ready for war."[527] Also, President Theodore Roosevelt, the twenty-sixth president of the United States, joined the US Army to participate in the Spanish-American War and helped form a new regiment known as the "Rough Riders." About the same time, Roosevelt invoked a now-famous deterrence message: "Speak softly, and carry a big stick," which he claimed was from a West African proverb.[528]

In 1900, Roosevelt, then governor of New York, first publicly used the phrase as the metaphorical means to hold state senators accountable. He clarified the expression:

If you simply speak softly the other man will bully you. If you leave your stick at home, you will find the other man did not. If you carry the stick only and forget to speak softly in nine cases out of ten, the other man will have a bigger stick.[529]

Therefore, leaders like Roosevelt and Washington understood that to prevent a potential aggressor from acting, we must demonstrate a willingness to have weapons and, if necessary, use them. Obviously, the most common national instrument of power is to field an armed force, which demonstrates deterrence through its size and readiness to fight. However, a host of national power levers other than our military, such as economic sanctions and diplomatic pressure, can be part of the dissuading tool kit. Unfortunately, the realm of effectively forestalling an enemy can be quite challenging, because selecting the best tools that discourage an aggressor from acting tends to be more of an art than science, which makes it a complicated concept to effectively employ.

Victor Davis Hansen, an American military historian and conservative commentator, perhaps explained the deterrence challenge best. "The problem with deterrence—apparently sometimes forgotten by our former presidents—is that it is not static, but a creature of the moment, captive to impression, and nursed on action, not talk," he wrote. "It must be maintained hourly and can erode or be lost with a single act of failed nerve, despite all the braggadocio of threatened measures. And, once gone, the remedies needed for its restoration are always more expensive, deadly— and controversial—than would have been its simple maintenance."[530]

There are many books solely dedicated to the deterrence concept. However, for the purposes of this book, I will briefly introduce the issue in three parts. I begin with a brief history of examples wherein deterrence failed to prevent past conflicts. Second, I introduce common tools to constrain adversary action, and finally, I recommend keys to effective deterrence planning with the intent of keeping the peace in a turbulent world.

Failed Deterrence

It is commonplace, especially among the political class, that, once the bullets begin flying and people die, fingers are inevitably pointed at those who allegedly failed to discourage the conflict. That happens with every war, because combat often results in great sacrifice, and someone must be held accountable—especially in the case of failure—to prevent conflict.

Consider evidence of the blame game thanks to past examples of failed deterrence.

The US blamed Japan for starting the war in the Pacific because Tokyo attacked the US fleet in Pearl Harbor on December 7, 1941. That was an unprovoked attack. However, we should ask whether the US and Japanese governments tried to do anything that might have stopped—deterred—the attack and eventual war before that fateful day.

In the early 1930s, Japan tried to solve its economic and demographic woes by invading Manchuria, China. Might Tokyo have been deterred from that invasion had other nations like the US provided economic aid to the Japanese? Once again, in early 1941, Tokyo and Washington negotiated for months prior to the Pearl Harbor attack. America, in those months prior to the conflict, tried to put a stop to Tokyo's expansionism using sanctions and embargoes. However, our economic penalties only angered the Japanese, and war became inevitable. Did deterrence fail with Tokyo because we used the wrong instruments?[531]

We should ask the same question about the Second World War in Europe. Earlier in this book, I discussed the impact of the Treaty of Versailles on the German people, which arguably completely humiliated and impoverished that population, making them ripe for the rise of the fascist Adolf Hitler. Once Hitler became chancellor in 1933, he gradually rebuilt Germany economically and militarily, and during that process, he severely tested the Allies. At first, the Führer's ambitions were met with appeasement, because the Allies wanted to avoid another war. However, giving into Hitler's demands only encouraged his aggression until he was strong enough to then launch the Wehrmacht into Poland on September 1, 1939. At that point, deterrence died, thanks to a strict diet of appeasement, and war once again engulfed Europe.

More recently, it seems as if Washington is blamed for military action across the globe, even when US military personnel aren't directly involved in the conflict. For example, Gerard Baker, a British writer and *Wall Street Journal* editor-at-large, blames President Joe Biden for failing to deter our enemies, which resulted in multiple serious foreign policy failures.[532]

Baker wrote:

In diplomacy, as in childrearing or teaching, to be effective, 'Don't,' [the word President Biden often used to deter/threaten our adversaries from acting] requires the expectation on the part of those being admonished that something bad will happen if they ignore the warning. That is the essence of deterrence, which had kept the U.S. and our allies largely safe for three quarters of a century.

He went on to explain that "most of the time our enemies [in the past] had good reason to believe that defying America involved a substantial risk—an existential risk in some cases."[533]

Certainly, under Joe Biden's leadership, deterrence often failed because his threat wasn't believable. Baker explained in his April 2024 article, "When Biden Says 'Don't,' America's Adversaries Do," that, under Biden:

So many lines have been crossed that the world is running out of red paint. His failure to deter can be measured in the terrifying number of historic geopolitical firsts recorded in the past three years: the first major ground war in Europe in nearly 80 years [Ukraine], the deadliest attack on Israel in its 75-year history [Hamas, October 7, 2023], the first time in its 45-year history that Iran's revolutionary regime has directly attacked [with missiles and drones] the Jewish state [April 13, 2024].[534]

Mr. Baker concluded, "If we continue to defer to rather than deter our adversaries, Beijing will surely respond [that is, attack Taiwan] like Iran, Russia, and terrorists worldwide when this president [Biden] says 'Don't.'"[535]

America must return to a regime of effective deterrence, perhaps something more akin to Teddy Roosevelt's aphorism, "Speak softly, and carry a big stick," which begins by taking inventory of tools that might dissuade our adversaries from aggression.

Tools Used to Create Deterrence

The 2022 NSS calls for an "integrated deterrence," which "represents a particular approach to the age-old problem of how to prevent various forms of state aggression using instruments of statecraft." That's why it is helpful to think of deterrence as a toolbox with many specialized instruments of statecraft available for the executive branch to collaboratively work with our foreign partners to prevent war.[536]

"Integrated deterrence" comes with cautions, according to RAND Corporation experts Michael J. Mazarr and Ivana Ke. First, we can go too far in the use of our military forces, "which has the effect of provocation rather than prevention." Second, deterrence is often very difficult to measure. Specifically, "It can be difficult to identify effects of specific actions on potential aggressor motivations or mindset."[537]

There are various types of deterrence, according to Mazarr and Ke, including "denial versus punishment, immediate versus general, and central versus extended." There are also factors that help us understand whether our deterrence applications work: aggressor's motivation, clarity, and defender's threats, and credibility of threats.[538]

Before addressing the planning of deterrence, it is important to identify in more detail the tools of statecraft that make up our toolbox.

Whole-of-government effort deterrence: Although the armed forces are often considered the chief instrument of deterrence, a better approach than Roosevelt's "big stick" is a whole-of-government effort that brings to bear all elements of national power, including diplomacy, economic investment, cybersecurity, trade, education, industrial capacity, technical innovation, civic engagement, and international cooperation.

That approach, akin to the concept of "integrated deterrence," requires, according to the 2022 NSS, "that other departments [other than the Department of Defense (DoD)] and agencies have the same priorities and the organizational culture and capacity to be full partners—and that DoD is effective in pursuing integration with those organizations." This strategy integrates deterrence across all domains, theaters, and the spectrum of conflict, and it especially seeks to recruit foreign allies and partners to the task. Further, it should tailor deterrence, because each situation is unique, and it should provide steps to reduce an "aggressor's perceived need to engage in aggression—and threats of consequences if it does so," according to RAND.[539]

Multi-war strategy deterrence: The previous chapter explained the necessity of embracing a multi-war strategy, especially given the number of serious threats facing America. Therefore, an aspect of an "integrated deterrence" in today's threat environment means we must have sufficient military capability for defending the homeland as well as maintaining deterrence against enemies in at least two regions, as well as forestall opportunistic aggression such as terrorism and cyberattacks. Of course, the president publishes that multi-region strategy, then Congress must fund the effort; otherwise, all is for nil.

Collaborative allies and partners' deterrence: The National Defense Strategy (NDS) outlines the deterrence roles the DoD must play. A "foundational" aspect of the department's strategy is the inclusion of allies and partners, as alluded to above. "Such cooperation requires moving beyond allies and partners providing access, basing, and overflight and toward demonstrating integrated and combined capability, interoperability in employing that capability, and the collective resolve to do so," states the NDS.[540] Further, the 2024 Commission on the National Defense Strategy (CNDS) states, "The unmatched U.S. network of allies and partners brightens the strategic environment considerably." However, CNDS calls for more effort to assist Taiwan, Japan, and partnerships in the Middle East.[541]

Robust defense industrial base (DIB) deterrence: Today, we have far too few people, companies, and financial investment in the production-capacity of arms and military platforms to meet the needs of our armed forces. That must radically change, which is a key deterrence instrument. Failure to restore the might of the nation's DIB erodes our credibility, undermines our support of allies and partners (especially in a crisis), and leaves our armed forces ill-equipped to fight and win a conflict.[542]

The DoD "has long failed to invest adequately in stocks of preferred munitions," states the 2024 CNDS. Therefore, according to a variety of war games with China, the US "would largely exhaust its munitions inventories in as few as three to four weeks, with some important munitions (e.g., anti-ship missiles) lasting only a few days. Once expended, replacing these munitions would take years."[543]

Unfortunately, our allies and partners aren't any better, and some are in worse shape. After all, many of them rely on the US DIB capacity, not on their domestic DIB. Consider that "no country in NATO," according to the CNDS, "has sufficient initial weapons stocks for warfighting or the industrial capacity to sustain largescale operations.... At the height of the fighting in Donbas [easternmost Ukrainian province], Russia was using more ammunition in two days than the entire British military has in stock."[544]

Economic and diplomatic measures that deter: During the first Trump administration, maximum, mostly nondefense pressure put on Iran discouraged the Islamic regime from hostile action, such as further inciting and supplying its terror proxies like Hamas. Also, in concert with European countries and the United Nations, those mostly economic and diplomatic sanctions helped pave the way to the Abraham Accords, a long-term peace and normalization effort among several Arab states and Israel.

Unfortunately, the Biden administration lifted or failed to enforce existing sanctions put in place by President Trump, such as those on Iranian oil exports, which turned into an economic bonanza for Tehran and allowed that regime to collect tens of billions of dollars each year thanks to the sale of energy to communist China. That money was in part used to fuel proxy terrorist groups and Tehran's own armed forces, especially the Quds Force, which employed those fresh funds to attack US interests across the region.

Further, President Biden's lifting of sanctions and reengagement with Iran regarding the regime's nuclear program, which Trump abandoned in 2018 (the Joint Comprehensive Plan of Action), encouraged Tehran's renewed terrorist threats and its nuclear program. Soon after lifting sanctions, Iran accelerated its uranium enrichment efforts and the UN watchdog, the International Atomic Energy Agency, reported more suspicious activities inside the regime's nuclear facilities regarding the possible weaponization of fissile fuel, inching the regime ever closer to the day it will have a nuclear-tipped ballistic missile to threaten the world.

Measuring deterrence effectiveness: Every toolbox should include instruments to measure success or failure. For example, an electrician uses a multimeter to confirm whether the power in the line has the appropriate current. Similarly, the deterrence practitioner must employ a feedback mechanism—a specialized tool—that registers whether his actions are having the desired effect.

The RAND study mentioned above identified a three-part, sixteen-factor measurement tool to report on deterrence effectiveness. That tool was derived from RAND's review of deterrence literature and informs the practitioner about the success or failure of his actions.[545]

That tool is summarized below.

First, "How intensely motivated is the aggressor?" The tool identifies factors such as the aggressor's "general level of dissatisfaction with status quo and determination to create a new strategic situation."

Second, "Is the defender clear and explicit regarding what it seeks to prevent and what actions it will take in response?" This question considers issues such as "precision in the type of aggression the defender seeks to prevent."

Finally, "Does the potential aggressor view the defender's threats as credible and intimidating?" This considers points such as the "actual and perceived strength of the local military capability to deny the presumed objectives of the aggression."

Obviously, this subjective tool isn't as precise as the electrician's multimeter. However, it does capture information across a variety of indicators as to whether the applied tools are in fact working.

In summary, "integrated deterrence" is dependent upon context and the application of tools. It is impossible to prescribe a one-size-fits-all approach because no two situations are identical. The best we can recommend is to consider all tools available to the federal government as candidates for application, while frequently reevaluating whether they are effectively dissuading the aggressor. After all, as Victor Davis Hansen said above, deterrence "is not static, but a creature of the moment…. It must be maintained hourly and can erode or be lost with a single act of failed nerve."[546]

Keys to Effective Deterrence Planning

America must take seriously the challenge to deter our adversaries. After all, we're faced with Russia threatening Europe, China pursuing territorial ambitions in the Indo-Pacific region, and countries like Iran and North Korea persistently issuing threats to our national interests. We need to do a better job of averting these threats as well as the other twenty-two identified by the GAO's survey outlined in the prior chapter.

As the RAND report indicates, the foundation for deterrence outcomes are the aggressor's motivations. We know that a weakly motivated aggressor is typically easy to stop. However, an intensely motivated and paranoid aggressor is nearly impossible to hold back. That's why we need to carefully analyze each threat and frequently reevaluate the application of our various deterrence tools, as Hansen recommends. This is especially important when considering crises that could quickly morph into broader, even global, conflicts.

The RAND study recommends five actions when planning deterrence. "The first step toward bolstering deterrence is to manage the motives of a potential aggressor," state the authors of the study. They continue, "Doing so often requires concessions, as well as steps to shape the surrounding geopolitical context to ease its concerns and also raise the political costs of aggression."[547]

RAND recommends actions when planning deterrence, mostly from a military perspective, because the Department of Defense was the sponsor of the original research. However, a whole-of-government deterrence strategy outlined in the NSS that accounts for all domains and levers of government is best.

Below I provide examples for each of RAND's five recommendations.

- **"Assess the motives of potential aggressors and ease security concerns."** Years ago, Russia's Vladimir Putin expressed concerns that Ukraine would become a member of NATO. At this writing, NATO and Ukraine have advanced Ukraine's path to alliance membership, which only encourages Putin to be more aggressive. Arguably, entertaining NATO membership for Ukraine and our significant, ongoing flow of aid to Kyiv doesn't relieve security concerns for Russia. The situation with China and Taiwan is quite different, however. China doesn't view Taiwan as a threat to its existence, but seeks to return Taiwan to Chinese control. Therefore, US support for Taiwan threatens Beijing only in that American aid to the island nation is retarding, at least for now, China's reunification intent. Although promises of American support to Taiwan may give Beijing pause, it doesn't ease security concerns for the communist Chinese. Thus, we're not effectively deterring Moscow and Beijing, because our efforts are not easing security concerns expressed by both regimes; as a result, we have the potential to trigger a hostile response.

- **"Work to create a context hostile to aggression."** In Europe, NATO constantly restates its commitment to Article V, a message to Putin that the alliance's intent is to aggressively respond to any attack on a member state. Meanwhile, in the Indo-Pacific, the US is bolstering the combat capabilities of many allies such as Japan, South Korea, and the Philippines; countries near China that amplify our deterrence across the region. Are we creating a situation through the posturing of our forces and work with allies that ultimately discourages Russian and Chinese aggression? Only time will tell.

- **"Seek clarity in what the United States pledges to deter and in its reaction to aggression."** The US and its allies need to publish their pledges promising to rush to defend both allies and partners if attacked. We should reinforce that message with annual multinational exercises, diplomatic conferences, and the forward placement of US military assets, especially strategic platforms like aircraft carriers, squadrons of jet fighters, and long-range ballistic missiles. Certainly, the US and allied responses to Russian and Chinese aggression in the air and at sea are important indicators of our published pledges to ward off aggression.

- **"Take specific steps that reinforce successful deterrence criteria."** The US and its partners should work on their DIB and push for more coproduction of key weapons and munitions. Meanwhile, the US and allies must demonstrate effective communications and crisis-management abilities across all domains. After all, our enemies are watching our every effort to spin up production of weapons and munitions and to enhance our interoperability through joint exercises with key foreign partners. Unfortunately, at least at the present, Russia and China discern that we're not prepared for global war because of our force size and lack of sufficient DIB. Meanwhile, both nations are rapidly expanding their DIB, which signals the possibility of future aggression, and they're ramping up joint exercises to improve military interoperability as well.

- **"Deploy or support capabilities that signal the seriousness of U.S. commitment."** Routinely rotating US forces into contested regions such as the South China Sea and in Eastern

Europe demonstrates US commitment and advances interoperability with key allies and partners. For example, the US and its allies routinely conduct freedom of navigation exercises throughout the South China Sea, an area claimed by communist China as sovereign territory. We also rotate US Army and Marine units into that region for joint exercises, and we do much the same in Eastern Europe, such as with Poland and the Baltic countries. Our maintenance of training facilities in Germany, such as the 7th Army Training Command at Grafenwöhr, is evidence of our commitment to defense. These actions all signal to our adversaries that we are serious about being prepared for war.

A whole-of-government approach to deterrence brings all elements—departments and agencies—into the necessary effort. Perhaps the National Security Council should assemble matrices using the above or a similar set of questions and responses to establish the tools to apply to the threats we're realizing across the world, thanks to our many antagonists.

Conclusion

America must refresh our "integrated deterrence" thinking regarding the contemporary strategic setting and our many threats. That includes the necessity to explore new deterrence frameworks that better fit those modern challenges. This is especially true given the number of adversaries, the rapid advancement in technology, and an explosive list of threats.

The next section of *Preparing for World War III* considers what citizens and local communities must do to prepare for the unthinkable.

Section V
PREPARING COMMUNITIES AND FAMILIES FOR THE UNIMAGINABLE

There are no secrets to success. It is the result of preparation, hard work, and learning from failure.[548]

Colin Powell (1937–2021),
American politician, statesman, diplomat, and US Army general

Our journey to this point has demonstrated that the state of the world is troubled, and the threat of a new global war is virtually certain—at least most people, according to surveys, believe that's the case. Therefore, in *Preparing for World War III* up to this point, we've explored past global wars to consider their causes and triggers, and reviewed the weapons and technologies of that future conflict. Then, in section IV, we outlined what we must do to prepare for that war as a nation and how, if possible, we should try to deter such a crisis. This section considers in two chapters how, as communities, families, and individuals, we ought to prepare if deterrence fails and war occurs—especially if it comes to our homeland.

Chapter 11 calls for all citizens to work together to help prevent (deter) global war, for example, by demanding specific action by political leaders to prepare the country, communities, and families for crisis. Aside from nation-state governments, what can we do at the state and local levels to be ready for such an outcome?

Chapter 12 goes to the heart of family preparations for times of crises. Ultimately, if the worst happens, the crisis can be about survival when all public services fail and the government cannot keep us safe. This is the time for neighborhoods to protect themselves and for families to hunker down to survive.

+ · · · + · · · + · · · + · · · + · · · + · · · + · · · + · · · + · · · + · · · +

Chapter 11

CIVILIANS IN COMBAT AND THE FUTURE FIGHT AT HOME

> Neither a wise nor a brave man lies down on the tracks of history
> to wait for the train of the future to run over him.[549]

> Dwight D. Eisenhower (1890–1969),
> Thirty-fourth president of the United States

This chapter considers the impact of past wars for noncombatants
and how changes on the future battlefield, thanks to technology,
might affect civilians. We also consider local and state government
efforts to prepare for war, particularly if the fighting comes to our shores,
which is an unfortunate possibility.

History of the Consequences for Civilians Caught in the Crossfire

President Eisenhower, who learned firsthand the lessons of war, warned us
to reflect on the past so to avoid being run over by "the train of the future."
That is especially important advice for noncombatants, civilians who, due
to no fault of their own, become victimized by war.[550]

This part of the chapter will dip into the history of war to help us
understand the stark realities of combat for civilians caught in the cross-
fire. I will first lead the reader through a historical survey on the topic and
then will suggest the impact the changing future battlefield might have for
noncombatants.

Civilians Caught in War, 1500–1789

Jeremy Black, a professor of history at the University of Exeter, United
Kingdom, wrote an article for *History Today*, "Civilians in Warfare." That
paper covers the period AD 1500–1789, and portrays how civilians have

always suffered in warfare, with no exceptions. Below are a few highlights from that survey.[551]

Early modern European governments focused on maintaining and supplying their armies. Also, at the time, among their civilian populations "was a greater willingness to accept both war and killing than we find in the west today," wrote Professor Black. He explained that "levels of violence could also be very high in daily life, while killing was accepted as necessary, both for civil society—as a punishment for crime, heresy and disorder—and in international relations."[552]

In that era, there was also a religion-based critique of just wars, which were related to fighting the nonbelievers, the infidels. After all, many Christians at the time relied on the Bible, especially the Old Testament, as justification for the use of violence, such as in the battles described in 1 and 2 Samuel and 1 and 2 Kings. The same can be said for Muslims, who turned to their scriptures like the Koran, to justify fighting Christians, whom they labeled infidels.[553]

Prior to the Reformation (early sixteenth century in Europe), Black wrote, "Warfare had been mainly a matter of dynastic conflict." However, wars soon evolved around two goals: the defeat of opposing armies and the destruction of "heretical civil societies." For example, "On March 1st, 1562, at Vassy [French: *Massacre de Wassy*], the Catholic Due [Duke] de Guise was involved in a dispute with a Huguenot [French Protestants who held to a reformed (Calvinist) tradition] congregation that led to the massacre of the latter." This was the first major event in the French Wars of Religion (1562–1598).[554]

The seventeenth and eighteenth centuries in Europe were marked by the increase in the size of standing armies, which led to a personnel and financial drain on those societies. Specifically, those countries levied heavy taxes and conscripted non-volunteer men to fill their militaries' ranks.[555]

Conscription was conducted in an arbitrary manner and drained civil society. For example, Britain filled its naval force by "impressments by the press-gang [conscription via intimidation and physical coercion]," and on the mainland, national armies often filled their ranks with criminals or would, like the Prussians, seize men after Sunday church services. Predictably, these harsh recruiting tactics resulted in very high desertion rates.[556]

The 1527 sacking of Rome, then part of the Papal States, garnered considerable attention throughout Europe. Evidently, the unpaid mercenary Imperial Army made up of mostly German Protestants and commanded by the Duke of Bourbon, who died at the time of the battle, was especially brutal. They stormed the lightly defended city, where they looted, killed, and held civilians for ransom.[557]

Soldier conduct was often cruel on civilians, especially when towns like Rome were stormed. It was common in the sixteenth and seventeenth centuries for troops to sack towns as an expression of anger and power. In fact, the Spanish Duke of Alba responded to the Dutch Revolt (1566–1648) by ordering the plundering of a town "as a warning to others to surrender when besieged."[558]

The Thirteen Years' War (1593–1606) between Austria and the Ottoman Turks (Muslims) was especially hard on the civilian population. That war saw the destruction of crops, which was meant to intimidate and weaken the opposing armies. Also, because of the war, and combined with epidemics and civilian refugees, the Hungarian plain was nearly depopulated.[559]

The Thirty Years' War (1618–1648) started as a religious conflict initiated by the Reformation within the Holy Roman Empire and fought in central Europe. It was a vicious fight notable for more than eight million casualties from battles as well as famine and an epidemic of typhus, which spread rapidly in areas torn apart by the violence.[560]

Occupying armies were also known for spreading disease. For example, the French and Austrian armies brought the plague to Italy in 1629. Venereal disease was spread by soldiers in the Italian Wars (1494–1559). Another disease-related tactic was to prevent civilians from fleeing besieged cities afflicted by plague, such as the Austrian siege of Mantua in 1630.[561]

Of course, all-male occupying forces contributed to the rate of illegitimate births as well, which in turn put pressure on a city's social welfare to cope with the growing bastard population.[562]

Often civilian militia became necessary when a country's regular army wasn't available to defend cities. These forces were prominent in civil wars. For example, in 1562, when the French Wars of Religion began:

Individual protestant parishes and colloquies [informal theological discussion groups] were set quotas of troops in an attempt to
mobilize Huguenot strength. Thus, the structure of the church was
to become the structure of the army [militia]. While the Huguenot nobility was responsible for the heavy cavalry, the churches
provided the infantry.[563]

Peasant and urban uprisings—guerrilla actions—were particularly
hard on civilians as well. The 1534 siege of the German city of Minister
was hosted by the Anabaptists (those who believed in baptism only for
people who confessed faith in Christ) and resulted in a high death toll
thanks to disease and starvation.[564]

By contrast with previous rebellions, the American Revolutionary War
(1763–1774) demonstrated unusual constraint with the American civilian
population because the British government and army wanted to restore
the colonies to royal rule. However, British raids on patriot-held towns
provoked civil outrage, such as the assault that destroyed Falmouth (now
Portland, Maine) on October 18, 1775.[565]

The British also came to understand that stationing a substantial
garrison in a colonial town encouraged further rebellion. Then again,
internally among the colonists, the tensions between the patriots and
crown loyalists often resulted in harsh treatment among the civilian
population.[566]

The conclusion from previous centuries of war is clear: Civilians inevitably pay a high price when conflicts roar into their communities.

Civilians in World War II

The civilian carnage was especially significant in World War II. Approximately sixty million to eighty-five million people, mostly civilians, were
killed during the Second War, the deadliest military conflict in history. It
is noteworthy that an additional nineteen million to twenty-eight million
deaths were attributed to war-associated famine and disease.[567]

Consider two diverse examples of the challenges civilians experienced
in World War II.

An article, "London at War," addressed the Second World War's effect
on life in London. Although London was never occupied by foreign troops,

it was bombed many times, which had a profound impact on the civilian population.[568]

Early stages of the Nazi blitz on London created widespread panic and chaos. As a result, thousands of Londoners fled the city and settled in the nearby Epping Forest or the Kentish Hopfield, "where they camped out under trees or in makeshift wooden huts." Further, "more than 10,000 ended up spending the war in the Chislehurst caves."[569]

Those "caves" are a network of intersecting man-made tunnels covering twenty-two miles in the London borough of Bromley. Beginning in September 1940, the caves acted as air-raid shelters and soon became an underground city with electric lighting, toilets, and washing facilities.[570]

Once the bombing started, the crisis of homelessness became acute. An estimated quarter million Londoners were rendered without homes during the first six weeks of saturation bombing, yet only seven thousand were ever officially rehoused by local authorities. That situation significantly undermined the population's will to keep resisting, and the divisive effects of the ongoing war contributed to the expanding black market and breakdown in labor relations as well.[571]

Obviously, Londoners who were the target of attacks suffered mightily, but on the other side of the world, civilians caught in another war zone also suffered—in some cases, at the hands of mostly Japanese service members.

For a description of the consequences of war for civilians in the Pacific arena, we turn to Matthew Hughes and Major General Matthew C. Horner, who wrote, "Where Soldiers Kill Civilians," a sobering account from World War II describing when American service members encountered Japanese resistance on Saipan, the second largest of the Pacific chain of Mariana Islands.[572]

The Americans landed on Saipan, June 15, 1944, to be opposed by Japanese fighters. They also met with the island's twenty-five thousand to thirty thousand civilians, who were Japanese and Korean settlers that became caught up in the fight until the ninth of July.[573]

The official report on the campaign stated:

[The] US had to deal with civilians, an 'unknown quantity' whose reactions to invasion "no one could predict." "At best, if they remained entirely passive, they would still present a problem utterly alien to our experience to date."[574]

Dorothy Richard, who wrote the American military's account of the administrative services at Saipan, said, "There was little of the civil affairs operation on Saipan of which the Americans could be proud." Evidently, the Americans made "no provision" for the erection of shelters for civilians, or "for their medical care."[575]

A Marine report about the US' military governance on Saipan stated there was a "natural difference of viewpoint between the forces trying to conquer or annihilate enemy personnel and destroy all property which might be used by the enemy and forces trying to conserve property which might be beneficial to the alien enemy civilian population."[576]

The US report also said:

Japanese soldiers killed their own people. Even without soldiers present, Japanese parents would kill their own children and their spouses, often cutting their throats; children would be bayoneted.[577]

Why? Evidently, Japanese authorities portrayed the US forces as brutal, and to "save" them from falling into the hands of the Americans, they "encouraged civilians to retreat with the battle; and they killed many civilians who refused to kill themselves."[578]

Alarmingly, according to the report:

Japanese soldiers had children in circles throw live grenades like balls. All of this was made easier by Japanese notions of honor relating to surrender that civilians as well as soldiers seem to have imbibed.[579]

All total, half of the civilians on the island died from a variety of causes.[580]

Civilians Affected by Twenty-first-century Ukraine War

Immediately on the heels of the start of the 2022 Russia-Ukraine war, the civilian population was seriously affected by the fighting. Vsevolod Konstantinov, a professor and head of the Department of General Psychology,

Penza State University, Penza, Russia, surveyed some of the refugees who fled the Ukrainian battlefields. His findings were published in the *Journal of Loss & Trauma*.[581]

"The Russian invasion of Ukraine has led to the world's largest refugee crisis in the 21st century," wrote Konstantinov. Specifically, more than 7.7 million Ukrainians fled the country for mostly eastern European destinations.[582]

Professor Konstantinov had the approval from the Commissioner for Human Rights to conduct an online survey about refugee well-being. A total of 238 Ukrainian refugees responded to the online survey, 63.4 percent female and 36.6 percent male. The other demographic information was typical of the region from which the refugees evacuated—Mariupol and elsewhere in the Donbas region.[583]

The Ukrainian respondents reported experiencing the following:[584]

- 67.6 % being under siege and artillery shelling
- 68.1% loss of property and housing
- 24.4% exacerbated health conditions, including chronic illness
- 64.3% job loss
- 12.6% death of loved ones/family members
- 61.8% (of respondents who lost property) higher incidents of alcohol use
- 91.7% deterioration of psycho-emotional status

Clearly, the toll paid by the Ukrainian civilians caught in the war zone was severe.

Historical Overview of Civilians Caught in War

David R. Meddings reviewed the impact of war for civilians for the journal *Medicine, Conflict and Survival*. Dr. Meddings, who works for the World Health Organization, claims in his article, "Civilians and War: A Review and Historical Overview of the Involvement of Non-combatant Populations in Conflict Situations," that between 35 and 65 percent of war-related deaths and injuries are civilians.[585]

Dr. Meddings identified the direct and indirect effects of armed violence on civilian populations caught in armed conflict zones. Specifically, based on information from the International Committee of the Red Cross (ICRC), armed conflicts "have by no means spared civilians and, in many instances, civilians have been directly targeted." ICRC data gathered since 1991 demonstrates that at least 35 percent of all victims of armed conflict are probable civilians, according to Meddings.[586]

An ICRC study considering the conflict in Cambodia found that the proportion of civilians injured in combat was 42 percent of the total, "and most often [victimization] was due to fragmenting munitions, such as the use of mortars to shell civilian inhabited areas."[587]

The indirect effects of armed violence on civilian populations are alarming as well. Dr. Meddling observed that "population displacement," like the situation with Ukrainian refugees, is always "associated with profound degradation in the health status of populations." The primary culprits of health crises are infectious disease and malnutrition.[588]

The same civilian populations suffer psychosocial effects thanks to living in a war zone, such as witnessing "armed threats, forcible confinement, mock executions and assassinations of prominent community figures."[589]

The report calls out the experience of women who suffered "either physical or sexual violence in a war zone." It states, "The use of sexual violence during periods of conflict has been examined from an anthropological perspective, and experience of physical and sexual violence has been found to be prevalent among women" in numerous studies.[590]

Children, especially unaccompanied youths, are another vulnerable group. They are subject to being recruited as combatants as well as to being separated from their families, which "diminishes children's ability to cope with situations of armed violence."[591]

Summary of Consequences for Civilians Affected by War

The above material identifies numerous consequences civilians suffered in past wars. A summary of those findings include:

Impact on Civilians Caught in War Zones

- Resources taken from the civilian population to maintain and supply armed forces
- Greater willingness of civilians to accept both war and killing
- Conscription drains civilian society of manpower

- Panic and chaos among civilians
- Civilians fleeing attacked cities for safe shelter
- Emergency shelters in short supply
- Black markets popping up in battleground areas
- Lack of public services resulting in austere conditions
- Medical care becoming scarce at best

Combatant Motivation Impacts Civilians

- War provides justification for violence against civilians.
- Faith of combatant may be used as justification to use violence against nonbeliever (so-called infidel) civilians.
- Some combatants take license to loot and abuse civilians.

Impact for Civilians Whose Communities Are Occupied by Combatants

- Often brutal treatment
- Destruction of civilian agricultural crops
- Potential for spread of diseases
- Possible increased rate of illegitimate births
- Joining militias and guerrilla groups to oppose occupying forces
- Civilian casualties often exceeding the rates among combatants
- Destruction of civilian property
- Enemy propaganda among civilian population possibly leading to noncombatants taking their own lives rather than being taken captive
- Denial of critical services

Civilian Losses and Health Harm in War Zone

- Civilians comprise at least 35 percent of all war-related deaths and injuries.
- Famine and disease often claim significant numbers of civilians.
- Physical and sexual violence are often perpetrated against civilian women.
- Civilians experience exacerbated health conditions:
  - o Chronic illness
  - o Substance abuse

o   Deterioration of psycho-emotional status
o   Profound degradation in health due to infectious diseases and malnutrition

The repercussions of war for civilians can be quite significant. However, modern technology may even worsen the situation for noncombatants caught in a future war.

Impact of Future Battlefield for Civilians

The consequences of World War III for civilians could be absolutely devastating.

I have already identified the technological revolution transforming our military and, by extension, the future war. Likely, the consequences of a high-tech war will not be completely understood until after the fact. However, below is an attempt to provide a perspective about the ramifications of that future war, which was described in the previous section of *Preparing for World War III* and could deliver a profound shock to our civilian population.

Generally, a global war will have several very significant consequences. It will shatter economies, produce massive humanitarian crises, and reshape the globe as we know it thanks to potential significant devastation, the possible realignment of nations, and shifts in geopolitical power.

Global war will also turn our intrinsically connected economies upside down, creating chaos in financial markets, disrupting most international trade, and threatening local market stability. Meanwhile, equity investors will see their holdings nosedive as shareholders panic and many sell and then move assets to safer havens. Also, as the markets tumble, currencies will wildly fluctuate. Nothing will be stable, and most banks will close their doors to account holders.

Global supply lines will also suffer severe disruption as trade agreements among adversaries collapse and sanctions are slapped on a host of nations. Critical food and medicine will stop flowing as demand skyrockets, as do prices, and shelves at local stores are quickly emptied.

The kinetic part of the future war begins with the adversaries using cutting-edge technologies across all domains, first severing cyber links and satellite connections to critical infrastructure and communications networks. There might even be a preemptive EMP attack that fries all electronics across a broad swath of countries.

The attacks on the nation's communication and infrastructure networks plunge power grids into darkness, water treatment plants fail to pump, public transportation is frozen in place, and all financial transactions are disabled because of computer and satellite failure.

One frightening possibility is the temptation to use nuclear weapons. After all, nuclear war, either limited or expansive, cannot be completely ruled out—an indication of a dramatic escalation that promises great devastation. Those weapons being in the hands of many nations today could immediately incinerate entire cities and regions. Of course, the long-term implications of nuclear war are sobering: cancer, genetic mutations, creation of radioactive areas, loss of massive swaths of real estate, and more.

Aside from the devastation of nuclear weapons, modern technologies have literally changed the battlefield and enlarged it to include areas that directly impact civilians. Drones and artificial intelligence platforms armed with sophisticated weapons that are deadly accurate target people and facilities, and many civilians will be killed and wounded.

The emergence of hypersonic missiles that travel many times the speed of sound, maneuver close to the earth, and deliver warheads with great precision are nearly impossible to defend against. They will in a flash devastate military and civilian targets, and noncombatants will become collateral damage.

The dominant military force may elect not to occupy the enemy country; rather, it might hold the enemy nation hostage with standoff weapons. However, if foreign forces do elect to occupy the homeland, expect the civilian population to suffer many of the same issues associated with past wars.

On a broader scale, throughout the areas impacted by the combat, expect the suffering and devastation to result in the displacement of millions of civilians. Those war refugees will seek safety, shelter, medical care, and food, quickly overwhelming any host nation's ability to support them. That could drive some countries into economic ruin as the infrastructure is overstressed and resources fail. Meanwhile, dire food shortages will become commonplace as warehouses of food are destroyed and transportation grinds to a halt. Soon food riots will crop up, and violence will become commonplace.

The savages of war and the crises thanks to dire food scarcity and domestic violence will all contribute to a global healthcare catastrophe. There just won't be enough space in hospitals, sufficient medicine, and enough care providers for those in need of treatment. Soon, the widespread lack of housing, clean water, and sanitation will lead to a surge in the spread of communicable diseases.

At some point, the attacks will stop and adjustments to a new reality will begin to set in. There will be little trust among nations, especially between the opposing sides in the war. Therefore, all forms of cooperation will suffer, which inevitably hinders our collective security, economies, and sharing of common domains like the seas, skies, and space.

There might also be distrust within the US between regions that have resources and areas that don't. This could prompt people to flow toward areas that have supplies. The destination regions will likely defend their resources, which could pit region against region and state against state—especially if, after the war, we don't have a strong central government to help solve the disputes.

The ongoing resentment and lack of trust will also make it more difficult to resolve future disagreements peacefully. That may well require nations to sustain large armed forces and intelligence services, therefore create a heavier long-term tax burden for the future citizen.

The above describes a dire global situation. Hopefully, we will never get to the point that another world war happens, especially one that is so widespread and that engulfs all domains. That being said, the next section outlines how local communities ought to prepare for the worst case: global war that enters our homeland.

Preparing for War's Consequences

States and local communities might not be able to influence national decisions to go to war. However, there are actions they must take to protect their citizens should the worst happen. Several of those preparations are outlined below.

Inform the population: One important action is to inform the population, much like the Swedish government began doing in World War II and recently started doing once again. In 2018, that government sent to all the country's households a public information leaflet advising the population what to do in the event of war. The twenty-page pamphlet, "If Crisis or War Comes," explains how citizens can "secure their basic needs such as food, water, and heat, what various warning signals mean, and how they can contribute to Sweden's 'total defence.'"[592]

The pamphlet includes illustrations of sirens, warplanes, and families fleeing their homes. It addresses dangers such as cyber and terror attacks, and features a page on how to identify fake news. The document states, "If you are prepared, you are contributing to improving the ability of the country to cope with a major strain."[593]

Such leaflets were first distributed in 1943 by then-neutral Sweden, which walked a tightrope in the Second World War. Subsequently, that government regularly issued public notices until the end of the Cold War (1991), and restarted the notification effort in 2018 as instability threatened once again.[594]

"Society is vulnerable, so we need to prepare ourselves as individuals," said Dan Eliasson, with Sweden's Civil Contingencies Agency. "There's also an information deficit in terms of concrete advice, which we aim to provide."[595]

The leaflet also provides a variety of information, such as how to cope if there is no heating, food, water, cash machines, or mobile phones. It warns about organizations trying to influence the masses through propaganda and outlines how to remain resilient. Finally, it explains that, in the event of armed conflict at home, "everyone is obliged to contribute and everyone is needed" for "total defence."[596]

The leaflet concludes that, if Sweden is attacked, "We will never give up. All information to the effect that resistance is to cease is false."[597]

Future war may well come to our homeland, requiring every able-bodied person to prepare themselves.
Photo by Piotr Wilk on Unsplash[598]

Certainly, educating the public with material like the Swedish publication is a great start. However, US local and state governments must carefully study the possible consequences of war such as those identified in the previous part of this chapter. Many of those challenges must be addressed well in advance of hostilities, while others can be put on the shelf and then placed into action as the situation occurs.

Consider some of the costs of war discussed in the previous parts of this chapter, which government ought to anticipate and address now. They are noted below with a brief explanation about the required action. The endnote with each recommendation is a great reference for further study. Also, I have elaborated on this issue in more detail in appendix C, "Preparing for World War III at Home."

Preparing people to deal with war: Various government agencies provide behavioral health resources that help folks prepare, respond, and recover from disasters. Of course, war is a significant long-term disaster that draws a variety of reactions. What is needed across the population facing war is resilience—the ability to bounce back, cope with adversity, and endure difficulties. Material and training are available for local government to use to help prepare the public for the disaster of war.[599]

Hardening public services against hackers: In 2024, US cybersecurity officials warned about state-sponsored malicious cyber actors affiliated with the People's Republic of China "that were compromising and maintaining persistent access to US critical infrastructure for future disruptive activities should a conflict with China arise." The US Environmental Protection Agency warns that cyberattacks can damage water structures like valves and pumps, interrupt how water is treated or stored, and increase chemical levels to dangerous amounts. Jen Easterly, director of the Cybersecurity and Infrastructure Agency, testified to Congress, "Unfortunately, the technology underpinning our critical infrastructure is inherently insecure because of decades of software developers not being held liable for defective technology."[600]

Hardening electronic systems against EMP attacks: EMPs are short bursts of electromagnetic energy caused by either a solar geomagnetic disturbance or a thermonuclear detonation in the atmosphere. That pulse can cause damage to electrical systems hundreds of miles away. Earlier, I explained that an adversary could ignite an atomic weapon above the US, creating an EMP effect that would fry most of the electronic systems below the blast. There are steps the government can take to protect our most sensitive electronics from an EMP burst, such as those details outlined in a 2019 document published by the National Coordinating Center for Communications entitled "Electromagnetic Pulse (EMP) Protection and Resilience Guidelines for Critical Infrastructure and Equipment."[601]

Building up stocks of emergency supplies: The federal government maintains the Strategic National Stockpile, a reserve of essential medical supplies. However, local governments may not have access to those supplies in an emergency and therefore ought to create their own reserves. After all, the federal government wasn't especially helpful during the COVID pandemic (2020–2022), and little has changed to suggest it will shift its support going forward.[602]

Planning how to deal with mass casualties: The federal government provides tool kits to help guide local and state jurisdictions as they develop a mass fatality plan, which also addresses infection/pandemics and other threats often associated with war.[603]

Arming citizens who are prepared to stand in the gap: The Swedish pamphlet introduced earlier calls for its citizens to "never give up." We've seen in history that when regular soldiers are not available to defend the city, then militia and minutemen such as during the American Revolutionary War were recruited from local civilians to stand in the gap. Of course, our National Guard, which reports to the state governor, represents that militia under most natural disaster circumstances. When even the National Guard is required to fight the nation's wars, other forces may become necessary. Although having armed auxiliary units might be opposed by some, it may become necessary to augment police and perhaps resist occupying foreign troops and/or marauding criminal gangs. Those militia-like units could be trained and armed by the police or National Guard, precluding the formation of local unorganized militia who would likely set their own rules and standards. State and local government ought to formally consider this alternative and put in place a mechanism for such local forces to enhance security requirements in times of war, especially if foreign forces occupy our land.[604]

The formation of "armed auxiliary units," whether independent of any government or hosted by state and local governments, must consider current and possible future laws.

First, there are no federal laws that address paramilitary activity. However, federal law (10 U.S. Code § 246) defines two classes of militia: the organized militia, known as the National Guard, and the unorganized militia who are not members of the National Guard.[605]

For purposes here, a "militia" is a fighting organization of nonprofessional or part-time soldiers who perform armed services during a time of need. When acting in lieu of government, militias tend to have limited capabilities, such as skirmishing, guarding fortifications, and conducting irregular operations. They often serve only in their local areas and as needed. Historically, they have served as a pool of available manpower in emergencies.

Second, Georgetown Law surveyed the fifty US states regarding constitutional provisions requiring the "subordination of the military [militia] to civil authorities." It found that forty-eight states do address the issue—for example, the state of Virginia's constitution declares: "In all cases the military [read militia] should be under strict subordination to, and governed by, the civil power." Therefore, private armies/militia that are not responsible to civil powers "may violate this constitutional command to the detriment of civil order."[606]

Third, in early 2024, US Senator Edward J. Markey (D-MA) and Congressman Jamie Raskin (D-MD) introduced legislation, "Preventing Private Paramilitary Activity Act," which would create a federal prohibition on paramilitary groups through civil and criminal enforcement. Both chambers of Congress must pass the bill before it becomes law. As of this writing, the bill has not passed either chamber.[607]

Capabilities in the Waiting

Consider consequences that ought to be planned for, funded, and then put on the shelf in the event they are required in war.

Reviewing FEMA's preparedness sheets: The Federal Emergency Management Agency provides significant material on its website to help citizens address various disasters and emergencies. Even though FEMA provides no information regarding war times, much of the material related to other types of disasters is quite helpful and should be used by local governments to inform their preparations for conflicts that enter our homeland. See more detail in appendix C.[608]

Addressing homelessness: Wars inevitably lead to homelessness, either because structures are destroyed or because people flee the battlefield seeking safe shelter. Local governments need a plan to house these residents. The US Center for Disease Control & Prevention provides significant material to inform local government officials charged with planning for homelessness challenges.[609]

Mitigating against the spread of diseases: Wars and most natural disasters dramatically increase mortality and morbidity due to communicable diseases. The major causes of communicable disease in war include infections from contaminated food and water, respiratory infections, vector and insect-borne diseases, and infections because of wounds and injuries.[610]

Addressing food shortages: The *2023 Global Report on Food Crises* states that war annually pushes many millions of people into acute food insecurity. The problem is exacerbated when hostile forces poison wells, burn crops, or in other ways deprive civilians of food. Even when foreign forces aren't present, local conditions in time of war can create food shortages. This is a problem local government should anticipate and address through plans and stockpiling food.[611]

Local and state governments have a moral obligation to plan for the consequences of disasters and war. There are many steps that ought to be taken today to harden infrastructure and stock necessities, and others that require detailed plans but should be tucked away for times when disasters and or war encroach on our communities.

Conclusion

This chapter reviewed the impact of past wars for civilians and suggested additional consequences that might arise in a future conflict thanks to the emergent high-technology war-making systems. It concluded with a host of recommendations about how local and state governments can be prepared to address should the worst occur.

The next chapter addresses preparations the individual and the local family ought to consider should the nation go to war, and especially how to mitigate the effects of conflict for the family especially if combat happens in the homeland.

Chapter 12

PREPARING YOURSELF AND YOUR FAMILY TO FACE WAR

We are driven by five genetic needs: survival, love and belonging, power, freedom, and fun.[612]

William Glasser (1925–2013),
American psychiatrist

This chapter explores the heart of individual and family preparations for the time of war, an outcome that threatens our basic needs. Ultimately, if the worst happens, the crisis becomes about survival when all public services fail and the government can no longer protect us. That develops into the hour for neighbors to protect one another, and for you and your family to make tough decisions about whether to flee, "bug out" (a familiar colloquial term among the "prepper" community), or just hunker down to survive.

Further, this chapter is written from a secular perspective. Although the topic of war and how to prepare for armed conflict has significant underlying philosophical and spiritual aspects, I have chosen here to focus primarily on the mechanics of preparing for the local consequences associated with human conflict on a grand scale. I will address the evangelical Christian perspective of living in times of war in the next section of this book.

It shouldn't be surprising that few people give more than a passing thought to preparing for the possibility of war. Why? Because there hasn't been a real attack here at home since the War of 1812. Yet, three in five Americans, according to a national survey, believe world war that could include our homeland is somewhat likely in the next five to ten years. That begs the question: Why don't more of us prepare for what seems to be a real possibility? The answer may surprise you: We don't believe what we tell pollsters; we don't know how to prepare ourselves for war in our backyard; or we expect government to take care of us in the event conflict comes to our shores.[613]

Let me disabuse you of the notion that any government—local, state, or national—will help us should war come to our homeland. I addressed that issue in the previous chapter. It would certainly be welcomed if our various governments did more of what I recommend. However, now, most elected "leaders" and their civil servants have failed dismally to address the outlined issues, and I have no reason to believe that will change. Further, I assume most Americans aren't sure how to prepare for such a war. So, this chapter provides a starting point for those of us who are serious about preparing ourselves and our loved ones for global conflict.

In three parts, this chapter reviews historical, sobering testimonies from others victimized by war. Subsequently, I identify a key question we must answer as war draws near, and then offer a couple of thought-provoking options. Finally, I summarize many of the actions/preparations we should seriously consider to get ready for that potentially stark situation.

Victims of War and How They Reacted

One-quarter of humanity—2 billion people—live in conflict areas, according to United Nations Secretary-General Antonio Guterres. Today, the world faces the highest number of violent conflicts since the Second World War. In fact, eighty-four million people were forced to leave their homes in 2021 because of conflict.[614]

The toll suffered by civilians caught in war zones should make others facing such a situation decide either to flee conflict or do more to prepare for the possibility that they, too, might encounter such an unimaginable scene.

Consider some grim testimonies from those caught in recent war zones. We begin with an overview of the conditions people might expect to experience in a future conflict area.

In the wake of the terrorist group Hamas' October 7, 2023, murderous attack into southern Israel, many people were killed and wounded by the coordinated strikes. Once Israel responded and attacked into Gaza, a great number of Palestinian residents quickly hid in bomb shelters, while others evacuated elsewhere inside Israel or fled to other countries.

The toll for those caught in the Gaza conflict areas was especially high.

Dr. Steven Marans, a child and adult psychoanalyst and professor at the Yale University Child Study Center, said:

> When we think about trauma in a war, in a conflict zone, I think it's important to remember that war brings a convergence or a realization of all of our worst nightmares about fears of loss, of our own lives, about the lives of people we love, damage to our bodies, loss of control and also the loss of a familiar anchor in the routine of daily life…. And so, the symptoms that we see here are really a reflection of some of the tremendous impact that these sudden unanticipated threats and realization of these nightmare scenarios are created in in wartime.[615]

The physical risks of being in a war zone can be significant, with the possibility of being killed or wounded. Besides that, most people are forced to breathe battlefield smoke and ash from fires, which degrades the nose and lungs. Dr. Ubydul Haque, an assistant professor of global health at Rutgers' Global Health Institute, studied how living in a conflict zone can affect human health. He found, after researching the Ukraine battlefield, that war-zone residents "have no access to medication, food, water, electricity, [and] heating." Further, he stated: "You know that during the war, their energy infrastructure was destroyed, and our study showed people had cold injuries that might make a lot of them permanently disabled." Add to those issues other illnesses, malnutrition, injury, or sexual violence, and recognize that most of them had trouble finding any medical attention.[616]

The mental health toll can be especially serious for people living in war zones, manifesting in issues like depression, anxiety, and post-traumatic stress disorder. Dr. Marans said we often underestimate the mental health challenges due to fears such as the likelihood of being injured or disabled.[617]

Consider some recent testimonies of people about life in war zones and the challenges that followed them into exile. Also, do not be so naïve as to believe these situations are unlikely to ever happen in America.

14-year-old Girl Flees War-Ravaged Burundi, Africa

The *Sydney Morning Herald* reported the story of a teenage girl in the east-central African nation of Burundi. Her family could only afford to send one person into exile, so they sent her on a dangerous journey—walking with a group of people. At the Rwanda border, they encountered armed men who demanded money.[618]

"They picked some of us from the group and said we needed to give them money," the girl said. "When we did not have money to give them, they took us into the forest."[619]

She was raped, became pregnant, and made her way to a refugee camp in Rwanda, where she eventually gave birth to a baby boy.[620]

Unfortunately, this girl's account of sexual violence is not uncommon. Children caught in war zones, according to Save the Children's annual report, are "far more likely to be raped, forced into child marriage or fall victim to other forms of sexual violence." Boys are especially "vulnerable to recruitment by armed forces or militia groups and abductions."[621]

Syrian Refugee from War in Beirut, Lebanon

Abdul Halim escaped the Syrian war zone to quickly become destitute. His wife left him, and he fled with two of his children to neighboring Lebanon, where he found himself penniless, struggling to survive on the streets of Beirut.[622]

"I tried to look for work, but no one would give me a job because I had my kids with me," Abdul explained. He continued:

> I walked the streets and saw there were schools and a lot of students, so I thought the best thing I could do was to sell pens. I went and bought a box of pens. And I left my son at home. And I took my daughter, who was this small. And I would carry her. What could I do? There was nowhere I could put her.[623]

One day, someone saw Abdul, daughter Reem in his arms, selling his pens. That person posted their picture on Twitter. The photo went viral, and a campaign was established to raise money for Abdul, which turned out to be enough to buy a bakery. Eventually, his shop employed twenty men, all Syrian refugees supporting their families.[624]

Abdul was extremely lucky. Most Syrian refugees from the civil war cannot find jobs, much less pay the rising cost of living in foreign countries.

Seven-year-old Fled War in Syria

Alia, a seven-year-old from Aleppo, Syria, who now lives in Damour, Lebanon, told an Italian nongovernment organization representative about her departure from Lebanon:[625]

> The last thing I remember of Syria, before we left, was when my mother was taking me from our place to our grandparents' [house]. The roads were full of dead corpses. I saw dead people with no heads or no hands or legs. I was so shocked I could not stop crying. To calm me down, my grandfather told me they were mean people, but I still prayed for them, because even if some considered them mean, they were still dead human beings.[626]
>
> Back at home, I left a friend in Syria, her name was Rou'a. I miss her a lot and I miss going to school with her. I used to play with her with my Atari but I could not bring it with me. I also used to have pigeons—one of them had eggs. I would feed them and care for them. I am worried about them; I really pray someone is still caring for them. But here I have a small kitten that I really love! I miss my home a lot. I hope one day we will be back and things will be just like before.[627]

Family Fled Ukraine War for Poland

A woman named Wictoria shared her story of fleeing in the face of war:

> We [Wictoria, Vova and son, Sasha] are from around Kyiv. When the war broke out, we were not only afraid of bombings, we knew that the only way for our son to function normally was to go to Poland, where doctors were always available.[628]

Their son, Sasha, had just turned fifteen at the time. Since he was two years old, he had been moving around only in a wheelchair. He suffers from SMA (spinal muscular atrophy). "He is a bright boy who is interested in everything related to the Internet," Wiktoria said. "He is studying remotely in a Ukrainian school and will soon have a well-deserved vacation."[629]

"When the war broke out, we didn't think long," Vova said. "We quickly packed our bags and moved to Poland, knowing that good people there would help us start a new life. They escaped from Ukraine during the heaviest shooting. The journey to Poland took four days.[630]

"There is no place on Earth we cannot leave to make our son's life easier. We were able to take a few pictures from our home in Ukraine, the rest is in our hearts and heads," Wiktoria said.[631]

Missionary "Sam": Work in Ukraine with Those Remaining in Active War Zone

Sam, a missionary sponsored by the North Coast Church, Vista, California, works to supply relief to Ukrainian families caught inside the war zone. Sam spoke of a family who lived with neighbors in a crowded church basement for more than three weeks under constant fire. He also traveled to many remote rural villages where there might be "only two people left" alive.[632]

"There is a bigger fear in leaving than there is for living in a war," said Sam. "Most of those who make the choice are over 50 years old perhaps, unlike young people, the mature citizens are concerned about starting all over again in a foreign place."[633]

Life for these older people is austere. Sam explained, "A lot of older people are being cared for by [other] older people and often there is no running water or electricity so diapers are a big need. Try washing reusable diapers with no water or having to use your limited bottled water to do that."[634]

Ukrainians Living in Russian-occupied Kherson

The British Broadcasting Corporation (BBC) profiled life for the average Ukrainian citizen who remained in Kherson, a city occupied by Russia six months after the start of the war. The following are some verbatim statements provided by residents and summaries of conditions documented by the BBC in the fall of 2022. Names are changed to protect their identities.

The Ukrainians who stayed behind had to be constantly on their guard. "You have to make sure there are no incriminating photos in your deleted [iPhone] folder," Boris said. Otherwise, you might be arrested. After all, many people "disappeared" because Russia cracked down on anyone considered loyal to Kyiv.[635]

Half of Kherson's pre-war residents of 280,000 left for safe havens in Ukrainian-controlled territory or abroad. The residents who stayed behind, according to Boris, adjusted to occupation, initially making their own rules, and avoided Russian occupiers at all costs.[636]

"For four or five months we felt we were living in a kind of libertarian society," Boris said. "Self-sustaining, self-regulating." However, that ended months after Kherson was lost and Russian secret service personnel arrived. Soon the propaganda started, with billboards across the city boasting "Kherson—Russian city."[637]

The Ukrainians tried to stay connected with Kyiv, however. Boris said, "Either you mobilize yourself or you just fall apart." There was the constant question in the back of everyone's mind: "Why does it take ZSU [the Ukrainian forces] so long [to rescue us]?"[638]

A major concern, especially among young men, was the threat of Russian conscription. At the time, fighting-age males from occupied Ukraine were recruited into the Russian forces and then expected to fight against their own countrymen.

The occupied Ukrainian's financial life was seriously affected by the Russians. Soon the Russian currency became the mainstay; welfare payments were only paid in rubles, and local shops were forced to accept Moscow's currency. The only operational banks were Russian, and only those carrying Russian passports could open an account or even hold local government jobs.[639]

The Russian occupiers tried to destroy every trace of Ukraine in the city. Specifically, "After the occupation, my whole life broke down," said Alex, a former teacher. "Russians went from apartment to apartment, destroying everything connected with Ukraine," he said. "At my home, they burned Ukrainian symbols and a lot of books."[640]

Eventually, Russian soldiers withdrew and turned over the city to pro-Moscow separatists. At that point, "The city turned into a ruin," said Daryna, a student who eventually fled the city. "It became a big market where everyone sold what they could to earn something [presumably to purchase food]."[641]

At the time, electricity and water were scarce, many homes were destroyed, and bodies lay unburied across the city's rubble, said Daryna. Meanwhile, many Ukrainians become so desperate to live that they worked for the *rashists*, a derogatory term for Russians.[642]

By the summer, locally grown vegetables were cheap to buy, but prices for food like meat and cheese rose quickly. The low cost of vegetables was due to farmers being cut off from selling their produce except locally while Russian-run supermarkets were stocked with expensive Russian products.[643]

Natalya, a pensioner, said, "Everyone who was able to leave has left, especially mums with kids." There was no gas for months and frequent electricity blackouts; life became a constant struggle, said Natalya. They could not get needed drugs because, according to Toma, a woman in her thirties, pharmacies are run by Russian authorities, who dispensed inferior products, if any.[644]

In summary, people caught in these difficult situations must decide whether to remain in the war zone or risk the perils of leaving for a safe haven. Even for those who escape conflicts, life can be very challenging.

Deciding Whether to "Bug Out" Before Home Becomes a War Zone

In modern times, Americans haven't faced the prospect of war being fought in their homeland. However, millions of people around the world today have faced the decision about whether or not to abandon their homes and communities to seek safety from hostilities. That is a difficult call to make, but sometimes, because of the imminent dangers, there is no other choice.

Certainly, in places like central Europe, the Middle East, and Africa, wars have driven millions of people away from their homes to seek safety in nearby countries. However, what if war comes to America? Where will citizens flee? Will they seek refuge outside their cities, like we saw in the case of Londoners in World War II? Will they seek refuge in less-populated, rural areas of the US where there is a better chance to survive? Perhaps, if war seems imminent and there is time, some Americans might voluntarily move overseas to countries likely to be safe from hostilities.

How do you know whether war will put your community at risk? The answer to that question has much to do with where you live. For example, you are at risk if you live near the epicenter of government, such as Washington, DC; close to an important military installation; not far from a place known to be rich in resources our enemy might need to sustain his occupation; or near a place vulnerable to attack for a variety of other reasons.

Therefore, you must decide whether to stay put or relocate inside the US or even go abroad.

Consider the Implications of Going Elsewhere in the US

Are you looking to relocate closer to family and friends or to escape city life for the countryside, believing that will be safer? After all, America has plenty of wide-open spaces, especially in the Midwest and Rocky Mountain areas—most are sparsely populated. However, along with fewer people, there are minimal services: food stores, doctors, electricity, running water, and much more.

Seeking a refuge might lead you to buy a few acres of land in the middle of nowhere and build a small house. However, will it have electricity and running water? Can you really live under more austere conditions? That's a very personal question.

I lived in Alaska years ago and knew people who made their homes in the wilderness, what Alaskans called the "bush." They seldom came to town to stock up on necessities. It is a tough, lonely lifestyle—one that's not for everyone. After all, most of those people had no electricity, not even generators; they lived on well water (if it did not freeze); they ate a lot of game (mostly moose, caribou, and some fish); and they heated/cooked year-round with the timber they cut and split themselves.

If that's too much for you, there are also relatively safe, albeit less-remote, places than the Alaskan bush inside the Lower 48 states where electricity and running water are likely available. However, other issues must be considered when weighing out this option as well.

It's best to have a dependable support system, especially if you elect to move to a remote refuge location. Think about living with family and or friends, say, in a larger house where the chores and expenses are shared. There is always the option of establishing a support group at a local church. But, bottom line: Everyone needs help at some point, and thinking through your relocation should include identifying your support system.

Other matters to assess regarding your potential remote location include adequate housing, access to food (well-stocked stores), and/or the opportunity to grow food and hunt—or even to raise chickens and a few cattle or hogs. After all, even the best-stocked pantry will run dry after a few months of feeding your family. You need access to a dependable supply of necessities.

You'll inevitably require medical and dental attention. Where is the closest doctor, clinic and/or hospital? How is your health? Do you require continuous care and special medicines?

Do you have the right skills and equipment to live in the new setting? In relatively remote locations, you'll need to do more for yourself, such as making minor repairs. Even more critically, you'll need to defend yourself and your family against wild animals and dangerous people. That's a tall order for the modern American.

Will you depend on a motor vehicle at your new location? If you live off the beaten path, is a repair shop nearby? Or can you repair your vehicle yourself, even if you have access to the needed parts? Where do you buy and/or store gasoline?

Does your new location have access to communication technologies? Most Americans have grown accustomed to having cell service and access to high-speed Internet. That isn't a given in many remote areas. Yes, assuming communication satellites are still flying, which is unlikely, you can use those links, but they require special equipment and a power source, and those tend to be quite expensive. Solar power may be a partial energy option, but even the best solar panels are slow to charge batteries, especially in the low-light winter days.

Do you have sufficient financial resources and access to them at the new location? Or will you have to find employment to provide for yourself and family? Are there jobs in the area that fit your skills?

Obviously, relocating within the US requires significant planning, and there are risks associated with each location. Yet, others may conclude that remaining inside the US is too risky, because this country will either be seriously degraded by war or, albeit unlikely, will suffer some form of foreign occupation, perhaps staffed by civilian overseers like in Ukraine and backed by threats against critical services, as well as a few "show" troops to enforce obedience.

Perhaps it occurs to you to relocate overseas. But where should you go?

Mikkel Thorup, founder and CEO at Expat Money, wrote an interesting article on the topic, "World War 3: Where Will Be Safe in a Global Conflict?" Mr. Thorup is an expat consultant who "focuses on helping mostly high-net-worth private clients to legally mitigate tax liabilities, obtain a second residency and citizenship, and assemble a portfolio of foreign investments including international real estate, timber plantations, agricultural land and other hard-money tangible assets."[645]

Let's assume for the moment you decide remaining in the US is no longer in your best interests. You seek a safe haven outside this country. Where should you consider relocating to, and what are the challenges in moving there?

Fortunately, Mr. Thorup offers some possibilities to consider. He suggests that in "uncertain times, countries like Uruguay, Brazil, Argentina, Paraguay, Panama, and Colombia" are attractive places of refuge. Why? They're a significant distance from the likely epicenter of conflict—the US, Europe, and China—and they boast "food independence, water independence, and energy independence," which are all key to survival.[646]

Latin America is a safe bet, not only because it's away from the likely battlegrounds, but also because much of the region maintains a neutral stance, according to Thorup. They also boast good economies and living standards, and aren't likely to be ground zero for a nuclear attack.

Below are Mr. Thorup's summaries for the six countries that top his list of potential future safe places. Admittedly, leaving for another country may not be possible for most, but it is an option to contemplate.

- **Uruguay**: Known for its political stability and progressive social policies, which make it an ideal place for expats looking for peace amidst chaos. Uruguay's strategic position outside major conflict zones and military conflicts with fertile land makes it an appealing choice, alongside being self-sufficient regarding basic necessities like food & water;
- **Brazil**: Brazil offers a vast environment with fertile land, ensuring self-sufficiency during crises. The country presents opportunities due to its vast resources and distance from key conflict areas. Rich natural resources make Brazil largely independent regarding energy production;
- **Argentina**: With rich agricultural lands, Argentina promises food security even under dire circumstances. The country sits well away from potential conflict zones;
- **Panama**: This Central American nation has significant financial advantages, attracting many expats and businesses. A hub

for expats, Panama offers a blend of modern conveniences and tropical charm;

- **Colombia**: Boasting a diverse economy, Colombia offers a variety of opportunities for those looking to relocate their wealth or business. An increasingly popular choice among expats due to its improving safety record and vibrant lifestyle. With its vast biodiversity and mountainous terrain, Colombia provides ample resources to ensure self-sufficiency;
- **Paraguay**: A lesser-known destination with promising prospects. Paraguay's low cost of living and welcoming attitude towards foreigners make it an attractive option. Paraguay is not only self-sufficient in terms of basic necessities but also maintains a neutral foreign policy. This country is likely well out of any nuclear fallout if things were to escalate in Europe.[647]

Admittedly, Mr. Thorup acknowledges that relocating one's business and home overseas is rife with challenges. However, he offers some insights for those ready to make the plunge.

He urges folks to consider a country that is a "safe haven during turbulent times," specifically one that is militarily neutral. He points out that countries with long histories—like Switzerland and the six Latin American countries identified above—can offer relative safety and are unlikely to become part of a future war.[648]

The relocation country ought to be far away from conflict zones, especially if there is a nuclear attack or it is subject to invaders. Likely, that means good candidates are countries far from Europe and China, which have a history of hosting conflicts and are more than likely going to be party to World War III.

Alternatively, some readers may wonder about relocating to a small island in the middle of the Pacific Ocean. Perhaps on first glance, the idea of living in a tropical paradise with only one season year-round is inviting—that is, until you begin to consider the unique challenges associated with island life.

Some Americans considering island life quickly reflect on their only experience, which might have involved a vacation at Oahu, Hawaii, or perhaps Puerto Rico and the Bahamas. These are great vacation spots, but lousy places to be in wartime. Why? Well, Mr. Thorup quickly cautions that moving to an island presents special challenges for survival, even though it is certainly likely to be isolated from the war zone.

He notes that because the majority of small islands lack sufficient arable land for growing crops, 90 percent of the food consumed by islanders must be imported. That becomes problematic in time of war, because international trade will likely be disrupted.[649]

Further, he points out, fresh water is a luxury on many small islands. After all, fresh water on an island comes from collecting rainwater or from desalination plants, which can become a vulnerability in times of crisis, either because there isn't enough rain due to drought or, even if you are fortunate enough to have a desalination plant, the parts to make necessary repairs might not be available and/or you might not be able to obtain the fossil fuel to run the facility.[650]

Most small islands also rely on fossil fuels for all power generation. Much like food, petroleum products must be shipped to the island; that transport could be seriously delayed as the global war rages. Also, for those looking to solar and wind power as an energy source, they typically represent a very small part of any island's total electric demands.[651]

Actions for Everyone Facing War

Whether you decide to leave or stay put, there are certain issues you need to consider. Even if you relocate to a "safer" place, many of these suggestions are relevant because there is no guarantee the war will not also reach your new location.

In addition, don't wait until you hear bombs and your power is cut off by a cyberattack to make a relocation decision. That may be too late.

Carefully think through the following actions necessary to survive in war, even if you're going abroad. No one knows how long the war might last and when, if ever, life might return to a new normal. So, think and decide about your preparations in detail.

Think through each of the following questions and the associated, recommended actions.

Question: *What should everyone consider, starting today, to prepare for a worst-case scenario like World War III?*

Recommended Action: Stay informed. The process of being prepared should there be a war is to stay informed, educated. Monitor global affairs and understand the evolving situation that will inform your decisions to prepare for the crisis and the possible timeline before disaster strikes. There are numerous specific actions to take before conflict comes to your doorstep.

- **Reinforce home security,** beginning with ensuring that your entry points are well protected and you have a reliable security system. Work with your neighbors to develop watch strategies and discuss how to share news among your friends and family.
- **Establish an emergency plan,** no matter the threat. That plan must have details and be updated on a regular basis. As a minimum, it should include communication protocols, evacuation routes, meeting (rally) points if ever separated from your group/family, and contingency arrangements. Meanwhile, emphasize sticking together and creating a safe space at your home, and an alternative refuge if your home is compromised or destroyed.
- **Maintain financial readiness,** because a constant threat of attack, much less a war, will be expensive. Expect the enemy to disrupt critical supplies both for our armed forces and your community. Therefore, anticipate massive shortages of food and water, and understand that what you can buy will skyrocket in price.
- **Arrange appropriate funds,** because you will need a lot of money (cash), whether you stay put or relocate. Particularly if you leave in a time of war, expect the costs of living to be very expensive. Also, don't expect to sell your valuables at the last moment to build up your liquidity. After all, most people aren't looking to buy them when their lives are threatened. Rather, take money out of the bank, especially before your neighbors do; otherwise, you will have to wait in long lines—and you might walk away empty-handed. Note, too, that wars typically destabilize currencies, another issue for serious consideration. Therefore, silver and gold coins are always a sure bet when government paper currency is not backed well or inflation gets

out of hand. Consider investing in bartering materials such as precious metals, alcohol, gasoline, propane, candy, and even ammunition for the dark times ahead.

• **Set up a secret room** (panic room) in your home or nearby, such as in an underground bunker on your property that is well camouflaged. It will buy you time to plan your next steps. You don't have to create a sophisticated fallout shelter with a special air-filtration system and stand-alone utilities stocked with months of supplies. However, you can convert a crawl space, attic, or closet into a secret room. Prepare a place now and improve on it with time. Keep in mind the space should have ventilation and, preferably, the walls should be reinforced by steel rebar. If your community is invaded by enemy forces and/or criminal gangs, they'll look for hidden spaces using techniques such as smoke or trying to burn down the structure. Therefore, consider anti-fire devices and equip the space with oxygen masks for all occupants if possible.

Question: *What should I do if my home is partially or totally destroyed?*

Recommended action: Keep a "bug-out" bag for each family member. That bag—a backpack or waterproof sack—should contain essential supplies to survive, including, as a minimum, food, water, tools, and a first-aid kit. Adjust the contents of the bag for the weather conditions and whether conflict is on the horizon. Packing a weapon might be wise as well.

Also plan where you would go if you lose your home, your primary secret room. Do your research of potential areas of refuge and safe houses, preferably places with minimal damage and away from the conflict. In addition, relocating to another city might not be a good decision, because you may find yourself quickly leaving that place as well. Better to locate to a small town or rural area, especially where you have family and/or friends.

Plot out an evacuation route to your alternative safe place very carefully. Your route should purposely avoid sensitive areas like military installations, industrial zones, and economic centers. Also, if you're driving, expect massive traffic jams, particularly if you're leaving at the same time as most others. Further, expect to run out of gasoline, so plan to store some—in ready-to-go containers and treated with a stabilizer—in a well-ventilated room and away from any source of ignition. Once you're on the road, don't expect filling stations to be open. When your back-up supply of gasoline is gone, you might consider siphoning gas from abandoned cars. Make certain you practice a siphoning technique under less stressful conditions and have the right equipment in your trunk.

If evacuation by car is no longer an option or gas isn't available, take what you can in backpacks—food, water, and medicine—and hurry to the safer destination. Always consider arming yourself and carrying the gear to protect yourself from the elements as you move to your alternative safe place.

Question: *How should I prepare myself and family for the possibility of war?*

Recommended action: Remain healthy and fit. Conditions associated with war tend to be very unhealthy and very stressful for everyone. Therefore, strive to be in top health and maximum fitness beforehand…and try to sustain that condition even as war comes.

Being in a warzone will test your physical and mental endurance and strength. It's important to be able to run and lift heavy weights, if possible, because you might be required to evade enemy combatants, carry loads, and help rescue loved ones trapped under rubble. Or you might need to help carry those who are injured or suffering from wounds. There's also the possibility that you will face hostile neighbors who haven't prepared for war and now expect you to help them, presenting a physical test as well.

Your emergency plan should include special survival training as well. For example, everyone needs to know what to do if the house is on fire, how to purify water, how to build an emergency shelter, how to administer first aid, how to forage for food, what to do to evade someone tracking you, how to defend yourself, and much more. Consider these details.

- **Train to administer first aid.** There are many ways you can become hurt or be killed in a warzone. Therefore, learn how to treat injuries, wounds and illnesses when medical professionals aren't available. Your life and the lives of others may depend on your first-aid skills such as cardiopulmonary resuscitation

(CPR), basic trauma care, and treatment of burns, lacerations, fractures, infections, etc.

- **Learn basic survival skills** because they give you a greater level of self-sufficiency. Find out how to improvise a shelter from natural materials. Know how to treat water to make it safe to drink. Learn how to find edible food, trap small game, and then prepare that game for eating. Add to this mix how to camouflage and escape or evade those who might be searching for you. Keep in mind that fire and related smoke give away your location, so learn to eat what is available raw or to be creative with your cooking.

Preparing for life in a war zone may take you out of your comfort zone, such as by living in an improvised shelter in the woods.

Photo by Caspian Dahlström on Unsplash[652]

- **Learn about self- protection.** Train everyone in your family/ group in hand-to-hand combat and the use of firearms. Take classes in hand-to-hand defense, because personal safety is paramount. There are plenty of YouTube videos that lead viewers through the steps of properly using a knife and gun against an adversary. Consider obtaining a concealed carry permit before the war to become familiar/comfortable with carrying a firearm. Practice with your firearm often to gain proficiency. Keep it clean and understand when to use it. Also, always keep enough ammunition on hand to sustain you during a critical situation. Further, be prepared for the possibility that, if people come to believe law enforcement will not return to your community in times of war, then some of them will feel free to act without fear of consequences. That's when you and your group are most in danger.

- **Form a group.** Your only hope for survival in a war zone is banding together in larger groups with people you trust. You also need to be in a group so you can band together to help perform necessary work (especially when there are sick and wounded), to keep watch, to find and prepare food, and to generally provide manpower.

- **Establish communications** and maintain it within your family and group. It's best to use "off-the-grid" devices so you can communicate without drawing attention. Two-way radios and shortwave receivers can be your lifeline, and they're relatively cheap. Have solar panels so you can recharge your radio/shortwave batteries. Also, don't count on cellphone service or even satellite telephones because they aren't likely to be in operation. Establish secret code words, duress codes meant to be used among your group if you get into a serious situation like being taken captive. Those secret words are a signal to those you trust so they will understand something about your situation.

- **Watch your steps.** Avoid danger areas to improve your chances of survival. For example, stay away from active fighting and high-priority targets. Keep in mind that major roads are likely used by your enemy. Also, be observant to avoid unexploded ordnance, suspected minefields, and improved explosive devices (booby traps), especially if you find yourself in an active war zone.

Question: *What items should you stock in your secret/safe place?*
Recommended Action: Stock up on the items identified below.

- **Food:** There is a real possibility that global war will bring massive famine and serious food disruptions. The problem isn't as much about the actual growth and processing of food as it is about the energy required, which includes manufacturing fertilizers that are energy-intensive to make. The energy requirements for shipping are always a dicey issue in war as well.

✓ **Purchasing food with long shelf life:** Numerous camping and survival outlets sell food that can be stored for years at a time. Calculate your anticipated requirements and supplement with other foodstuffs that provide sufficient proteins to keep you and your family healthy.

✓ **Gardening:** Survival gardens certainly become popular in wartime, but you will not be able to grow enough food to meet normal caloric requirements without sufficient fertilizer and equipment. Consider buying a seed kit for that garden and seal it for protection from the elements.

✓ **Learn how to forage and hunt for game:** The forests have plenty of ready-to-eat foods if you know what to look for. Certainly, you should be prepared to hunt for game, catch fish, and cook the food. It might surprise you what you might eat if you're hungry enough.

✓ **Food prep:** You'll need cooking equipment, fuel, plates, utensils, can openers, and more stored in your safe place with the other food supplies. Also, think about how you will dispose of waste, and be alert to refuse that will attract rats and other scavengers that are often plagued with diseases.

✓ **Water:** You will need filtered water bottles, containers to store clean water, and water-filtering systems. Also consider large barrels with spigots to help dispense potable water. Most everyone who has watched enough adventure movies understands that boiling water kills the bacteria and is therefore safe to drink. That's an important alternative when your public water system is likely to be constantly disrupted by cyberattacks for temporary or long-term stops in service. Therefore, your ability to store potable water is critical to survival. Also, know the location of water sources near your home or refuge location: a stream, lake, or well. Be very careful when collecting water because, to paraphrase a fable, "The lion waits for the gazelle at the watering hole." You cannot be too cautious.

- **Tools and utilities:** Depending on your situation, you may need a generator, fuel (gasoline or diesel), a camping stove and appropriate fuel (propane is a good long-term option), flashlights and batteries, matches, candles, and a variety of hand tools for small repairs such as a hammer, a hunter's knife, a hatchet, a small saw, nails, a screwdriver, and much more.
- **Hygiene items:** Shampoo, soap, toothbrush and paste, toilet paper and feminine hygiene products will also be necessities. Learn the alternative options to these manufactured products and how to safely use them.
- **Clothing:** Although climate is situational, you'll need comfortable and protective clothing, including boots and jackets. Multiple changes of clothing for each person are necessary, and think about what you'll need to launder them as well. Remember, there are health dangers associated with wearing dirty clothing for extended periods.
- **First-aid supplies:** We previously reviewed the necessity of first-aid training. Your stock of medical supplies needs to include bandages, antibiotics, ointments, pain relievers, disinfectants, splints, and more. Also have ample supplies of prescription medications on hand, as well as, basic medical manuals for reference.

No doubt, global conflict will dramatically increase the requirement for medical care and supplies. Hospitals, if they continue to operate, will likely focus on acute cases. Therefore, your home first-aid kit must be more robust than usual and equipped to address animal bites, bladder and kidney infections, diarrhea, pneumonia, tetanus, and more. There are outlets that sell antibiotics for emergency use or for overseas travel.

Also consider, subject to the threat, acquiring personal protective equipment such as gas and oxygen masks, protective suits, gloves, and eyewear to protect you from chemical, biological, and radiological threats.

- **Sanitation:** Expect just like your water purification plant will shutter for unknown periods, the same will happen with your sanitation treatment facilities. Therefore, you need to consider alternatives such as pedal-powered off-grid washing machines and compositing toilets for waste. Of course, there are simpler solutions such as camping toilets or simply digging a trench in your yard and control odors, prevent insects from breeding in the waste by applying either quicklime or hydrated lime. Also, keep your slit trenches away from your water supply to avoid contamination, which could result in dysentery.

- **Energy:** Energy is important to survival as well. You need it to cook your meals (when safe), help you stay warm in the winter, and help you see in the dark. Maintain an ample supply of batteries, but also consider obtaining solar panels that charge batteries and small battery-based generators. You may also consider cooking gas like propane and a robust supply for your gasoline or diesel generators and your car.

- **Entertainment:** Stock up on entertainment aids because you and your family will likely spend considerable time waiting, doing nothing. Card games, amusement materials, books, and other items can help maintain morale.

- **Documents:** Keep your personal documents in a safe, fireproof place: birth certificates, passports, vehicle registration, insurance, and digital copies of investments etc.

Question: *What associations with family, friends, neighbors, and others should you develop before war?*

Recommended action: Earlier, I indicated you need to stay with a group because being isolated in a war zone is a death sentence. Build alliances with like-minded people before the first bullets fly and consider pooling resources, doing cross-training, and sharing knowledge for mutual support and encouragement.

Question: *Once war comes to your area, what must you remember to survive?*

Recommended action: Remain informed much like during the pre-war period, meaning you need some form of monitoring broadcasts, such as a radio receiver. Also, stay alert and aware of any potential threats in your area and develop the means to share information with all members of your group.

Why?

You need to appreciate what is on the horizon geopolitically, but also the local situation with the enemy. Build a network to share the latest local information about threats within your group and more broadly. It is important to stay connected, especially with family and friends.

Avoid large crowds because they draw attention and present a greater risk of danger. Avoid creating a predictable pattern others, especially your enemies, might notice.

Always plan an emergency exit, even from routine situations. Identify alternative hideouts and safe houses in your area.

Do not call attention to yourself. Specifically, make certain you don't draw attention to any valuable items on your person like jewelry or special equipment. Avoid being at or doing something that might garner unnecessary attention, such as you and your family being the only people in the neighborhood who aren't losing weight because you wisely stocked your secret room. Eventually, your neighbors will come knocking, the hungrier they get.

Question: *What should you do with your assets?*

Recommended action: It is a good idea to prepare your financial matters before the war. There are some common-sense matters to consider regarding your assets.

Once the war begins, money will tend to lose value because government will flood the market with newly printed bills. This will accelerate inflation, perhaps to hyperinflation as was in the case in Germany post-World War I, which made the German mark (currency) virtually worthless.

Hide your tangible assets: gold, silver, copper, weapons, watches, glasses, alcohol, food, ammunition, and more. Keep in mind that cryptocurrencies crumbled in value as gold surged after Russia invaded Ukraine in 2022. Your tangible items can be very useful as barter, because cash may become almost useless.

Before the war, buy bonds from the country you believe will win, especially the nation you expect will pay back its debt. In 2008, the US dollar gained strength because much of the world believed America was a good investment. Also, when Russia invaded Ukraine, the US dollar strengthened as the ruble fell.

Meanwhile, hoard cash if you believe we're facing just a temporary period of uncertainty. Although cash will lose value, it is better than actual losses on the stock market. However, some stocks and real estate historically do well in wars. For example, the S&P 500 has performed well through all the wars since Vietnam. Meanwhile, real estate is also a good asset class during wartime. It tends to hold its value through wars and matures with each economic recovery. Of course, that assumes your property is not confiscated by an invading enemy.

Conclusion

This chapter is full of practical ideas for civilians facing the prospect of being caught in a war zone. It began with some heart-rendering accounts of people who fled or stayed in war zones and the consequences for them either inside hostile areas or at their refuge location. The second part addressed the key question for all of us: Do I remain at home or flee to safety either elsewhere in the US or overseas? Finally, I provide some recommended actions to prepare for staying at home as you anticipate the war or the effects such as loss of services might have for your community.

The next section of *Preparing for World War III* provides the Christian guidance on being faithful in incredibly stressful situations. The book ends with a glimpse at the prophetic implications of a possible future global war and whether that conflict will indeed usher in the end times.

Section VI
CHRISTIAN AND PROPHETIC IMPLICATIONS FOR WORLD WAR III

And you will hear of wars and rumors of wars. See that you are not alarmed, for this must take place, but the end is not yet. For nation will rise against nation, and kingdom against kingdom, and there will be famines and earthquakes in various places.

Matthew 24:6–7 (ESV)

This section is for those who are anxious about the spiritual aspects of our coming global conflict. Specifically, you might ask whether the future global war will usher in the coming Antichrist to wrestle control over the world. Is there evidence World War III is the platform for the forces of evil, Satan and his demonic army, to prepare for the end-times battlefields spelled out in biblical prophecy? If so, what should Christians do as the indicators of such a conflict grow more evident?

Chapter 13 outlines the Christian's biblical responsibilities as the world collides into World War III. No doubt, some of us believe the Rapture is about to happen and true believers will escape the ravages of the coming high-tech Armageddon. However, what if the coming global conflict is not God's plan for initiating the biblical end times, and the Rapture of the Church is yet farther into the future? Just maybe things aren't bad enough yet that the Lord is ready to pull the plug on this world and wrap up the story of humankind forever.

Chapter 14 makes the case that the next world war could in fact lead this globe into the prophetic end times. Only the Lord knows for sure, but there are certainly indicators both in biblical prophecy and in plain sight that might persuade many of us to reach that conclusion. However, there is still the possibility that the next global war is but another step forward and the end times remain in the future. Also, for those who believe China, Russia, and the US will fight the end-times battles, consider an alternative view.

Chapter 13

CHRISTIANS PREPARING TO SERVE DURING WORLD WAR III

A time to love, and a time to hate; a time for war, and a time for peace.

Ecclesiastes 3:8 (ESV)

This chapter addresses Christians' (believers in Christ's offered salvation) biblical responsibilities as the world likely collides into World War III. No doubt, some Christians hope the Rapture will soon happen and the true believer will escape the ravages of the coming high-tech Armageddon-like war. However, what if the coming global conflict isn't God's decision point to usher in the biblical end times, and the Rapture of the Church is yet farther into the future? Just maybe things aren't bad enough that the Lord is ready to sundown this world and end human history.

In four parts, this chapter digs into the mix of Christians and war. We begin with some real-to-life vignettes of Christians who lived through war and what they discovered from that experience. Next, we consider what the Bible says about armed conflict and under what circumstances it can be justified. We examine what the Scripture says about the Christian participating in combat as a soldier and complete this portion of our journey with a summary of the Christian civilian's responsibilities in conflict areas.

The Christian has a special role to play in the future war.

Photo by Ben White on Unsplash[653]

Christians Trapped by War

Christians are often targeted for abuse across the world today, according to Open Doors, a nonprofit organization that tracks persecution of the Church. That group has found that more than one in seven Christians face persecution for their faith, and hardship is becoming dangerously violent in many countries for believers.[654]

Unfortunately, this isn't a new phenomenon. Christians caught inside conflict areas often suffer more than others because of their faith. Below are testimonies of believers who suffered in war because of their faith or survived the ordeal because of their trust in Jesus Christ.

American Missionary and World War II POW[655]

Darlene Deibler Rose was a missionary with her husband in Papua New Guinea prior to World War II. Her testimony of God's power and presence during the worst adversity is inspiring. She shared her story in a book, *Evidence Not Seen: A Woman's Miraculous Faith in the Jungles of World War II.*

Soon after the Japanese attacked Pearl Harbor, the Imperial Army took Darlene and her husband, Russell, captive and immediately separated the men from the women. At their last time together, Russell reminded Darlene of the paraphrased verse Hebrews 13:5, "Remember one thing, dear: God said that He would never leave us nor forsake us."[656]

Life as a prisoner of war (POW) was extremely hard: rampant diseases, dysentery, malaria, little food, and brutal treatment by the Japanese.

Despite the terrible living conditions, Darlene walked by faith, battled for the Lord, and never gave up hope.[657]

Her most spiritually stretching experience happened one day when a Japanese official assigned her to solitary confinement and intense interrogation. There, she was forced to sign a statement and was given her (presumably) last meal before what she assumed would be her execution. But no, her life was spared, which she didn't understand until much later.[658]

Evidently, sometime before being sent to her presumed death for allegedly being a spy, Darlene had confronted Mr. Yamaji, the head of her POW camp and a cruel man who often beat prisoners for minor infractions. Mr. Yamaji had learned of Darlene's husband's death and summoned her to his office. At the meeting, she asked for permission to speak, and to Yamaji's surprise, Darlene shared the gospel.

"[Jesus] died for you, Mr. Yamaji, and He puts love in our hearts—even for those who are our enemies. That's why I don't hate you, Mr. Yamaji. Maybe God brought me to this place and this time to tell you He loves you."[659]

Darlene wrote that her message so deeply affected the Japanese official that he ran to another room to cry. Sharing the gospel with her captor evidently saved her life,[660] because when Mr. Yamaji heard that Darlene had been taken to another camp and was to be executed as a spy, he personally lobbied on her behalf and saved her life.

Years after the war, Darlene heard that Mr. Yamaji had shared the gospel over Japanese radio.[661] So, even amid war's darkness, Christ can shine through the witness of those caught in the harsh realities of a prison camp.

Christian Faith Saw POW through Seven Torturous Years

Sam Johnson of Texas (1930–2020) was a highly decorated US Air Force pilot, a prisoner of war in Vietnam, and, later in his life, a US Congressman. However, he is best known for his testimony of faith in Jesus Christ while serving those seven years as a POW.[662]

On April 16, 1966, Sam Johnson was on his twenty-fifth combat mission over North Vietnam when his F-4 Phantom fighter jet was shot down. While ejecting from the aircraft, he suffered a broken right arm, a dislocated shoulder, and a broken back. He was immediately captured and put before a firing squad. As he faced those about to execute him,

Sam said, "Jesus, I love you." Then he heard a *click, click, click* from his would-be executioners, but their rifles did not fire. His life was spared. Evidently, using a mock firing squad was a common technique borrowed from the North Koreans to soften up a POW before interrogation.[663]

Sam spent the next seven years in captivity, with half of his time there being in solitary confinement. His captors treated him terribly. The tragic details of his POW experience are documented in *Captive Warriors—A Vietnam POW's Story*. In that book, Sam described his diet of rice and pumpkin soup, and he gave an account of being isolated from others in a three-by-nine-foot cement cell crawling with bugs, spiders, mosquitoes, and rats.[664]

Despite his loneliness and despair, Sam gave "his all to the Lord." He spoke of sensing God's presence, which gave him strength and courage to go on. He reflected on Bible verses and stories he had learned as a child, and he sang hymns that had been tucked away in his memory. He found freedom in speaking with the Lord from his place of isolation.[665]

Throughout the ordeal, Sam said he felt that God was "by his side." Finally, the long nightmare ended on February 12, 1973, when Sam and many others were released from captivity.[666]

Sam's favorite passage of Scripture is familiar to most Christians:

He gives strength to the weary, and to him who lacks might He increases power. Though youths grow weary and tired, and vigorous young men stumble badly, yet those who wait for the Lord will gain new strength; They will mount up with wings like eagles, they will run and not get tired, they will walk and not become weary. (Isaiah 40:29–31, NASB)

Oldest Christian Community Caught in Syrian Civil War[667]

The Apostle Paul came to salvation on the road to Damascus (Acts 9), and Peter likely preached in the same city (Acts 9:27). A few years ago, that Christian community was caught in the middle of Syria's bloody civil war.

The Christian community in that nation at the time made up 10 percent of its overall population. Although the believers tried to remain neutral in the war, they were distrustful of President Bashar Assad's regime and were constantly threatened by al Qaeda Islamist extremists who joined the rebel ranks.

Many tens of thousands of Christians fled to neighboring Turkey and Lebanon. However, a few remained behind for a while, such as George, a fifty-one-year-old former car dealer who spoke with a reporter on the condition of anonymity.

"When I saw Bashar's forces killing, beating and torturing Syrian citizens," George said, "I was standing with the FSA [Free Syrian Army]. But when I saw that a lot of the Free Syrian Army doing the same, I changed my position again." Soon thereafter, George fled the country for Turkey, in part because he feared the Islamist extremists.[668]

George's words expressed a common concern among fellow believers. "If you're a Christian, you're worried," said Dr. Nadim Shehadi with the British think tank Chatham House. "The Christians have maintained a neutrality which can be seen as being on the side of the regime or vice versa."[669]

By contrast, Amjad Hadad, a Syrian Christian, took up arms. The thirty-seven-year-old said that Christian silence doesn't mean support for Assad. On the contrary, he said. "We are fighting beside our Sunni brothers, Alawites, Shiites, Jews and Druze, and all other sects and minorities against the Syrian regime." He added, "We are part of the Syrian people, we shared with these people joy and happiness and beautiful days and now we must share with them in these difficult days."[670]

Russia Accuses Ukrainian Evangelicals of Being American Spies[671]

In March 2022, Russian forces occupied the Ukrainian city of Melitopol, and one of the first things the invaders did was turn on evangelical churches, pastors, and congregations.

Throughout all of Russian-occupied Ukraine, enemy soldiers closed churches that didn't have Russian President Putin's approval, which was only granted to the Russian Orthodox church.[672]

Evangelical churches were especially targeted for closure. Mikhaylo Brytsyn, pastor of Grace Evangelical Church, said that on Sunday, September 11, 2022, he was conducting a worship service and suddenly the building was stormed by twenty armed men with masks. They wore military uniforms and were very brutal.[673]

Pastor Mark Sergeev of New Generation Church was told by enemy soldiers, "You have to stop this. You have to stop these [church] meetings."

Pastor Sergeev's response to the Russian soldiers' demands for him to stop preaching was, "I'm a pastor. I cannot stop the will of the people."

They replied with a threat: "If you will not stop, you're going to see the blood."[674]

Since the Russians took over Melitopol, all evangelical congregations have been labeled undesirable and most of their members have been forced to flee. However, the few who remain continue to gather in secret and risk arrest, imprisonment, or death.[675]

Pastor Brytsyn said the Russians who stormed his church in September 2022, fingerprinted the church members, copied their identification papers, made pictures of each person, and took their addresses. "We were accused of being an extremist organization," he said. "We were accused of being German spies and then American spies."[676]

More broadly, the Russian military destroyed many churches across every seized Ukrainian city. Specifically, at least 206 evangelical churches have been expropriated or destroyed, according to the Institute for Religious Freedom.[677]

Steven Moore, the founder of Ukraine Freedom Project, said, "When the Russians come into a town in an occupied area, they see Protestant churches, they say, this is an American religion. You must be an agent of the American government."[678]

He continued:

So they go to the churches. They shut them down. They frequently torture the pastor, and, sometimes, they murder believers for their faith. And we know of 29 Christian leaders who have been murdered in Ukraine by the Russians.[679]

Pastor Sergeev called for those in the West to send help. "In the name of Jesus, let us defeat and destroy this enemy!" he cried. He went on:

I wanted to say to the whole English-speaking world, we have so many Protestant churches in Ukraine, and they have to understand that so many pastors were killed. We need weapons because

Russia cannot stop. Pray for Ukraine. Still pray. It's only us—what I can ask you to do, really.[680]

Whether taken as prisoner or having your life threatened, the war experiences outlined here are not the worst. The take-away is that war is hellish for everyone, but can be especially hard for those who profess Christ.

What Scripture Says about War

War is a common theme throughout the Bible; most often it's either used as a metaphor for spiritual battle or to describe actual conflict. Scripture indicates that armed conflict is a result of sin, obviously disobedience to God's plan for humanity. The purpose of war is to seek peace and reconciliation; in fact, violence and aggression are condemned in the Word. However, there are times when battle is necessary, such as for self-defense and to protect the innocent, albeit as a last resort. Further, when those conditions are met, believers are called to seek God's guidance and trust Him for protection.

Different types of war described in the Bible include *wars of conquest* (Joshua 6, Judges 4, and 1 Samuel 17), *civil wars* (Joshua 20:14 and 2 Samuel 3:1), and, of course, *heavenly battles* (Revelation 12:7). The bottom line for war is killing, which, in moral law (Exodus 20:13), is condemned—but not when it applies to an enemy in a just war.

God commands some wars; in those cases, killing is not a sin. You will recall that God told the Israelites to take the Promised Land, and in that process, Joshua became the "commander of the army of the Lord," who conquered and killed the enemy first at Ai (Joshua 8:1–2) and then beyond.

Other Israelite leaders, such as King Saul and later King David, were called upon to vanquish their enemies such as the Philistines (2 Samuel 5:23–25). Therefore, they were following God's direction when they engaged in war, killing the enemy.

The arrangement between God and humanity regarding war has changed since Old Testament times, however. Arguably, modern nations aren't commanded by God to launch wars—and, much like in Joshua's case, no contemporary army commander is given a war plan by God. However, war continues to this day.

God hates war, but it is sometimes necessary to maintain order and defeat evil, as evidenced in His command to Joshua to take the Promised Land by force. Of course, the first conflict predates Joshua and is recorded to have occurred in Heaven between Satan and his evil army against God and His angels. We read in Revelation 12:7:

> Then war broke out in heaven. Michael and his angels fought against the dragon, and the dragon and his angels fought back. (NIV)

At the center of battle/war are important biblical concepts such as justice, peace, mercy, and courage:

- **Justice:** War can be the instrument to bring about justice by defeating evil and protecting the innocent
- **Peace:** The goal of war is often to bring about peace by defeating evil.
- **Mercy:** Although war involves violence and destruction, the Bible emphasizes the importance of showing mercy and compassion to one's enemies.
- **Courage:** Warriors are called to be courageous by trusting in God and standing up for what is right.

Today, it is clear from the Scriptures that God sanctions government authorities to enforce moral laws, and, under certain situations, war becomes necessary. Unfortunately, because of humanity's disobedience, war will be present on the earth until the return of Christ. We know that because of what Jesus states in Matthew 24:6:

> You will hear of wars and rumors of wars, but see to it that you are not alarmed. Such things must happen, but the end is still to come. (NIV)

War is a defining activity of humankind. The Scripture grants government the authority to conduct war to protect its citizens from evil and uphold law. Therefore, maintaining a military force is necessary for government, just as police are for internal security and prisons for offenders.

Most Christians hold the view there is such a thing as just war. That belief dates to Christian theologians Augustine of Hippo (AD 354–430), also known as Saint Augustine, and Saint Thomas Aquinas (1225–1274), who are responsible for formulating the theory of just war. That theory (Latin: *bellum iustum*) essentially aims to ensure war is morally justifiable. The criteria for the theory are twofold: *jus ad bellum* (Latin for the "right to go to war") and *jus in bello* (Latin for "right conduct in war").[681]

The basics of those criteria are, first, a just cause, which means war should only be waged in response to "certain, grave and lasting damage inflicted by an aggressor"; the motive must be "advancement of good or avoidance of evil"; and the objective "must be to bring peace." Further, "revenge, revolt, a desire to harm, dominate, or exploit and similar things are not justification for war."[682]

The second just war requirement is that other means of settling the conflict "must be exhausted first." Specifically, "there must be serious prospects of success; bloodshed without hope of victory cannot be justified"; declaration of war must be "by a legitimate authority"; the conflict "must not cause greater evil than the evil to be eliminated"; civilians "must not be intentionally harmed"; and "prisoners and conquered peoples must be treated justly."[683]

What about a contemporary scriptural perspective for just war? John MacArthur, pastor-teacher of Grace Community Church in Sun Valley, California, outlines a scriptural justification for war in his blog article, "What Does the Bible Say about War? Is There Ever a Just Reason for It?" He offers three parts to that justification.[684]

First, "God considers human life precious." Pastor MacArthur explains. "God created us with the unique privilege of bearing his image (Genesis 1:26–27)." Therefore, as God's image-bearers, "we are designed to reflect God's ruling, creative, and moral nature and character." However, Adam's fall soiled our likeness to God with sin. Yet, God affirms the special value of human life (Psalm 8:4–6, Matthew 10:29–31, Matthew 12:12, and James 3:8–10).[685]

Second, "God commands protection of human life." We see in Genesis that God mandates protection of human life by calling for punishment of those who murder "his image," wrote MacArthur. The Lord states in Genesis 9:5–6:

And for your lifeblood I will surely demand an accounting. I will demand an accounting from every animal. And from each human being, too, I will demand an accounting for the life of another human being. Whoever sheds human blood, by humans shall their blood be shed; for in the image of God has God made mankind.[686] (NIV)

Thus, God made clear after the Flood a "renewed appreciation for human life," which is why He "commands the death of those who murderously shed another's blood."[687]

And third, "God commissioned government to punish evildoers." Civil authorities are commanded to bear the sword "as avengers and execute wrath on those who practice wickedness," according to Pastor MacArthur. In Romans, we read that the Apostle Paul "declares that God empowers governments to punish those who do evil." Specifically, Romans 13:1 states, "Let everyone be subject to the governing authorities, for there is no authority except that which God has established" (NIV). Also, 1 Peter 2:13–14 states that God calls on government to ensure order in society:

Submit yourselves for the Lord's sake to every human authority: whether to the emperor, as the supreme authority, or to governors, who are sent by him to punish those who do wrong and to commend those who do right.[688] (NIV)

Therefore, wrote Pastor MacArthur, these verses grant government the responsibility to punish those who "commit deadly atrocities." That includes waging war when morally necessary.

Christian Soldiering

Today, there is no theocracy, and God hasn't handed battle plans to modern man as he did with Joshua. However, our world is marked by constant war because of humanity's fall. Yet, the Bible does not condemn the soldier for participating in just wars. In fact, the New Testament illustrates the type of faith all Christians should demonstrate by comparing it with the obedience of a Roman centurion (a soldier) in Matthew 8:10: "When Jesus heard this, he was amazed and said to those following him, 'Truly I tell you, I have not found anyone in Israel with such great faith [a comment about the soldier's faith]" (NIV). Evidently, men of war like this Roman centurion aren't condemned for participating in the profession of arms.

The Apostle Paul also illustrates a spiritual truth using the example of a soldier in 2 Timothy 2:3: "Join with me in suffering, like a good soldier of Christ Jesus" (NIV). Even John the Baptist doesn't condemn soldiers who asked him, "And what should we do?" In Luke 3:14, John simply said to the soldiers "Don't extort money and don't accuse people falsely—be content with your pay" (NIV). He said nothing about their profession or service.

So Christians must decide for themselves whether serving in the military is right. However, according to the Scriptures, killing an armed enemy in the context of a just war is not sinful.

Many years ago, as a second lieutenant fresh out of West Point, I was stationed along the demilitarized zone separating South Korea from the communist North Korea. At the time, I wrestled with the issue of being a Christian and an infantry officer expected to be prepared to kill. Fortunately, I had the occasion to learn from numerous godly senior soldiers who helped me understand the issue from the Scriptures.

One of those men was retired Lieutenant General William K. Harrison, who had served as the chief United Nations negotiator at Panmunjom, Korea, and later was the president of the Officers' Christian Fellowship (OCF), an evangelical ministry to military officers. General Harrison spoke at OCF conferences and authored an insightful booklet on the topic, *May a Christian Serve in the Military?* His testimony and the booklet helped me to conclude that being a Christian and a combatant were consistent within a just war scenario.

The following are a few excerpts from General Harrison's booklet. He addresses in his writing the biblical material outlined above, but adds other insights worth mentioning below.

General Harrison admits to wrestling for some time with the issue of being a Christian in the military:

> As it must to every Christian soldier, this question presented itself to me. It was something that could not be ignored but had to be solved. As I studied the history of war and military operations I was struck with the horror of war.[689]

He began his analysis by taking inventory of some men from history who were also both Christians and soldiers. His summary was quite impressive:

> Abraham, who fought the four kings; Joshua, who served the Lord; David, who killed Goliath and then led his armies in war and who then received from God one of the greatest promises ever given to man; and those who in the eleventh chapter of Hebrews are described as having through faith in God subdued kingdoms, waxed valiant in fight, and turned to fight the armies of the aliens. In our own national history, all know that George Washington and Robert E. Lee were simple Christians, and yet among the great soldiers of history.[690]

General Harrison recalled the four soldiers mentioned in the New Testament. Two were mentioned above. The third is the soldier at the foot of the cross of Christ, who said, "Truly this was the Son of God!" (Matthew 27:54, ESV). And the fourth was one of the Gentile soldiers to whom God sent Peter to introduce the gospel message (Acts 10). General Harrison wrote, "There is no indication that any of these soldiers discontinued their military service, nor is there any command in the New Testament that a Christian should not be a soldier." In fact, Paul states in 1 Corinthians 7:20, "Each person should remain in the situation they were in when God called them" (NIV), which includes the profession of serving in the armed forces.[691]

Military service is quite like the operation of police power, which is recognized in both the New and Old Testaments. "It seems to me rather obvious that, in a community where individual freedom of will exists, order and security can be maintained only by force in the final analysis. Persuasion can go only so far," wrote Harrison. "If a criminal insists on pursuing his criminal way, force is the only known method of protecting the law-abiding citizen."[692]

A nation's armed forces are an extension of the police system. "Its legitimate purpose is to ensure the peace and security of the nation from outside aggression and in case of domestic insurrections," Harrison said. "Just as policemen must be especially armed and trained, so must soldiers."[693]

Just prior to His crucifixion, Jesus told His disciples to prepare themselves for His departure. Specifically, He said, "But now, he that hath a purse, let him take it, and likewise his scrip: and he that hath no sword, let him sell his garment, and buy one" (Luke 22:36, KJV). Why did the Lord give His disciples this directive? We find the explanation beginning with Romans 1:18, "The wrath of God is being revealed from heaven against all the godlessness and wickedness of people, who suppress the truth by their wickedness." (NIV). God gave humankind "up to all of those personal moral evils which cause the troubles in society, among which is war," said Harrison. We live in such a world, and, unfortunately, we must defend ourselves against such evil.[694]

The Bible is also prescriptive about the composition and conduct of a nation's armed forces. For example, not only are Christians allowed to be policemen and military combatants, but the Bible also addresses inherent issues, including age qualifications of those who serve; soldiers' training and pay; women in combat; exemptions from service; and rules of engagement.

Christians as Civilians in War

Christians that find themselves in a war zone have the same responsibilities to help and reach the lost as those who live in circumstances of peace. The difference is arguably that those in a hostile environment are in a pressure cooker of life unlike most any other and must exercise a special kind of faith.

Christians should prepare for that conflict following the same prescription outlined in the previous chapter. However, the difference is spiritual preparation, which requires walking daily by faith with a vibrant prayer life that carries believers up to and throughout the conflict.

Spiritual Preparation for War

But I say, walk by the Spirit, and you will not gratify the desires of the flesh. For the desires of the flesh are against the Spirit, and the desires of the Spirit are against the flesh, for these are opposed to each other, to keep you from doing the things you want to do. But if you are led by the Spirit, you are not under the law. (Galatians 5:16–18, ESV)

War is among the toughest of life's experiences, thus demands that Christians recognize the times and prepare accordingly. As Galatians says above, believers should "walk by the spirit." But how does one walk by the spirit in a time of war?

The previous chapter addressed the secular response to war, which is to prepare for crises by having plans, getting equipped and trained, stocking up on survival supplies, and making tough decisions such as whether to stay in place or seek refuge elsewhere.

Christian civilians facing war at home must also prepare themselves to address the brewing crisis from a biblical perspective centered on hope in God by "equipping" themselves for war. That means turning to God's word for guidance and prayer. That is why it's important to have an intimate relationship with God the Father and Jesus Christ before the conflict begins.

Developing that spirit-guided life begins with a good understanding of the Father and His concern for you. One of the most comforting Scriptures for Christians caught in war is Psalm 46, which helps us better appreciate our Lord and put the dire situation (armed conflict) and our lives into perspective. After all, that psalm was the inspiration for such inspiring songs as Martin Luther's "A Mighty Fortress Is Our God" and Katharina A. von Schlegel's "Be Still, My Soul."

In Psalm 46:11, we are encouraged by the reminder that God is our protection, He provides immediate help; He is our refuge and strength. We should learn to rest in Him amidst the chaos of war. The first stanza in "A Mighty Fortress Is Our God" screams about life's struggles and God's help:

> A mighty fortress is our God, a bulwark never failing;
> Our helper He, amid the flood of mortal ills prevailing:
> For still our ancient foe doth seek to work us woe;
> His craft and pow'r are great, and, armed with cruel hate,
> On earth is not his equal.

Psalm 46:1 reassures the believer that "God is our refuge and strength, an ever-present help in trouble" (NIV), which means He is our defense and offense. He has authority over all the world—including wars.

In fact, we're safe trusting in Him because we belong to Christ, who has all authority on earth (Matthew 28:18).

Psalm 46 encourages believers facing the tragedy of war. Specifically, verses 2 and 3 call for us not to fear, even if "the earth give way and the mountains fall into the heart of the sea" (NIV). Thus, take courage when all around you is crumbling.

We're also called to recognize our relationship with God, Jesus Christ. Psalm 46:4–7 instructs believers to go to the temple of the Lord. For Christians, our temple is Jesus Christ, and the Spirit of God dwells in us (1 Corinthians 3:16–17). Christ is the vine and we are His branches; we're attached to Him, and from Him we draw spiritual nourishment and the power to continue (John 15:5).

We should recognize that "the Lord almighty is with us; the God of Jacob is our fortress" (Psalm 46:7, NIV). Therefore, we are urged to fear God; "stop trusting in mere humans" (Isaiah 2:22, NIV); be bold witnesses for Christ; and seek refuge in Him (Luke 23:28).

Also, remember that the sky is always darkest before the dawn. Metaphorically, we're to rely on Christ, our light, to see into life's darkness because we cannot find our way without Him. Therefore, Psalm 46:10 encourages us to rest in Him: "Be still, and know that I am God; I will be exalted among the nations, I will be exalted in the earth" (NIV).

Then, with assurance that Christ is our "refuge and strength," our temple, and that He is always "with us," we're then to walk by faith in the face of war. What does that look like in the future World War III?

Christians: A Special Calling of Obedience

In time of war, we should support our government. Romans 13:1–2 tells us, "Let everyone be subject to the governing authorities, for there is no authority except that which God has established. The authorities that exist have been established by God" (NIV). These verses indicate that God ordains our government; therefore, we should submit to His authority and serve in the capacity as we are called unless the governing authorities demonstrate they violate the word of God (Acts 5:29).

This is not a cry for so-called Christian nationalism. However, it is an appeal for obedience in Christ and for us to willingly submit to the authority granted the government (Romans 13). But that submission comes with a caveat. Specifically, we're to advocate for the government to understand and exercise without abuse its God-given role.

Consider an illustration of a Christian looking to the government to recognize its stewardship responsibility under God's direction. For example, the proper understanding of God granting authority was articulated by Reverend W. R. Watkinson of Ridleyville, Pennsylvania, who asked the director of the US Mint to inscribe America's coins with the words, "In God We Trust." Why? Watkinson wrote, on November 13, 1861:

> No nation can be strong except in the strength of God, or safe except in His defense. The trust of our people in God should be declared on our national coins. Will you cause a device to be prepared without delay with a motto expressing in the finest and tersest words possible, this national recognition?[695]

Should Christian Civilians Take up Arms?

Sometimes the government fails to defend its citizens, and in those times, it may become necessary for those citizens, civilians, to fight for themselves and their neighbors. Certainly, in our colonial march to independence, Americans were called to arms by the Black Robed Regiment of pastors, an illustration of citizens taking up arms during dangerous times.

The Black Robed Regiment was a courageous and patriotic group of colonial-era clergy whom the British blamed for American independence. Those clergymen spoke boldly concerning the issues of the day; wearing their black clerical robes while in the pulpit, they preached the Word of God without fear or favor. They told the congregants what and whom they should elect based on the Scriptures, because they understood that to have a good government, the people must first be good citizens.

Lieutenant General Jerry Boykin, the retired Army officer and executive vice president for the Washington, DC-based Family Research Council, is the person who called my attention to the Black Robed Regiment. "Pastors are supposed to be spiritual warriors, and that includes within the culture," he said. "And that hasn't changed since the creation of this nation."[696]

It was the "Black Robed Regiment that preached the message of biblical separation from the British crown," Boykin said. "We would still be a British colony if not for the Black Robed pastors who encouraged separation from the crown." Then he said, "Today's pastors need to follow in the tradition established by the Black Robed Regiment...to be bold enough to preach unpopular messages. The people in the pews must hear the biblical truth."[697]

Should we fall into a World War III, some iteration of the former Black Robed Regiment might provide direction to the Body of Christ as they face the lack of protection in the face of catastrophic situations. In fact, that may require people in the pews to take up arms in defense of themselves and their communities.

Prayer: Focus on Leadership, Troops, and Protection

President Harry S. Truman reminded Americans:

> But all of us - at home, at war, wherever we may be—are within the reach of God's love and power. We all can pray. We all should pray. We should ask the fulfillment of God's will.[698]

Truman's call to prayer is consistent with 1 Timothy 2:1–2, which states:

> I exhort therefore, that, first of all, supplications, prayers, intercessions, and giving of thanks, be made for all men; For kings, and for all that are in authority; that we may lead a quiet and peaceable life in all godliness and honesty. (KJV)

When we pray, we should ask God to provide our leaders wise and godly counsel, godly character, and biblically based decision-making.

We should pray for those defending us from the enemy. After all, Proverbs 11:11 tells us, "By the blessing of the upright the city is exalted: but it is overthrown by the mouth of the wicked" (KJV). Those standing in the gap for us, our armed forces, and police warrant God's protection as they carry out their mission.

We should also pray for our own protection from the enemy, as well as for God's direction in our circumstances. In difficult times, we should pray for physical health, the ability to fight depression, protection from evil, and opportunities to encourage others suffering.

Don't Neglect Spiritual Relationship with Christ; Avoid Fear

In troubled times, it might be challenging not to be overcome by fear and, as a result, take our eyes off Christ. However, in those tough times, we should keep short accounts and constantly examine ourselves to maintain our integrity and proper relationship with Christ. Remember Psalms 34:4: "I sought the Lord, and he answered me and delivered me from all my fears" (NIV).

Share Christ with a Troubled World

War affects everyone, and in many cases, those found in tragic situations are very open to spiritual matters. Christians have answers to life's anxieties and should share the peace of God with those filled with fear. Remember the example of missionary Darlene sharing the gospel of Jesus Christ with Mr. Yamaji, the prison superintendent who evidently came to Christ? We are called to obedience and may not understand God's purpose until much later, if ever.

We read in John 16:33, where Christ said, "I have told you these things, so that in me you may have peace. In this world you will have trouble. But take heart! I have overcome the world" (NIV). Earlier in the book of John, Christ also said, "Peace I leave with you; my peace I give you. I do not give to you as the world gives. Do not let your hearts be troubled and do not be afraid" (John 14:27, NIV).

"War is cruelty," said Civil War General William Tecumseh Sherman. "There is no use trying to reform it. The crueler it is, the sooner it will be over." [699] The suffering and often wanton destruction of conflict demonstrates humankind's sinfulness. Therefore, the Christian caught in the throes of war is called to act against such injustice and use God's promise of peace amidst life's anxieties to explain the gift of salvation in Christ—even our enemies, as in the case of Darlene.

In Such Times Our Duty Is to Pray

- **Pray for the protection of the innocents.** After all, war destroys and often creates catastrophic crises, especially among innocent civilians. Pray that God will protect men, women, and children who live in daily mortal danger.

- **Pray for war refugees caught in the fight.** Some people are forced to leave their homes because the structures were destroyed; others leave because combatants chased them away. These people rendered homeless may have no food, water, medicine, and are desperate for help, much like a stray, injured animal. Pray these people will find aid, and if you can, assist them generously.
- **Pray for those suffering pain and loss.** As discussed throughout this book, war claims a price in life and blood. Pray for those who are grieving the loss of family and friends and for those suffering injuries and sickness due to the war.

Spirit-filled Christians know God is a "mighty fortress…amid the flood of mortal ills," a metaphor for war. We have a special role in those times and a calling to share His promises.

Conclusion

This chapter in four parts addressed Christians who prepare for and are caught in a war zone. We reviewed some testimonies of believers who have been caught in various conflicts, and considered what the Bible has to say about armed conflict. We briefly examined the just war theory and whether Christians can serve as combatants. The final portion of this chapter reviewed recommendations for Christians and their responsibilities in conflict areas.

The final chapter in *Preparing for World War III* considers the prophetic implications of the coming conflict and whether that future war might in fact lead to the prophetic end times.

Chapter 14

WORLD WAR III AND PROPHETIC END TIMES

We are like people under [a] sentence of death, waiting for the date to be set. We sense that something is about to happen. We know that things cannot go on as they are. History has reached an impasse. We are now on a collision course. Something is about to give.[700]

Reverend William Franklin "Billy" Graham (1918–2018), American evangelist, Southern Baptist minister

T his chapter argues that Scripture indicates that a future world war will usher this globe into the prophetic end times and the Second Coming of Jesus Christ. However, the problem for us today is that we don't know whether there might be multiple global conflicts ahead, meaning the one that appears to be on our immediate horizon may not necessarily be the final conflict spoken of in the Bible. Further, the geopolitically threatening situation with today's "axis of evil" countries could well fade and be replaced by a situation that's much worse.

In four parts, this chapter addresses the above issues. First, the Word is in fact clear that the world will be engulfed in a global war that brings in the prophetic end times, but we have no idea about the future much less the timing of the return of Jesus Christ. Second, biblical prophecy provides some indicators of that end-times scenario. Admittedly, many scriptural indicators appear to be evident today. However, we don't know whether those markers match the intensity promised in the Bible. Third, we know something about the end-times antagonists from biblical prophecy, but have no clear indication of whether they're necessarily the present-day rogue regimes in China, Russia, and Iran. Finally—and this may upset many Westerners—America is not found in biblical end-times prophecy.

At this point, for those who are anxious for the promised Rapture of the Church (1 Thessalonians 4:17), I encourage you to reconsider chapter 12 of this volume and begin to prepare for the next war. I'm not convinced we are necessarily close to the prophetic end times. If I am correct, then we must also prepare to execute our responsibilities outlined in chapter 13 to fulfill Christ's calling as we live for Him in this anti-Christian, upside-down world.

Jesus will return, but we don't know whether the next war will usher in the prophetic end times.
Photo by Pisit Heng on Unsplash[701]

Final World War and Prophetic End Times

There is no doubt world war is in our future. Scripture clearly states in Matthew 24:4–31 that global war will precede the Second Coming of Jesus Christ. But when will it happen?

We don't know the precise timing. We do, however, have clues, such as those found in Matthew 24:6–7:

[There will be] wars and rumors of wars but see to it that you are not alarmed. Such things must happen, but the end is still to come. Nation will rise against nation, and kingdom against kingdom. There will be famines and earthquakes in various places. (NIV)

Unfortunately, that description could represent the situation at virtually any point in the past century. Warfare seems inevitable, given humanity's fallen condition. However, we should understand that Jesus foretold of an escalation of conflicts preceding the end times. Evidently, Christ has not returned up to this point, so we wait and expect things to continue to get much worse.

Part of the issue about predicting the details about the end times is that nothing in Scripture says how many world wars are in our future.

After all, I see no evidence that World Wars I or II are mentioned in the Bible. All we know from God's Word is that the final global war will bring about the end times.

We do have some clues of that future conflict, however. The Bible describes that period as being fraught with intense tribulation and upheaval marked by wars, famines, natural disasters, and persecution of believers. No doubt, similar indicators have been evident for some time, but the Word does not provide a metric against which to measure today's woes and their intensity.

In Revelation 6, we read that the Apostle John speaks of this future tumultuous era, the seven-year Tribulation following the Rapture prior to Christ's return. Then we read about His actual return in chapter 19. Specifically, the prophet John said, "And I saw heaven opened, and behold a white horse; and he that sat upon him was called Faithful and True, and in righteousness he doth judge and make war" (Revelation 19:11, KJV). Verse 19 of chapter 19 continues, with John stating that he "saw the beast, and the kings of the earth, and their armies, gathered together to make war against him that sat on the horse, and against his army."

This means the kings of this world and their armies will be arrayed for battle against Christ in the final world war. Of course, the victor in this conflagration is Christ, who seizes the Antichrist and his False Prophet, and casts them and their armies into the lake of fire (Revelation 19:20–21).

The Righteous Christ, the King of Kings, defeats Satan and his armies. Immediately, the thousand-year reign of Christ commences, followed by Satan's release and his final rebellion. Christ ends that rebellion with fire from Heaven that consumes all (Revelation 20:7–10).

Then we read:

And God shall wipe away all tears from their eyes; and there shall be no more death, neither sorrow, nor crying, neither shall there be any more pain: for the former things are passed away. (Revelation 21:4, KJV).

Every believer looks forward to that day. However, although World War III will happen, it might not be the conflict that kicks off the prophetic end times. Only the Lord knows the exact circumstances and the timing of that final world war.

Regardless, we must remember Christ's admonition in Mark 13:37 to "Be on the alert!" (NASB).

What Are the Signs of the Prophetic End Times?

The following will help clarify whether the war on our horizon is the final conflict described in the Bible. We simply need to compare what the Scriptures say with what we begin to see around us once World War III begins to materialize.

The biblical end times are described in several passages in the Old and New Testaments. For example, in the book of Revelation, we read about the events leading up to the return of Jesus Christ. Those events include a series of judgments—catastrophic plagues referred to as the seven seals, seven trumpets, and seven vials.

Certainly, 2 Timothy 3:3–4 provides a stark description of conditions during the "last days." For some of us, the words signal what most of us are seeing today:

> For men shall be lovers of their own selves, covetous, boasters, proud, blasphemers, disobedient to parents, unthankful, unholy, without natural affection, trucebreakers, false accusers, incontinent, fierce, despisers of those that are good, traitors, heady, high-minded, lovers of pleasures more than lovers of God. (KJV)

Unfortunately, those signs have become rather common across history, especially over the past century. So, in themselves, their presence today doesn't necessarily mean we're living at the end of time. In fact, Jesus provides a caution about jumping to such a conclusion. He states in Matthew 24:24:

> For there shall arise false Christs, and false prophets, and shall shew great signs and wonders; insomuch that, if it were possible, they shall deceive the very elect. (KJV)

Therefore, true believers—the "elect"—must be cautious and heed Jesus' warning in John 14:21:

He that hath my commandments, and keepeth them, he it is that loveth me: and he that loveth me shall be loved of my Father, and I will love him, and will manifest myself to him. (KJV)

Our conundrum, upon seeing evidence of many of these indicators today, is knowing when they are bad enough to herald the end times. After all, Mark 13:32 states, "But of that day and that hour knoweth no man, no, not the angels which are in heaven, neither the Son, but the Father" (KJV). Christ provided a further caution in Matthew 24:5–8:

For many shall come in my name, saying, I am Christ; and shall deceive many. And ye shall hear of wars and rumors of wars: see that ye be not troubled: for all [these things] must come to pass, but the end is not yet. For nation shall rise against nation, and kingdom against kingdom: and there shall be famines, and pestilences, and earthquakes, in divers places. All these [are] the beginning of sorrows. (KJV)

We also see in Scripture there will be heavenly evidence of the end times. Specifically, Luke 21:24–26 states:

And they shall fall by the edge of the sword, and shall be led away captive into all nations: and Jerusalem shall be trodden down of the Gentiles, until the times of the Gentiles be fulfilled. And there shall be signs in the sun, and in the moon, and in the stars; and upon the earth distress of nations, with perplexity; the sea and the waves roaring; men's hearts failing them for fear, and for looking after those things which are coming on the earth: for the powers of heaven shall be shaken. (KJV)

Therefore, it should be self-evident that we must watch for the signs of the end times, but trust that God alone knows the last days. In the meantime, we are to be going about the Lord's work as outlined in chapter 13, living for Christ in these troubled days.

Also, consider that, as bad as things might get here on earth, there is always the possibility of global revival that prompts the Lord to put the coming end times on pause. After all, a global war could so devastate humanity that people, in desperation, will turn their hearts back to the Lord. History has seen numerous examples of mass revival amid great apostasy, turning around the direction of entire nations onto a more righteous pathway.

Who Are the End-Times Antagonists?

Present-day China and Russia captivate the attention of many students of prophetic Scripture because they seem to satisfy scriptural descriptions of those who launch the world's final global war. That is possible, but not knowable. Let me explain.

Some people would have us believe God encrypted the identity of contemporary China and Russia into his prophetic Word. Admittedly, it is interesting to search the Scriptures to try to correlate God's Word to contemporary situations. However, that's a dangerous practice and misuses the Word of God.

Years ago, I wrestled with this issue, and turned to an American biblical scholar and author, Dr. Michael S. Heiser, for answers. He cautioned Christians about trying to contemporize the Scriptures.

The material in this part of the chapter comes with slight modifications from my 2018 book, *Alliance of Evil*, which declared we were in a new cold war with China and Russia. Dr. Heiser's words were appropriate then and perhaps are more to the point today for this book. That's primarily because many people now agree with me that we're in a new cold war with China and Russia, and that those antagonists pose a true existential threat to America and the West, which will likely lead to a future global war.[702]

"I don't see any modern state as the focus of any biblical prophecy," Dr. Heiser explained. He acknowledged that "Israel of course plays a role because Armageddon is cast as a battle at…Mount Zion/Jerusalem, but these other modern states didn't exist. What we think of as Russia and China aren't even in the table of nations [in the biblical times], so it's doubtful people in the first century even knew they existed."[703]

"If we interpret scripture in its own context [not ours] we have to look at it quite differently," Heiser writes. He continues:[704]

You could say, "Well God knew about all those countries and countries that would become countries." Sure. God knew lots of things—like the brain is really the locus of intellect and emotions, not the kidneys or heart [as the ancients believed]; like a woman's hair had nothing to do with fecundity [capacity to produce off-spring], like the Earth really wasn't round and flat with a dome over it, like Jerusalem really wasn't the actual geographical center of the Earth, though Ezekiel calls it such—but God didn't correct the men he chose to produce scripture on these matters.… So why would I presume God would encrypt modern geo-political information into a first century (or much older) text? Wasn't the whole idea that the writers were supposed to be communicating to their own audience?[705]

This issue comes down to understanding God's intent with Scripture, according to Heiser. In a 2015 presentation available on YouTube, "The Naked Bible," Dr. Heiser seeks to clarify some fundamental misunderstandings about the Bible. For example, he states, "The Bible is not a paranormal event.… The writers were not zapped by God who took control over their minds in a trance and then wrote the text." God worked through human circumstances after having prepared the writers throughout their lives. Writing God's Word was "a providential process," not "a paranormal event."[706]

Heiser then states that inspiration does not involve modern content, because "God's word is written for us not to us." It is also "the product of culture that produced it" to convey a theological message in the language of the day that is consistent with the ancient world." Therefore, Heiser insists, "Let the Bible be what it is and resist the urge to be what it isn't."[707]

Heiser's views do not dispute end-times prophetic Scriptures, but they caution modern Bible students against reading into the ancient text something God unlikely intended. Frankly, even though contemporary geopolitical events seem to fit what ancient prophets like Ezekiel and the Apostle John wrote, let's not be too dogmatic.

Heiser then proposes:

How is it sound hermeneutical method to think prophecy was about countries and peoples the biblical writers knew nothing about? If someone can show me how that approach is sound, then it changes things. I've just never come across a coherent way to do that. I prefer to read scripture in its own context, not a foreign context. It's a simple strategy, but it's the one that is most coherently defended.[708]

Non-seminarians like me likely aren't familiar with the "hermeneutical method." So, I visited compellingtruth.org, an organization that boasts that its purpose is "presenting the truth of the Christian faith in a compelling, relevant, and practical way." That site explains hermeneutics as follows.

Biblical hermeneutics is the field of study related to the interpretation of the Scriptures. Because Christians have historically lived based on the teachings of the Bible, and because "All Scripture is given by inspiration of God, and is profitable for doctrine, for reproof, for correction, for instruction in righteousness, that the man of God may be complete, thoroughly equipped for every good work." (2 Timothy 3:16–17 NKJV), a proper interpretation of the Bible's contents is vital. As the Apostle Paul wrote in 2 Timothy 2:15, the Christian's goal is to "Be diligent to present yourself approved to God, a worker who does not need to be ashamed, rightly dividing the word of truth.[709]

Biblical hermeneutics involves many principles of literature that have developed over time. For example, one principle involves first identifying the genre of that passage of study. Genesis included much narrative content. Many of Paul's writings are letters. The Psalms are poetic while the Proverbs are wisdom literature. Each genre is understood in unique ways that help readers better understand the meaning of the passage.

Three important guidelines related to biblical hermeneutics include observation, interpretation, and application. Observation focuses on what the text says—the who, what, when, why, and how? Interpretation seeks to understand the meaning of the passage along with various controversies regarding passages or topics. Application then applies the original, historic understanding of a biblical passage to a contemporary context.

Of great importance in this process of biblical hermeneutics is to interpret Scripture according to its original setting. This includes the historical context, grammar, genre, literary context, and more. Rather than asking, "What do these words mean to me?" proper biblical hermeneutics first seeks to understand what the passage meant when written. Only after this does the reader or interpreter look to discover how the original intent of the writing applies to one's own personal context.

In more recent years, postmodern literary theory has attacked this historic biblical hermeneutic, emphasizing "reader response" more than or instead of the author's original intent. While application and human emotion are important elements to spiritual growth, this does not negate the importance of understanding Scripture from its original perspective. Both inductive study as well as modern application must serve as part of a healthy biblical hermeneutic.

Finally, a biblical hermeneutic is of great importance because of the power of the Word of God. Hebrews 4:12 (NKJV) teaches, "For the word of God is living and powerful, and sharper than any two-edged sword, piercing even to the division of soul and spirit, and of joints and marrow, and is a discerner of the thoughts and intents of the heart." Scripture offers much power for those who would study its contents and look to apply its principles to their lives today.

Another interpretive tool is exegesis, which refers to drawing truths out of the Bible. This is like hermeneutics in that we should check the context of the verses, chapter, and the entire book of the Bible to capture a more complete understanding. Then we should consider the original language as well.

Alternatively, "eisegesis" refers to the practice of reading things into the inspired text, as opposed to drawing things out. This can be a dangerous practice because it imposes one's own preferred views upon the Bible. Although the interpretive effort may be sincere, it is influenced by the inevitable flaws of humankind and should be avoided especially if we are dogmatic about those interpretations.

Now, consider some of the scriptural interpretations allegedly pointing to China and Russia as major players in the end times. Then apply the explanation of the hermeneutical method above to either confirm or reject these interpretations.

There are two common arguments to support the view that China, for example, is involved in the end-times prophetic scenario.

China: The "Kings from the East" in Revelation 16 Who Join the Battle of Armageddon

Revelation 16:12–16 states:

And the sixth angel poured out his vial upon the great river Euphrates; and the water thereof was dried up, that the way of the kings of the east might be prepared. And I saw three unclean spirits like frogs come out of the mouth of the dragon, and out of the mouth of the beast, and out of the mouth of the false prophet. For they are the spirits of devils, working miracles, which go forth unto the kings of the earth and of the whole world, to gather them to the battle of that great day of God Almighty. Behold, I come as a thief. Blessed is he that watcheth, and keepeth his garments, lest he walk naked, and they see his shame. And he gathered them together into a place called in the Hebrew tongue Armageddon. (KJV)

This passage in Revelation describes the Battle of Armageddon, which occurs at the end of the Tribulation. Leading up to the battle, the Euphrates River will dry up, allowing the "kings from the east" to march toward Israel. Some people interpret those kings to be the modern nation of China. Thus, the massive Chinese army, which is part of a global coalition, crosses the dried riverbed and sweeps westward to join up with the forces of the Antichrist.

It is impossible to know for certain whether this Scripture means modern-day China. Certainly today, that nation has a massive military and is an economic world power. (See appendix B.) We know that under Chinese President Xi, the Chinese military is rapidly expanding its influence across the world—but will that expansion at some point include an attack on Israel at the Battle of Armageddon? We just don't know.

Besides, if one studies a map of the track of the Euphrates River through present-day Syria and Iraq, it isn't clear why any army today, especially one originating in current China, would take a cross-land route to Israel. The ancient Silk Road crosses the Euphrates River north of Baghdad, and presumably an army dependent on that route would have to do the same. But a modern army with ships and aircraft would not elect a ground movement.

China: Major Contributor to the 200-Million-Man Army
in the Battle of Armageddon

Revelation 9:15–17 reads:

> And the four angels were loosed, which were prepared for an hour, and a day, and a month, and a year, for to slay the third part of men. And the number of the army of the horsemen were two hundred thousand thousand [200 million]: and I heard the number of them. And thus, I saw the horses in the vision, and them that sat on them, having breastplates of fire, and of jacinth, and brimstone: and the heads of the horses were as the heads of lions; and out of their mouths issued fire and smoke and brimstone. (KJV)

A two hundred-million-man army is hard to imagine, even in the contemporary world of nearly eight billion souls. However, for those looking for an explanation of how such a massive army might be assembled, they understandably look to China, which has a large (3.3 million members—active, reserve, and paramilitary) standing armed forces, a far cry from two hundred million, however.

Interpreting this Scripture to point to contemporary China is problematic for several reasons, not the least of which is that it says nothing about an army from the east. Rather, the verse speaks of a demonic horde riding "horses." Further, the battle of Revelation 9 occurs after the sixth trumpet judgment, and the battle of Revelation 16, which involves the "kings of the east," occurs about three and a half years later. The timing is not right for such an interpretation.

Besides, no one has ever seen a two hundred-million-man army. I've seen and been part of large army formations and have some appreciation for the logistics associated with huge ground forces. Frankly, two hundred million men and their equipment cannot fit inside the Valley of Armageddon. The triangular-shaped Plain of Jezreel (Valley of Armageddon), is 36 miles by 15 miles, or 540 square miles, which means 370,370 soldiers and their equipment must fit into each square mile. There must be a better explanation for this Scripture.

Claims That Russia Is an End-Times Player

Even the leader of the Russian Orthodox Church believes humanity is approaching the end times, and Russia is a factor. In November 2017, Patriarch Kirill at Moscow's Christ the Savior Cathedral said, "One must be blind not to see the approach of the terrible moments of history about which the apostle and evangelist John the theologian spoke in his Revelation." He explained that the apostle's apocalyptic vision is being brought about by sinful behavior.[710]

Russian clergy are serious about the coming apocalypse. Archpriest Vesevolod Chapalin said it is Russia's God-given mission to stop America. "It is no coincidence that we have often, at the price of our own lives… stopped all global projects that disagreed with our conscience, with our vision of history and, I would say, with God's own truth," the archpriest told Interfax in 2014. "Such was Napoleon's project; such was Hitler's project. We will stop the American project too." Then, Chapalin said, Russia would lead the world against the forces of the Antichrist in an apocalyptic struggle. Who is that leader?

Russian philosopher Aleksandr Dugin sees Russian President Vladimir Putin as an Eastern Orthodox czar leading the war against the Antichrist in an apocalyptic struggle. In fact, Putin is our *katechon*, Dugin explained. The Greek word *katechon* is used in 2 Thessalonians 2:6–7 to describe a force that holds back the "mystery of iniquity." To Dugin, the "mystery of iniquity" is the secularized West.

Does that mean that Putin is Gog?

Ezekiel's Gog and Magog Point to Russia

Ezekiel 38:1–3 states:

And the word of the Lord came unto me, saying, Son of man, set thy face against Gog, the land of Magog, the chief prince of Meshech and Tubal, and prophesy against him, and say, Thus saith the Lord God; Behold, I am against thee, O Gog, the chief prince of Meshech and Tubal. (KJV)

Gog is a person from the land of Magog and the leader of Tubal and Meshek and a confederacy of nations: Persia, Cush, Put, Gomer, and Beth Togarmiah (Ezekiel 38:5–6). Gog has plans to attack Israel, and it's clear that the Lord is against him and he will be defeated (Ezekiel 38:4, 19–23; 39:3–5).

"Magog" is identified as a land "in the far north" of Israel, which many Bible commentators interpret as Russia. Or it could be a general reference to barbarians near the Black and Caspian seas. It is true geographically that Russia is to Israel's north and that, by association, "Rosh" is a reference to Russia and "Meshek" could be Moscow or people of the Black Sea (also north of Israel) and "Tubal," could be in central Turkey.

Therefore, the area referenced in Ezekiel 38–39 is territorially now referred to as Russia.

Dr. Heiser takes great umbrage with this view. He writes in *The Unseen Realm*:

The prophetic description in Ezekiel 38–39 of the invasion of "Gog, of the land of Magog" (Ezekiel 38:1–3, 14–15) is well known and the subject of much interpretive dispute, both scholarly and fanciful. One of the secure points is that Gog will come from "the heights of the north" (38:15; 39:2). While many scholars have focused on the literal geographic aspects of this phrasing, few have given serious thought to its mythological associations in Ugaritic/Canaanite religion with Baal, lord of the dead.

An ancient reader would have looked for an invasion from the north but would have cast that invasion in a supernatural context. In other words, the language of Ezekiel is not simply about a human invader or human armies. An ancient reader would also have noticed that this invasion would come at a time when the tribes had been united and dwelt in peace and safety within the Promised Land—in other words, since the period of exile had ended.

The battle of Gog and Magog would be something expected after the initiation of Yahweh's plan to reclaim the nations and, therefore, draw his children, Jew, or gentile, from those nations. The Gog invasion would be the response of supernatural evil against the messiah and his kingdom. This is in fact precisely how it is portrayed in Revelation 20:7–10.

Gog would have been perceived as either a figure empowered by supernatural evil or an evil quasi-divine figure from the supernatural world bent on the destruction of God's people. For this reason, Gog is regarded by many biblical scholars as a template for the New Testament anti-Christ figure.

While Magog and "the heights of the north" are not precisely defined in the Gog prophecy, the point is not about literal geography per se. Rather, it is the supernatural backdrop to the whole "northern foe" idea that makes any such geographical reference important. For sure ancient Jews would expect that the reconstituted kingdom of Yahweh would be shattered by an enemy from the north—as it had before. But ancient Jews would also have thought in supernatural terms. A supernatural enemy in the end times would be expected to come from the seat of Baal's authority—the supernatural underworld realm of the dead, located in the heights of the north. Gog is explicitly described in such terms.[711]

Russia Will Lead an Alliance of Nations against Israel

Ezekiel 38:13 states that when the aggressors (often identified as being led by Russia) move against Israel, other nations will join their alliance, such as "Persia (modern-day Iran), Put (modern-day Sudan), Cush (modern-day Libya), Gomer (part of modern-day Turkey), and Beth Togarmah (another portion of modern-day Turkey or possibly Syria)."[712]

Some commentators believe this war is one of the events leading up to the beginning of the Tribulation. Others believe it will occur close to the midpoint of the Tribulation, since Israel will be "dwelling without walls, and having neither bars nor gates" (Ezekiel 38:11)—in other words, Israel will feel secure at that time, possibly because of the covenant they have signed with the Antichrist (Daniel 9:27). Either way, this battle is distinct from the Battle of Armageddon, which occurs at the end of the Tribulation.

God promises to destroy Gog's army: "And I will bring him to judgment with pestilence and bloodshed; I will rain down on him, on his troops, and on the many peoples who are with him, flooding rain, great hailstones, fire, and brimstone" (Ezekiel 38:22, NKJV). The bodies of the fallen army of Magog will be buried, but it will take over seven months to complete the macabre task (Ezekiel 39:12, 14). This supernatural judgment will have the effect of preserving Israel and turning many hearts to God: "Thus I will magnify Myself and sanctify Myself, and I will be known in the eyes of many nations. Then they shall know that I am the LORD" (Ezekiel 38:23, NKJV). Many will be saved during the tribulation (Revelation 7), and the fulfillment of Ezekiel 38–39 will be one means by which God will bring people to a knowledge of Himself.

There is much we do not know for certain about Ezekiel's prophecy, including the timing of these events. However, it is possible contemporary Russia could be involved and will in fact lead an end-times league of nations to seize Israel's land. The prophet Ezekiel comforts Israel in much the same way as Moses had centuries ago: "For the LORD your God is He who goes with you, to fight for you against your enemies, to save you" (Deuteronomy 20:4, NKJV).

There are likely other Scriptures and interpretations that place both Russia and China in active roles in the prophetic end times. However, whatever those passages and their interpretations, they're based on speculation and employ questionable hermeneutic methods.

Emergent Alternative Non-State Antagonists

Put aside named nation-states like China and Russia playing a role at the end times to consider the modern phenomenon of the non-state antagonist. The emergence of globalization has created new centers of world power, especially in the information age, with social media and nongovernment organizations like the United Nations, the World Health Organization, corporations with budgets larger than most nations, and various international deep-state groups like the World Economic Forum.

These modern phenomena have taken on a life of their own and are not respecters of borders and sovereign governments, but claim to speak for all humanity. In fact, such non-state entities, thanks to globalization, may well become the future antagonists as opposed to actual nation-states that make way for the prophetic end times.

Understand that "globalism" is a synonym for "globalization," the system of global economic interconnection most often embraced by liberal groups like labor unions and climate-change alarmists. They claim global-ization is a dispassionate concept associated with increasing connectivity that makes life better for all humanity. Unfortunately, it is far more sinis-ter and potentially humankind's future nemesis.

The world's leading globalists are networked self-consumed elitists and backed by many naïve supporters who seek to control everything and everyone on earth. They manipulate the masses with sophisticated information campaigns using social media, education, and psychological manipulation.

The core governing philosophy of globalists is aligned with fascism, socialism, and Marxism—always endorsing group over individual—all the while espousing a utopian vision of the world to the gullible masses. These self-righteous elites could well become the future antagonists that war among themselves and thus touch off the prophetic end times.

I encourage readers to consider my 2016 book, *The Deeper State, Inside the War on Trump by Corrupt Elites, Secret Societies, and the Builders of an Imminent Final Empire*. That book exposes the globalists' agenda and how they seek to take over the world. It is quite possible that these non-state globalist entities fight among themselves using nation-state militaries as proxies that create the scenario that leads the way for the Antichrist and then the end times outlined in the book of Revelation.

I want to conclude this exploration of the prophetic word vis-à-vis a future world war by addressing the question: Why isn't the United States found in the prophetic Scriptures?

Where Is America in the Prophetic End Times?

Today, the United States remains a world power, which opposes the "axis of evil." Our current significant role as a nation in world affairs is no guarantee we will continue to be a player, especially in the biblical end times. After all, as many Bible scholars argue, America is absent from the end-times prophetic Scriptures. What happens to America, and does that necessarily influence the roles, if any, China, and Russia play in the end times?

Dr. David R. Reagan, the founder of Lamb & Lion Ministries, explains that the absence of America in biblical prophecy is based on pure specula-tion. For example, Isaiah 18 speaks of a people "tall and smooth" who are "feared far and wide," which some authors believe refers to a nation divided by a great river, such as the Mississippi River (the United States).[713]

One of the more popular Scriptures used by some to support the belief about the demise of America before the end times is Ezekiel 38, which the prophet describes as an invasion of Israel launched by a nation "from the remote parts of the north." This nation is considered Russia by some authors, but America is not suggested here.

Some of the same authors go on to claim that the passage in Ezekiel 38:13, "the merchants of Tarshish and all its villages," is a reference to Britain and English-speaking nations such as the United States. Apparently, Tarshish was once a seaport town near current-day Cadiz, Spain. Many years ago, so goes the conjecture, people from Tarshish moved to England and then eventually to the United States. Thus, "the young lions of Tarshish" mentioned in Ezekiel 38 is thought to apply to contemporary America. Further, in the final conflict when Israel is invaded by "Gog of Magog," the young lions of Tarshish say, "What are you doing?" Americans are allegedly monitoring the conflict from afar and ask the question, but evidently have no influence over the war's outcome.

Other Bible speculators claim that Revelation 12:13–17 identifies the US as the "wings of a great eagle" that helps Jews escape the Tribulation. Why? The "great eagle" is, some claim, a tipoff that the United States, which is identified by the bald eagle, the emblem of the United States, rescues the Jewish remnant in Israel by an airlift out of the grip of the Antichrist.

Finally, according to Dr. Reagan, another widely used passage to identify the United States in biblical end-times prophecy is Revelation 18, specifically the phrase "Babylon the great." Dr. Reagan says that chapter is about the last Gentile empire that dominates the earth at the Lord's Second Coming and it is not the United States.

There is evidently, based on the above examples, no meaningful mention of the US in Bible prophecy. That leaves us with only generalizable prophecies applicable to all nations, including the US, that will be judged at the end times and as a result cease to exist.

There are two alternative explanations as to why America falls out of the spotlight, according to Dr. Reagan: economic catastrophe and destruction. The economic destruction is not that hard to believe, given today's economic conditions and, especially, America's high debt ($35+ trillion), the ongoing issuance of fiat currency by the US Federal Reserve, the fact that America is a service-based economy that overconsumes, the rise of the giant and very competitive Chinese economy, and much more.

America could also be militarily destroyed—especially if we continue our naïve, hubristic ways. Yes, another nation, Reagan suggests Russia (or perhaps China), launches a preemptive nuclear attack on America, allegedly because our country is the only one willing to defend Israel in the end times. He suggests that Ezekiel 39:6 is key here in that the fire—perhaps the nuclear-tipped ballistic missiles launched from Russian submarines—falls on "those who inhabit the coastlands in safety," to wit, the United States. Once again, that is possible, but what mitigates against such a view is that Russia would cease to exist, given the certainty that the US would destroy Russia with nuclear weapons as well.

There is also the possibility that the Rapture (1 Thessalonians 4:17) removes so many American Christians that it quickly leads to the demise of the nation. The logic goes something like the following: All American, born-again Christians, who make up perhaps a third of the US population, or one hundred million souls, suddenly disappear from the face of the earth. That event causes the American economy to implode, and suddenly the country is militarily weakened to the point of impotence. This theory depends on born-again Christians being in many of the critical national security roles and their sudden disappearance results in the collapse of America's national defense.

Are these rational explanations? You decide. However, no one really knows.

The analysis of the Scripture outlined above should create enough doubt for you to question the reliability of those arguing with great confidence that China, Russia, and the United States are end-times players. Further, whatever you conclude after reviewing this analysis has no bearing on the ultimate reliability of the Scriptures. None. What this analysis suggests is that humankind, no matter how smart and in tune with the Scriptures, just doesn't know the details of the end times—concerning what nations, time, and events will be involved.

Yes, I believe the Scripture will be fulfilled exactly as it states. I do not know the details of the end times, and I sincerely doubt any other human does, either. So, what then must we do?

274 • PREPARING FOR WORLD WAR III

Arguably, as I indicated in the introduction to this chapter, we need to focus on the present. We need to be prepared to address the issues outlined in chapters 12 and 13. Yes, we should keep our eye on the indicators of end-times prophecy, but refuse to be so heavenly focused that we are no earthly good to God's plans for the present.

Conclusion

This chapter in four parts addressed significant issues facing our world. Yes, it appears a global war is at our doorstep, but no one knows whether this will be the final war that sets into motion the prophetic end times. Certainly, the Bible identifies indicators of that future era, but we have no clue as to the Lord's true timing. It is a misuse of the Scriptures to declare that China and Russia are the true end-times antagonists. In fact, the end-times antagonists could well be non-state globalists vying among themselves that leads to the arrival of the Antichrist. Then, as disappointing as it may be to Americans, there is no biblical evidence that the US is a player at the end times.

What is certain today is that the contemporary geopolitical situation presents many markers that seem to fit popular interpretations of end-times Scriptures, but at best those views are based on speculation clouded with uncertainty. Therefore, although we should be mindful of those Scriptures, our primary effort ought to be focused on the Great Commission (Matthew 28:16–20) while remaining watchful for the signs of the end times outlined in 2 Timothy 3, and heed what the Lord Jesus states in Matthew 24:36: "But of that day and hour knoweth no man, no, not the angels of heaven, but my Father only" (KJV).

AFTERWORD

If we don't end war, war will end us.[714]

H. G. Wells (1866–1946),
English writer and historian best known for science fiction novels

H umans are motivated to act before war begins, if in fact they fully appreciate the cost of such a conflict. The populations of Germany and Japan mostly supported their leaders at the beginning of the Second World War. However, it is unlikely they would have endorsed such an adventure if they had known the full extent of the cost in advance. The unanswered question at the time just prior to World War II is whether it would have been possible for the citizenry of Japan, Germany, and Italy to stop their leaders from launching such a foolish adventure. That is unlikely.

In some way, this hypothetical about the situation leading up to the Second World War reminds me of the thinking behind the Allies' strategic bombing in that war. At the time, did the Allies fully appreciate the implications of the European theater's bombing campaign would have on the German citizens, much less the Nazi regime?

History demonstrates that the bombing campaign had the opposite effect than the one the Allies intended. Rather than hurrying the Nazi's decision to abandon war, the population in Germany at the time became numb to the pain and encouraged their government's resilience to keep up the war effort. That begs a contemporary question: Are today's alliance of evil governments like China and Russia and their respective populations ready to withstand the pain and sacrifice associated with yet another global conflict?

That is a discouraging concern, especially for the West, which hopes to deter such a future war. After all, it should trouble everyone that the use of our most sophisticated weapons could significantly devastate our collective way of life. Why, then, might our enemies take such a risk? Evidently, it appears that this time they dismiss the lessons from past wars and believe they have a real possibility of winning, which means the destruction of the United States as a world power and its Western-oriented international order. That is quite an enticing trophy!

For that reason, the next global war could be quite different from the past, not just because of the incentive (humble the US and change the world order), but because of the level of devastation modern technology affords both sides. Further, and especially for the Christian community, the possible widespread devastation and evil outcome of the next global conflict could be so utterly horrendous that it is understandable why some Christians anticipate that war will bring about the prophetic end times.

That is why *Preparing for World War III* provides plenty of rationale and grist for nation-states and average citizens to aggressively deter global war. However, if that effort fails, we must be prepared for that fight, hoping to come out the other side to then rebuild civilization from the ruins or welcome the end of this world—that is, assuming that conflict ushers in the prophetic end times.

In summary, *Preparing for World War III* in fourteen chapters across six sections makes the case that our world is careening toward another massive conflict—a global war—and the one at our doorstep just might be different than the previous two global conflicts because of the level of devastation.

Section I demonstrates that much of humanity and the various governments are in fact thinking about global war. After all, there is a mad rush across most nations to arm up with the most sophisticated war-making technologies. That buildup is echoed by the clamoring of nation-states to align themselves with like-minded partners, thus the world is polarizing once again, much like it was in the post-Second World War era known as the Cold War.

Section II explores the histories of the previous two world wars to discover the causes and indicators of those conflicts and what happened during those eras that laid the foundations for subsequent tensions. That effort outlines numerous lessons from those past wars that inform the value of proper deterrence and how to prepare before a future conflict if in fact deterrence once again fails.

Section III indicates that the primary causes of the Second World War are present today and likely will encourage the world to stumble into another global tragedy. In fact, that war will be unlike the past international conflicts because of the proliferation of modern technology and how, this time, battlefields will engage all domains—air, land, sea, cyber and space—and potentially be the most destructive ever experienced in history. Given that reality, this book includes a chapter that identifies three potential scenarios for that worldwide conflict and the likely effects of combat for America's homeland. This time, we should anticipate that our nation will be directly impacted by the conflict, which could be quite devastating.

Section IV addresses our level of preparation for such a conflict and our deterrence effectiveness. In both cases, the US is left wanting, because we have seriously under-invested in the right, and enough, weapons platforms and personnel, albeit as our collective antagonists are rapidly readying themselves for a devastating blow against our country and Western allies. Meanwhile, our "integrated deterrence" strategy misses the mark by failing to sufficiently discourage our adversaries from moving in a dangerous direction toward conflict.

Section V is all about preparing for that future conflict. What is the true nature of the threat for our nation and the implications for government at all levels, national to local? There are concrete recommendations on how our various levels of administration must prepare for war. Also, we take a deep dive into what average American citizens must do to prepare themselves, their families, and their neighborhoods for the unthinkable—conflict that directly affects our communities, both thanks to the loss of public services and access to food, but also the possibility of foreign forces arriving in our homeland or at least holding us hostage from afar using sophisticated weapons.

Section VI is directed at the Christian community. Often, Christians are targeted for additional persecution in times of war because of their faith. That special attention, however, doesn't mean we should necessarily avoid war, much less abstain from becoming combatants. Further, crises present special opportunities wherein Christians are called to exercise their God-given responsibilities. Why? We have eternal hope and the promise for the future, which we are obligated to share with the lost. Finally, global conflict must be considered from a prophetic perspective, and the Christian has a unique view as to the inevitable outcome of the final world war,

278 • PREPARING FOR WORLD WAR III

which is the Second Coming of Jesus Christ and all that portends from the Scriptures.

Global war is an unpleasant thought! However, ignoring the prospect is not only naïve but incredibly irresponsible. Nations that properly prepare for the unthinkable are more than likely to either deter such a conflict or, if that fails, better weather it than others.

Unfortunately, war has consistently been part of humankind's long history on earth. We know from the Scripture it will continue to creep into everyday life until the return of Christ. Therefore, our mandate ought to be deterrence, yet we should always be prepared by making sure that, when efforts to forestall war inevitably fail, our resources, training, and resilience are sufficient to ensure our survival and our ability to rebuild.

Ultimately, there will be a future world war that ushers in the prophetic end times. It is not clear if the next global conflict will be that final war. If it is the end, then the Scriptures and the indicators outlined in chapter 14 of this book will light up our skies, thus it will be hard to deny. However, if that war is but another interlude in history that devastates our populations and our countries, then we must be prepared to survive and rebuild as we patiently wait for the final era. In either case, the Christian's mandate is clear: to advance the gospel of Christ until He calls us home.

APPENDICES

APPENDIX A

Modern Weapons and Their Capabilities

Technology is rapidly changing the face of the modern battlefield. This appendix begins with some of the major emergent changes and then takes a deeper dive to explore what capabilities are being developed over the next decade plus.

The future will provide capabilities that will shock most of us.
Photo by Thibault Dandré on Unsplash[715]

Near-term, Emergent Capabilities for the Battlefield

Rocket artillery: Ground forces are upgrading their rocket artillery with significant advancements in accuracy and range, almost reaching the capabilities previously attributed to short-range ballistic missiles. Therefore, rocket artillery with new payloads makes the system more flexible, especially with the expected integration of more guidance methods such as GPS-guided cannon shells like the Excalibur, named after the mythical sword of King Arthur. Beyond rocket artillery are the soon-coming electromagnetic railguns, which will increase weapon potency thanks in part to projectile hypersonic speeds and compressed reaction time.

Anti-ship missiles: Maritime supremacy is a critical aspect of modern warfare, which depends on global weapons and technology. Notably, the marriage of technology and naval weapons is the proliferation of long-range missile systems that reach across international maritime boundaries. Most significant within this class are modern anti-ship missiles that include the R-360 Neptune (Ukrainian), Long-Range Anti-Ship Missile (US Navy & Air Force), BrahMos (Russian), YJ-21 (Chinese) and 3M-22 Zircon (Russian).

Directed energy weapons: No longer are directed energy weapons just found in science fiction novels. Many countries are heavily invested in them, some nations have tested them in combat situations, and some are nearing production. Their initial role will be for short-range air defense and counter-rocket, artillery missions. Some of the systems in the mix include Peresvet (Russian), Iron Beam (Israeli), and Self-Protect High Energy Laser Demonstrator (US Air Force).

Small-arms weapon: Even small arms are experiencing technological advances such as the US Army's Next Generation Squad Weapon. The NGSW is a new rifle, light machine gun, equipped with a fire-control system and 6.8 mm cartridge.

Robot dogs of war: The Ukraine army is using robotic "war dogs" on the battlefield to deliver critical equipment. The British robotic dog, Brit Alliance Dog (BAD2), is equipped with remote-sensing technology and a thermal-infrared camera for tricky landscape. It can also conduct reconnaissance.[716]

Armor vehicles: Ground forces are experiencing the introduction of some sophisticated armor platforms such as Russia's Armata family of armored combat vehicles—i.e., tank, infantry-fighting vehicle, a self-propelled artillery piece, and other variants. Of course, the most prominent of these is the T-14 main battle tank Armata variant.

The T-14 is a radical departure from previous Soviet and Russian tanks, to include the T-90. The T-14 is fitted with numerous advanced features and puts a premium on crew survivability, a significant change from past armor. For example, it has an unmanned turret and the crew is physically separated from the ammunition magazine. The vehicle boasts passive laminated armor combined with reactive armor and an active protection system. In fact, the Afghanit active protection system radar detects, tracks, and intercepts incoming projectiles.[717]

Hypersonic weapons: The US Department of Defense (DoD) is working on a variety of hypersonic weapons that can move at least five times the speed of sound and have unpredictable flight paths. One American version is the X-51 Waverider, an unmanned scramjet aircraft launched from a B-52 or F-35. This platform could allow the US to successfully attack a heavily defended target from a great distance. Other nations such as China are developing similar hypersonic systems, and Russia claims it has already employed a hypersonic weapon in its war with Ukraine.[718]

Space weapons: The DoD claims China and Russia pose a significant risk to space assets, through cyber warfare, electronic attacks, and ground-to-orbit missiles capable of destroying satellites. As early as 2020, the Pentagon's annual report stated China claims that country has operational anti-satellite missiles, which puts America's significant inventory of satellites at risk.[719] Meanwhile, Russia is developing a nuclear-powered satellite that has the potential to cripple US satellites with electromagnetic pulses.[720] Currently (as of May 2023), there are 7,560 active satellites in orbit, and most (5,184) belong to the United States. That number is expected to grow to more than 24,500 by 2031, a 70 percent increase that is mostly due to commercial growth.[721]

Futuristic Capabilities for the Battlefield

The above systems are either on hand now or arriving soon, while the following systems are futuristic. These paint a scarily dangerous picture of the future battlefield.

Camouflage that works: BAE Systems' ADAPTIV camouflage masks the vehicle's infrared signature and shields detection. That system is proposed for ships, helicopters, and ground systems. The ADAPTIV camouflage is a honeycomb, ghostlike system that makes the vehicle invisible to enemy thermal imaging devices.[722]

Molten metal penetrator: The US Defense Advanced Research Projects Agency (DARPA) is working on the Magneto Hydrodynamic Explosive Munition (MAHEM), a magnetic flux generator to fire "a projectile without the traditional use of chemical explosives creating a more efficient and precise launch system." This system uses "molten metal to penetrate enemy armored vehicles increasing lethality and effectiveness on the battlefield."[723]

Area denial system: The Taser Shockwave is a large-scale "area denial system designed to help assist with riot control situations." More specifically, it is "a large modular system for firing numerous TASER X26 stun guns in a 20-degree arc with a 25-foot range." It is capable of being daisy-chained for use in a large area.[724]

Heavily armed ground robotic system: The Modular Advanced Armed Robotic System is a heavily armed robot intended to go where the commander fears to send his soldiers. The MAARS can be armed with a 400-round M240B machine gun, a grenade launcher, and can help evacuate wounded soldiers. It can move at 7 MPH and operates with a 12-hour battery system.[725]

Unmanned combat vehicle: BAE Systems has a prototype unmanned combat vehicle, Black Knight Unmanned Combat Vehicle, that looks like a small tank and has tank-like firepower. It is designed for high-risk situations for human operators. Although it has challenges associated with GPS and sensors, it can deploy via military transport and is armed with a 30mm cannon and 7.62 coaxial machine gun.[726]

Super-soldier system: Lockheed Martin's Human Universal Load Carrier system is "a hydraulic-powered exoskeleton suit intended to support soldiers on the battlefield and allow them to transport heavy loads for extended periods of time without the usual exhaustion that would come with such a task."[727]

Science fiction-like microbugs: DARPA is working on harnessing insects with military hardware such as cameras and tracking devices. Since the 1940s, the US government has sought to strap a circuit board on the back of a beetle, which makes them cyborg bugs to do the government's bidding. Evidently, DARPA is making progress.[728]

Almost perfect sniper weapon: Precision-guided firearms use the missile lock-on system from a fighter jet and apply it to long-range rifle systems. Specifically, the link helps guide the sniper's bullet to its target by accounting for human error.[729]

Very smart bullets: DARPA is working on the Extreme Accuracy Tasked Ordnance, "a self-steering, guided bullet designed for military snipers to support improved accuracy." The smart bullet can home in on a target and change course in midair to compensate for changes in wind speed. This potentially gives the novice marksman near-pinpoint accuracy at long ranges.[730]

Stealth tank: The Polish Obrum PL-01 Stealth Tank has a modular ceramic-aramid shell capable of a full range of protection from most projectiles. This fifth-generation tank is practically invisible to both infra-red and radar-detection systems.[731]

Stealth destroyer: The Zumwalt class destroyer is a multi-role battle-ship with stealth capabilities that presents a counter low-radar cross-section and a wave-piercing hull to make it less detectable. The destroyer boasts an advanced gun system that combines a 155mm naval gun capable of firing a long-range land attack projectile over 80 nautical miles.[732]

Naval electromagnetic rail gun: The Office of Naval Research has in development an electromagnetic rail gun "capable of firing projectiles at over 4,500mph and smashing through concrete structures 100 miles away." The challenge is to overcome the power requirements.[733]

Hololens for combatants: Microsoft has a US Army contract to supply Hololens devices. That system, Integrated Visual Augmentation System, will assist soldiers in combat by using augmented reality. It will allow soldiers to see through smoke and around corners, and acquire information from their immediate environment.[734]

In conclusion, most of us find the above "futuristic" technologies fascinating. However, the problem for futurists like the nineteenth century's George Orwell, author of *1984*, and others who envision the application of future technologies is that mankind's imagination isn't nearly sharp enough to truly anticipate how automation and science might develop over the next decade, much less the next century. Therefore, expect that today's futurists are wrong, much like Orwell's predictions fell flat, and that future applications of technology will develop in ways we cannot even imagine. That said, tomorrow's battlefields will be very different than today's combat environment, and likely much more deadly. Hopefully, that level of lethality will be so threatening that humanity will totally abandon any thought of war because of the potential risk of annihilating all life on earth.

APPENDIX B

Comparison of Military Capabilities

Five primary sources were used to compile this comparison of military capabilities across the armed forces of the United States, the Russian Federation, and the People's Republic of China. First, Janes is a public service organization that hosts the world's most complete collection of open-source intelligence, which includes orders of battle for all the world's militaries.[735] Second, the United States Department of Defense's (DoD) annual report to Congress (2023), *Military and Security Developments Involving the People's Republic of China*, details the latest unclassified information about the People's Liberation Army (PLA), China's armed forces.[736] Third, I referenced the website Globalfirepower.com, a "unique analytical display of data concerning 145 modern military powers."[737] Fourth, certain numbers regarding ballistic missiles was sourced from the website Missiles of the World, a project of the Center for Strategic and International Studies. Finally, the numbers for active and reserve duty strengths came from armedforces.eu[738]

This capabilities comparison is not comprehensive in part because national systems capabilities across the three countries (US, Russia, and China) are not evenly matched, and/or the information may not be available for each nation. Therefore, the few blanks in the chart are intentional, because the corresponding information is not available or clear. Further, understand that the five sources used for this analysis seldom agree on the exact numbers of identified systems or categories.

US aircraft carrier at dock
Photo by Michael Afonso on Unsplash[739]

Capability areas	Specific capabilities by area	United States	People's Republic of China	Russian Federation
Personnel	active personnel	1,358,500	2,035,000	1,000,000
	reserve personnel	799,500	2,000,000	2,000,200
Direct ground combat	army	10 divisions with 28 brigade combat teams (BCT); National Guard has 27 BCTs	82 combined arms brigades	12 mechanized divisions; 33 mechanized brigades; 3 tank divisions; 3 tank brigades
	air assault	3 BCTs (part of 28)	3 brigades	
	airborne	3 BCTs (part of 28)	7 brigades	5 airborne divisions; 2 airborne brigades
	marines	24 US Marine Corps battalions	8 marine brigades	
	tanks	2,300	4,000	10,344 (T-90A); (T-90M); (T-72B3); (T-72); 160 (T-80); (T-80BVM)
	infantry fighting vehicles	4,000	1,970	1,500 (MT-LB); 358 (LMV-SF); 100 (BTR-70); 560 (BTR-80); 208 (BMP-2M); 639 (BTR-82AM); 800 (BTR-82A); 300 (BMP-1); 1800 (BMP-2); 640 (BMP-3)
	artillery	2,883	4,227	10,195 26 different indirect fire systems

Capability areas	Specific capabilities by area	United States	People's Republic of China	Russian Federation
	MLRS (rocket artillery)		2,544	2,146
Special operating forces (SOF)		72,000 with 5 SOF elements	15 SOF brigades	8 special-purpose (commando and reconnaissance) brigades 1 special- purpose (commando and reconnaissance) regiment
Fire support for ground operations	army artillery	1 artillery battalion/brigade with multiple launch rocket systems	15 artillery brigades	23 artillery brigades; 12 missile brigades
	marine artillery	1 artillery battalion/regiment with MLRS		
	attack helicopters	750	211	394 Mi-24, 8, 35, 28 & KA-52, 50
	air force fire support	150 bombers & Warthog & C-130 Hercules		
	navy fire support	cruise missiles, naval gun fire, rotary & fixed wing aircraft		
ISTAR	ISTAR/C4ISR aircraft	550	222—The PLA operates EW/reconnaissance aircraft and AWACS; each platform is a variant and some purchased from the Russians.	187 across 22 airframes
	ground & sea-based ISTAR	clear advantage over potential adversaries		C4ISR systems, UAVs, and navigation satellites form the backbone of Russia's network-centric assets.

Capability areas	Specific capabilities by area	United States	People's Republic of China	Russian Federation
air defense	navy	capable of downing both drones and missiles		
	army	Patriot system for theater & ballistic missile defense (15 battalions +)	1 air defense brigade with each army	335 S-300, S-350, S-400, Pantsir
	other			Peresvet mobile laser system is likely to defeat airborne targets such as unmanned aerial vehicles and ballistic missiles.
air force aircraft	air force	9,907	2,478	Russian Aerospace Forces deploys 2,800 both fixed and rotary wing.
	attack/ fighter	2,063	1,283	1,001
	bombers	150	500	424
	tankers	455	8 PLA has tankers with variant of H-6 bomber, IL-78 Midas & developing Y-20 tanker.	12
	transport/ utility aircraft	718	500	294
battle-force ships	total	300	395 ships by 2025; 435 by 2030	210
	carriers & amphibious warfare ships	11 nuclear-powered aircraft carriers and 9 helicopter carriers	2 aircraft carriers & 3 amphibious assault ships	3 - 3rd aircraft carrier has electromagnetic catapults and began sea trials in 2024
	destroyers	75 Arleigh Burke-class guided-missile destroyers	49	14

Capability areas	Specific capabilities by area	United States	People's Republic of China	Russian Federation
	cruisers/ corvettes	15 Ticonderoga-class cruisers	72	83
	frigates	0	42	12
submarines	total	68	61; 80 by 2035	65
	attack submarines	50	53	10
	cruise missile submarines	4		
	strategic missile submarines	14	6	12
naval aircraft	total	1,400	600	400
	anti-submarine warfare platform (ASW)	400 various platforms.	Has an ASW capability but unknown number of assets.	Most of Russia's ASW assets were produced in Soviet period.
missile defense	homeland missile defense	limited ground missile defense ground-based midcourse defense at two sites (AK and CA)—not intended for large, sophisticated threats	developing tiered system; successful ground-based mid-course test (2023)	Russia is modernizing its missile defense shield to engage targets in launch/boost, mid-course, and terminal phases of flight. S-500 used against high-altitude, high-velocity targets at long ranges.

Capability areas	Specific capabilities by area	United States	People's Republic of China	Russian Federation
	regional defense capability	Aegis ballistic missile defense system, Standard Missile-3, Terminal High Altitude Area Defense, Patriot surface-to-air missile system	Russian S-400—32 launchers	S-400 used against ballistic and cruise missiles. S-350 used against short- and medium range SAM systems. S-300F & S-300FM used by Russian Navy part of maritime missile defense.
	sensors	pace tracking, space-based, various radars (AN/TPY-2, early warning radars, COBRA DANE, BMD SPY-1, Sea-Based, SPY-1)	A variety of satellite networks and ground-based systems that track targets	A variety of satellite networks and ground-based systems that track targets
information warfare	cyber	Willing to use military force to protect cyber domain (defend nation, prepare to fight & win nation's wars, protect cyber domain with allies & partners)	Cyberspace is a "critical security domain" to China. It directed the PLA to accelerate building cyberspace capabilities. Today, it is widely acknowledged as having one of the world's most advanced cyber armies. The PLA views cyber operations as a basis of modern warfare.	There is a Cyber Command within Russia's Land Forces' command tasked with countering threats in cyberspace and improving protection of infrastructure, especially mission-critical facilities.

Capability areas	Specific capabilities by area	United States	People's Republic of China	Russian Federation
Space warfare	role of space for armed forces	US heavily reliant on space-based assets to include intelligence, surveillance, reconnaissance, communication, global position-ing, functioning of weapon systems, aircraft, and datalinks	China's space pro-gram is controlled by the PLA. China has invested heavily in ground- and space-based sensors. Has a satellite network that provides communication, navigation, imag-ing, radar support	Russia has a signif-icant spacecraft capability: military satellite commu-nications, warning of missile attacks, navigation system, meteorological & cartographic work, use of outer space for military purposes.
	space-system vulnerability	US notes China & Russia present counterspace capabilities that put our system at risk	vulnerable to counterspace capabilities as well	vulnerable to physical & electro-magnetic attacks
	anti-satellite systems		researching using unmanned space platforms for space and earth attack combat missions; poten-tial to make a direct-ascent ASAT system; capability to use lasers to "blind" enemy satellites	MiG-31 Foxhound interceptor, or 81 Blue, is part of an anti-satellite system as is its direct-ascent anti-satellite weapon system 14A042 Nudol has been tested numerous times.
Nuclear capable	strategic launch platforms	662 of 700 per-mitted deployed ICBMs, SLBMs, and heavy bomb-ers under START	designated bomb-ers and missiles for delivery of nuclear warheads	In 2018, Russia declared it is using 517 deployed strategic delivery launchers.
	nuclear warheads	1,419 deployed of 1,550 permitted under START	440 (projected to grow to 1,000 by 2035)	1,420 deployed warheads from an arsenal of 4,489 warheads

Capability areas	Specific capabilities by area	United States	People's Republic of China	Russian Federation
	ICBM land-based	Minuteman III ICBM 397 deployed (261 non-deployed & 57 non-deployed empty launchers)	350	330 missile systems with around 812 warheads
	SLBM sea-based	14 Ohio-class submarines, each with 20 Trident II missiles (max of 160 warheads)	6 Type 094 Jin-class SSBNs; each carries 12 SLBM	Delta IV and Borey class (Project 955/955A) with around 600 warheads in total
	strategic bombers	36 B-52H (air-launched cruise missiles) & 12 B-2 Spirit (gravity bombs)	Unknown number	Air force uses Tu-95MS ("Bear-H"- and Tu-160 ("Black-jack") heavy bombers as part of nuclear triad and are being upgraded to employ Kh-101/102 air launched cruise missiles.
	tactical deliver aircraft	F-16 & F-15E 160-200 B-61 tactical nuclear gravity bombs	Unknown number	Unknown number
Ballistic missiles				
	short-range ballistic missiles	395 HIMARS/ ATACMS	750-1,500	Deploys the Iskander (SS-26 "Stone"), a SRBM & OTR-21 Tockhka, capable of both nuclear and conventional missions.

Capability areas	Specific capabilities by area	United States	People's Republic of China	Russian Federation
	interme-diate/ medium-range ballis-tic missiles	0	150–450	Claims it does not deploy MRBM although is suspected of developing a system.
	hypersonic glide vehicle	Tested	Tested	Tested: RS-26 Avangard is a silo-based liq-uid-fueled ICBM with an HGV.
Biological		Stopped develop-ing BW in 1969 & signed Biological Weapon Conven-tion 1972; it does conduct defensive BW research.	Joined BWC in 1984 and insists it complies. However, 2023 US DOD annual report on China's military states PRC "continues to engage in biolog-ical activities with dual-use applica-tions, which raise concerns regard-ing its compliance with the Biological Weapons Conven-tion (BWC)."	Former Soviet Union invested heavily in BWs and produced agents. Today, those former facilities remain subordinate to Russian MoD, which does not participate in international BW projects and disallows foreign visits.
Chemical		US used CW in WW I; signed CWC in 1993; last of CW destroyed 2023.	Insists it does not possess CWs. However, a 2001 US DoD report states, "Beijing is believed to have an advanced chemical war-fare program, including [R&D], production, and weaponization capabilities."	In 1987, claimed to have ceased CW production. Russia inher-ited enormous stockpiles of CW agents such as 40,000 tons of nerve, blister, and choking agents. Whis-tle-blowers claim Russia continued "third-genera-tion" CW research and production until 1992.

APPENDIX C

Preparing Yourself for War at Home

Chapter 12 outlined numerous recommendations for readers seriously interested in preparing themselves and their families for the impact of war, much less a natural disaster. It is sobering that almost three in four Americans do not have a natural disaster preparedness plan, and almost half (48 percent) have no emergency supplies at home. Although most emergencies are not catastrophic like war on the home front, they do, according to one study of the issue, tend to involve: "[a financial crisis that] drains your savings and disrupts your income; widespread utility failure that leaves your area without power or water; severe weather events that cause extensive flooding; or infectious disease outbreaks that lead to mandatory home quarantine measures." What is clear is that disasters, like war, are unpredictable; however, preparation is not.[740]

Start early to prepare yourself and family for the unthinkable.
Photo by Unsplash in collaboration with Josue Michel[741]

Federal Emergency Management Agency

One of the best places to begin preparing for emergencies is with the Federal Emergency Management Agency (FEMA), which has ten regional offices across the country that leverage the federal government's efforts to respond to disasters. Although FEMA does not address the hypothetical of a war coming to our homeland, it does address the loss of key services and how to plan for natural disasters.

I recommend visiting FEMA's website, https://www.ready.gov/resources, which provides material to help you think about your preparations. For example, the "Build A Kit" page addresses being prepared with sufficient food, water, and other supplies in the event of a disaster. There are many other lists and recommendations. Obviously, these materials are focused on natural disasters and not on long-term loss of services, much less occupation by a foreign army. However, review this material before advancing to other more extensive references.

Another helpful free aid is the *Home Prep Guide: What You Need to Last 2 Weeks in an Emergency*, published by *The Epoch Times*. This guide identifies five areas of preparation: food and water; health and hygiene; shelter, warmth and tools; communication and power; and financial preparedness and important documents. See the endnote for the URL to access this guide.[742]

Where to Find Supplies and Training?

Where does one go for more information about preparing for disasters, or worse, preparing for World War III? That is a fair question—and it's a bit overwhelming because so many websites related to the subject are available today.

My research sent me to a long list of "prepper" sites on the Internet. These represent a cottage industry offering lots of advice and merchandise to help you prepare yourself and your family for future disasters—or to simply to live off the grid.

I come to this topic with significant off-the-grid experience as a former Eagle Scout and an Army Ranger who has spent years in Arctic Alaska as an infantry officer. Even now, I routinely vacation in the Wyoming wilderness. So I know something about living in the elements, first aid, foraging, hunting, and survival-related skills.

After studying many of the prepper websites, however, I found it difficult to identify the "best" and recommend specific sites for further consideration. That's because I don't know the people behind the sites; I'm not familiar with their level of expertise or the reliability of their products. However, as I pointed out in chapter 12, it is prudent to prepare for emergencies and for the worst, a future war.

Your preparation adventure becomes one of personal preference. Whether you're interested in cultivating survival skills, assembling a kit for simple emergency preparedness, or more extensive off-the-grid self-sufficiency, the Internet offers numerous websites that suggest information, resources, and guidance for these and a host of other topics.

I recommend you begin by studying FEMA's lists, consider the areas mentioned in chapter 12 of this book, and then investigate the prepper sites. Ask friends and families about resources they found helpful and reliable. However, begin with a plan that addresses, soup to nuts, what you must do to prepare…and then begin the process.

Keep in mind that you don't need to buy everything at once. Just begin with a few essentials, then gradually build your preparedness for the worst-case scenario. Eventually, you will have developed a well-equipped safe space and the proper training for whatever is thrown at you in the future. Please don't wait until the last moment; that guarantees failure!

NOTES

1   Albert Einstein, brainyquote.com, accessed August 31, 2024, https://www.brainyquote
    .com/quotes/albert_einstein_122873?src=t_world_war_iii.

2   Somchai Kongkamsri, "four soldiers carrying rifles near helicopter under blue sky," Pexels,
    accessed September 11, 2024, https://www.pexels.com/photo/four-soldiers-carrying-rifles
    -near-helicopter-under-blue-sky-20258.

3   Richard Fisher, "China's Hegemonic Ambitions, From Taiwan to the Moon: Richard Fisher,"
    American Thought Leaders, *Epoch Times*, October 5, 2024, https://www.theepochtimes.com
    /epochtv/chinas-hegemonic-ambitions-from-taiwan-to-the-moon-richard-fisher-5733995.

4   Kevin Bonsor and Sascha Bos, "Hypersonic Speed Explained: How Hypersonic Planes
    Work," Howstuffworks, September 27, 2023, https://science.howstuffworks.com/transport
    /flight/modern/hypersonic-plane.htm.

    Note: This article states: "NASA's experimental space plane, the X-43A, set a new
    speed record for jet-powered aircraft on November 16, 2004. In the uncrewed test flight,
    the plane reached Mach 10—10 times the speed of sound or about 6,600 miles (10,600
    kilometers) per hour."

5   Paul Robeson, brainyquote.com, accessed August 31, 2024, https://www.brainyquote.com
    /quotes/paul_robeson_326906?src=t_world_war_iii.

6   Stephen Wertheim, "World War III Begins with Forgetting," *New York Times*, December
    2, 2022, https://www.nytimes.com/2022/12/02/opinion/america-world-war-iii.html.

7   Blake Stilwell, "Why President Truman Fired the Most Prestigious American General of
    His Time," military.com, April 5, 2022, https://www.military.com/history/why-president-
    truman-fired-most-prestigious-american-general-of-his-time.html.

8   "General Douglas MacArthur and Members of His Staff During Korean War," Harry S.
    Truman Library & Museum (public domain), accessed September 6, 2024, https://www
    .trumanlibrary.gov/photograph-records/2007-448.

9   William J. Clinton, "Remarks on the 50th Anniversary of D-Day at Utah Beach in Nor-
    mandy," The American Presidency Project, June 6, 1994, https://www.presidency.ucsb.edu
    /documents/remarks-the-50th-anniversary-d-day-utah-beach-normandy.

10 David E. Rosenbaum, "Spending Can Be Cut in Half, Former Defense Officials
    Say," *New York Times*, December 13, 1989, https://www.nytimes.com/1989/12/13/us
    /spending-can-be-cut-in-half-former-defense-officials-say.html.

    Note: Lawrence J. Korb, a former assistant defense secretary in the Reagan administra-
    tion, agreed with McNamara, saying that transferring funds to the domestic sector "can have
    a dramatic impact on our economic well-being and our competitive position in the world."

11 George W. Bush, "National WWII Memorial Dedication Address," American Rhetoric,
    May 29, 2004, https://www.americanrhetoric.com/speeches/gwbww2memorial.htm.

12 Courtney Kube and Mosheh Gains, "Air Force General Predicts War with China in 2025,
    Tells Officers to Prep by Firing 'a Clip' at a Target, and 'Aim for the Head'," NBC News,

January 27, 2023, https://www.nbcnews.com/politics/national-security/us-air-force-general-predicts-war-china-2025-memo-rcna67967.

13 Maite Knorr-Evans, "What Did Elon Musk Say about the Possibility of World War III?" AS.com, October 24, 2023, https://en.as.com/latest_news/what-did-elon-musk-say-about-the-possibility-of-world-war-iii-n/.

14 Ibid.

15 Saila Lewis, "Rhetoric of World War III Escalates amid Global Conflicts Alarming Experts and Public Alike," Trendy Digest, February 23, 2024, https://trendydigests.com/2024/02/23/rhetoric-of-world-war-iii-escalates-amid-global-conflicts-alarming-experts-and-public-alike/.

16 NASA, "View of Earth and Satellite," Unsplash, https://unsplash.com/photos/view-of-earth-and-satellite-yZygONrUBe8.

17 Douglas MacKinnon, "Do Our Leaders, 'Experts' and Pundits Want World War III?" The Hill, April 6, 2024, https://thehill.com/opinion/international/4577779-do-our-leaders-experts-and-pundits-want-world-war-iii/.

18 Kim Sengupta, "Defence Secretary Warns of Further Wars with Russia, China and Iran in Next Five Years," *The Independent* (UK), January 15, 2024, https://www.independent.co.uk/news/uk/politics/grant-shapps-nato-middle-east-ukraine-china-taiwan-defence-b2478918.html.

19 Armani Syed, "In First Post-Election Speech, Putin Threatens NATO with World War III," *Time*, March 18, 2024, https://time.com/6957938/russia-election-putin-speech/.

20 "U.S., U.K., Russia, Ukraine: U.S. and U.K. Preparing to Relax Restrictions on Strikes Inside Russia," Worldview, Stratfor.com, September 12, 2024, https://worldview.stratfor.com/situation-report/us-uk-russia-ukraine-us-and-uk-preparing-relax-restrictions-strikes-inside-russia?id=030c4e7823&e=f60ad9ba4b&uuid=505e88bc-86b3-40e3-abe9-3333d66a8a22&mc_cid=3fe3336b25&mc_eid=f60ad9ba4b.

21 "Prominent Pro-Kremlin Businessman Konstantin Malofeev: It Is High Time for Russia to Use Tactical Nuclear Weapons," MEMRI.org, Special Dispatch No. 11554, September 12, 2024, https://www.memri.org/reports/prominent-pro-kremlin-businessman-konstantin-malofeev-it-high-time-russia-use-tactical.

22 "Russia Signals Its Official Stance on Using Nuclear Weapons Is About to Change, Accusing the West of 'Escalation'," CNBC.com, September 3, 2024, Russia hints at changing stance on using nuclear weapons (cnbc.com).

23 Rachel Dobkin, "Putin Ally Insists 'Nuclear War is Inevitable'," Newsweek.com, May 26, 2024, Putin Ally Insists "Nuclear War Is Inevitable" (newsweek.com).

24 "With an Updated Nuclear Doctrine, Russia Looks to Slow Western Support for Ukraine," Worldview, Stratfor.com, September 27, 2024, https://worldview.stratfor.com/article/updated-nuclear-doctrine-russia-looks-slow-western-support-ukraine.

25 Matt Pottinger and John Pomfret, "Xi Jinping Says He Is Preparing China for War," Foreign Affairs, as published by FDD, March 29, 2023, https://www.fdd.org/analysis/2023/03/30/xi-jinping-says-he-is-preparing-china-for-war/.

26 Ibid.

27 "Stress in America," American Psychological Association, March 2022, https://www.apa.org/news/press/releases/stress/2022/march-2022-survival-mode.

28 Valerie Bauman, "Nearly Half of Americans Believe the U.S. Will Become Involved in a World War within the Next 10 Years—and Women, African Americans and Democrats

are the Most Worried, New Survey Finds," Dailymail.com, April 12, 2019, Nearly half of Americans believe the US will become involved in a world war within the next 10 years | Daily Mail Online.

29 Ibid.

30 Ibid.

31 Jamie Ballard, "Most Americans Think There Will Be Another World War within the Next Decade," YouGov.com, March 21, 2024, https://today.yougov.com/politics/articles /48981-most-americans-think-another-world-war-within-the-next-decade.

32 Ibid.

33 Ibid.

34 "With Highest Number of Violent Conflicts Since Second World War, United Nations Must Rethink Efforts to Achieve, Sustain Peace, Speakers Tell Security Council," United Nations Meetings Coverage and Press Releases, SC/15184, January 26, 2023, https://press .un.org/en/2023/sc15184.doc.htm.

35 "Are We Heading for World War Three? Experts Give Their Verdicts," Sky News, January 26, 2024, https://uk.news.yahoo.com/heading-world-war-three-experts-124500382.html ?guccounter=1&guce_referrer=aHR0cHM6Ly9zZWFyY2gueWFob28uY29tL3NlYXJjaaD9 mcj1tY2FmZWUmdHlwZT1FMjEwVVMwRzAmcD1XSEFUK1dPUkxEK0xFQURF UlMrU0FZK0FCT1VUK1BPU1NJQklMSVRZK09GK1dPUkxEK1dBUitJSUk&guce _referrer_sig=AQAAAL86p4U7GEz0ToQbuiXVwRltMb57VxTn13KLhCUsMsTFOD vtH7unIGTUlU6ue7AQEpGgKrLfmnK5hq0_Ur5-ImctrNpOkKjUe97FTyZDl-F0_D Wu_ZnGgU0oElyCNiybCP-3GGh-0s_E9_lC--6LYp0rNpmqVPD25hfA0-fj9pO4.

36 Ibid.

37 Ibid.

38 Ibid.

39 Ibid.

40 Sophie Heading and Ellissa Cavaciuti-Wishart, "These Are the Biggest Global Risks We Face in 2024 and Beyond," World Economic Forum, January 10, 2024, https://www.weforum .org/agenda/2024/01/global-risks-report-2024/.

41 Ibid.

42 Ibid.

43 Jose Caballero, "Global triggers: why these five big issues could cause significant problems in 2024," The Conversation, January 3, 2024, https://theconversation.com/global-triggers -why-these-five-big-issues-could-cause-significant-problems-in-2024-219371

44 "Xi awarded 3rd term as China's president, extending rule," Associated Press, March 10, 2023, https://apnews.com/article/xi-jinping-china-president-vote-5e6230d8c881dc17b 11a781e832accd1

45 Jill Lawless, "Over 50 countries go to the polls in 2024. The year will test even the most robust democracies," Associated Press, January 10, 2024, https://apnews.com/article/global -elections-2024-preview-cb77b0940964c5c95a9affc8ebb6f0b7#

46 Nick Marsh, "Is China's economy a 'ticking time bomb'?" BBC, August 30, 2023, Is China's economy a 'ticking time bomb'? (bbc.com)

47 Caballero, op. cit.

48 Pierre Emmanuel Ngendakumana, "Germany must be ready for war by 2029, defense minister warns," Politico, June 5, 2024, Germany must be ready for war by 2029, defense minister warns – POLITICO

49 "Fear of China, Russia and Iran is Driving Weapons Sales: Report," Al Jazeera, March 11, 2024, https://www.aljazeera.com/news/2024/3/11/fear-of-china-russia-and-iran-is-driving-weapons-sales-report

50 Joshua Posaner, "German tanks and troops in Lithuania have one goal: Scare off Russia," Politico, June 3, 2024, German tanks and troops in Lithuania have one goal: Scare off Russia – POLITICO

51 MacKinnon, *op. cit.*

52 James Rothwell, "Prepare for war, says Norway's top general," Daily Telegraph (London, England) January 24, 2024.

53 Ibid.

54 "Fear of China, Russia and Iran is Driving Weapons Sales: Report," *op. cit.*

55 Kitty Donaldson, "UK Urges China to Explain 'Biggest' Peacetime Military Build-Up," Bloomberg.com, April 24, 2023, https://www.bloomberg.com/news/articles/2023-04-24/uk-urges-china-to-explain-biggest-peacetime-military-build-up.

56 Ibid.; Fisher. *op. cit.*

57 Ibid.; "Rankings," armedforces.eu, accessed September 7, 2024, https://armedforces.eu/countries.

58 "Rankings," armedforces.eu, accessed September 7, 2024, https://armedforces.eu/countries.

59 Ben Westcott, "Australia Plans Major Changes to Military Amid China's Build-up," Bloomberg.com, April 24, 2023, https://www.yahoo.com/news/australia-plans-major-military-changes-024217342.html?fr=sycsrp_catchall.

60 Jessie Yeung, "Japan Prime Minister Kishida Makes Surprise Visit to Ukraine to Meet Zelensky," CNN, March 21, 2023, https://www.cnn.com/2023/03/20/asia/japan-ukraine-kishida-zelensky-intl-hnk/index.html.

61 "Global Military Spending Surges amid War, Rising Tensions and Insecurity," SIPRI, April 22, 2024, https://www.sipri.org/media/press-release/2024/global-military-spending-surges-amid-war-rising-tensions-and-insecurity.

62 Scott Sacknoff, "With the World on Edge, Defense Stocks Soar," *Defense News*, August 8, 2024, With the world on edge, defense stocks soar (defensenews.com).

63 Stephen Cobb, "an-aerial-view-of-a-large-metal-object," Unsplash, https://unsplash.com/photos/an-aerial-view-of-a-large-metal-object-ls82dpWdpk4.

64 "Global Military Spending Surges amid War, Rising Tensions and Insecurity," *op. cit.*

65 Kayla Tausche and Haley Britzky, "More Than 20 of 32 NATO Allies Spending at Least 2% of GDP on Defense, Stoltenberg Says," CNN, June 17, 2024, https://www.cnn.com/2024/06/17/politics/nato-allies-spending/index.html, and "Global Military Spending Surges amid War, Rising Tensions and Insecurity," *op. cit.*

66 Ibid.

67 Ibid.

68 Rob Schmitz, "With War on Its Doorstep, Germany Plans a Major Military Buildup," NPR, March 22, 2022, https://www.npr.org/2022/03/22/1087859567/germany-military-buildup-russia-invasion-ukraine.

69 Ibid.

70 Ibid.

71 Ibid.

72 Ibid.

73 Taegan Goddard, "An Anxious Asia Arms for a War it Hopes to Prevent," *New York Times*, March 25, 2023, https://www.nytimes.com/2023/03/25/world/asia/asia-china-military-war.html.
74 "World Military Expenditure Reaches New Record High as European Spending Surges," SIPRI, April 24, 2023, https://www.sipri.org/media/press-release/2023/world-military-expenditure-reaches-new-record-high-european-spending-surges.
75 Xiao Liang and Dr. Nan Tian, "The Proposed Hike in Japan's Military Expenditure," SIPRI, February 2, 2023, https://www.sipri.org/commentary/topical-backgrounder/2023/proposed-hike-japans-military-expenditure.
76 Ibid.
77 Ibid.
78 "Global Military Spending Surges amid War, Rising Tensions and Insecurity," *op. cit.*
79 Ibid.
80 Goddard, *op. cit.*
81 Ben Westcott, "Australia Plans Major Changes to Military Amid China's Build-up," Bloomberg.com, April 24, 2023, https://www.yahoo.com/news/australia-plans-major-military-changes-024217342.html?fr=sycsrp_catchall.
82 Ibid.
83 Ibid.
84 "Global Military Spending Surges amid War, Rising Tensions and Insecurity," *op. cit.*
85 Oriana Skylar Mastro, "China's Agents of Chaos," *Foreign Affairs*, November/December 2024, https://www.foreignaffairs.com/united-states/china-agents-chaos-russia-mastro?utm_medium=newsletters&utm_source=twofa&utm_campaign=The%20New%20Battle%20for%20the%20Middle%20East&utm_content=20241025&utm_term=EWZZZ003ZX.
86 "Global Military Spending Surges amid War, Rising Tensions and Insecurity," *op. cit.*
87 Caitlin McFall, "Top Russian Official Lands in Iran amid US, UK Concerns over Alleged Nuclear Deal," Fox News, September 17, 2024, Russia's Shoigu lands in Iran amid US, UK concerns over alleged nuclear deal | Fox News.
88 Nan Tian, et al, "Trends in World Military Expenditure," *SIPRI Fact Sheet*, April 2024, https://www.sipri.org/sites/default/files/2024-04/2404_fs_milex_2023.pdf.
89 Ibid.
90 "Global Military Spending Surges amid War, Rising Tensions and Insecurity," *op. cit.*
91 Ibid.
92 Ryan C. Berg, "China and Russia engage Latin America and the Caribbean differently. Both threaten US interests," Atlantic Council, February 12, 2024, https://www.atlanticcouncil.org/in-depth-research-reports/issue-brief/china-and-russia-engage-latin-america-and-the-caribbean-differently-both-threaten-us-interests/
93 "Global Military Spending Surges amid War, Rising Tensions and Insecurity," *op. cit.*
94 Ibid.
95 Ibid.
96 Joseph Humire, "The New Sino-Iranian Alliance Taking Over Latin America: Joseph Humire," American Thought Leaders, *The Epoch Times*, October 10, 2024, https://www.theepochtimes.com/epochtv/the-new-sino-iranian-alliance-taking-over-latin-america-joseph-humire-5737722?utm_source=Morningbrief&src_src=Morningbrief&utm_campaign=mb-2024-10-11&src_cmp=mb-2024-10-11&utm_medium=email&est=AAAAAAAAAAAAAAAAY%2B0peBILkJLo77wDvWRKH%2Fp0zle%2FQzAkSnnTu5OdEYzwv2cm.

97 Ibid.
98 Ibid.
99 Ibid.
100 Mohamed Elerian, brainyquote.com, accessed August 31, 2024, https://www.brainyquote
    .com/quotes/mohamed_elerian_416057.
101 Henry Kissinger, *World Order*, (Penguin Press, 2014), https://www.amazon.com/s?k=henry
    +kissinger+world+order&i=stripbooks&adgrpid=1344704078175821&hvadid=84044
    199248142&hvbmt=be&hvdev=c&hvlocphy=66645&hvnetw=o&hvqmt=e&hvtargid
    =kwd-84044889954265%3Aloc-190&hydadcr=22567_13494438&msclkid=ddb8aa717
    6751ad474b3cc09eb0fb60a&tag=mh0b-20&ref=pd_sl_8serx1heb7_e
102 Michael J. Mazarr et al, "Understanding the Current International Order," RAND, Octo-
    ber 19, 2016, https://www.rand.org/pubs/research_reports/RR1598.html.
103 Vladislav Klapin, "red yellow and green flags," Unsplash, https://unsplash.com/photos
    /red-yellow-and-green-flags-9mE5MQfXInE.
104 Mazarr, *op. cit.*
105 "Which Countries Have Authoritarian Governments in 2024?" *World Population Review*,
    accessed August 31, 2024, https://worldpopulationreview.com/country-rankings/what
    -countries-have-authoritarian-government.
106 G. John Ikenberry, "Power and LKiberal Order: America's Postwar World Order in Transi-
    tion," *Relations of the Asia-Pacific*, Vol. 5, Issue 2, January 1, 2005, https://doi.org/10.1093
    /irap/lci112.
107 Ibid.
108 Ibid.
109 Ibid.
110 Ibid.
111 Stewart M. Patrick, "World Order: What, Exactly, Are the Rules?" *Washington Quarterly*,
    Vol. 39, Issue 1, May 3, 2016, https://www.cfr.org/blog/world-order-what-exactly-are-rules.
112 Ibid.
113 Ibid.
114 Ibid.
115 Ibid.
116 Ibid.
117 Ibid.
118 Ibid.
119 Heather Stephenson, "U.S. Foreign Policy Increasingly Relies on Military Interventions,"
    Tufts Now, October 16, 2023, https://now.tufts.edu/2023/10/16/us-foreign-policy
    -increasingly-relies-military-interventions.
120 Volker Wagener, "25 Years Later, What Happened During the Kosovo War?" DW, June
    10, 2024, https://www.dw.com/en/25-years-later-what-happened-during-the-kosovo-war
    /a-69318675#:~:text=It%20was%20the%20first%20intervention%20by%20the%20NATO
    ,for%20the%20first%20time%20since%20World%20War%20II and Patrick, *op. cit.*
121 Patrick, op. cit.
122 Ibid.
123 "China: Nuclear and Missile Proliferation," In Focus, Congressional Research Service, Octo-
    ber 3, 2024, china-nuclear-and-missile-proliferation-oct-3-2024.pdf (documentcloud.org).
124 Ibid.

125 Ibid.
126 Ibid.
127 Ibid.
128 Ibid.
129 Ibid.
130 K. Moak, "The Washington Consensus Versus the Beijing Consensus," *Developed Nations and the Economic Impact of Globalization*, (Palgrave Macmillan, 2017), https://doi.org /10.1007/978-3-319-57903-0_9 Note: "The Beijing Consensus could become an alternative to Anglo-American neoliberalism, presented by some in the West as a 'one-size-fit-all' model for all developing countries. That neoliberal model, dubbed by John Williamson as the Washington Consensus, turned out to be more harmful than helpful to the countries that received loans from the IMF and WBG. The Beijing Consensus, a term coined by Joshua Cooper Ramo, has created a Chinese economic miracle, lifting it to become the second largest economy in the world and over 700 million people out of poverty within less than 40 years. Contrary to some pundits in the West predicting an imminent economic collapse, the Chinese economy continues to grow at an annual average of 6.5% and contributes to over 30% of global economic growth since 2008."
131 Patrick, *op. cit.*
132 Ibid.
133 Ibid.
134 Ibid.
135 Fisher, *op. cit.*
136 Ibid.
137 "U.S.: Washington Creates Team to Combat Chinese Hacking into Telecommunications Companies," *Situation Report*, Rane, October 14, 2024, https://worldview.stratfor.com /situation-report/us-washington-creates-team-combat-chinese-hacking-telecommunications -companies?id=030c4e7823&e=f60ad9ba4b&uuid=00aff29d-75cf-468e-9940-d47e08afec 70&mc_cid=b03d6845a3&mc_eid=f60ad9ba4b.
138 Ibid.
139 Ibid.
140 Ibid.
141 Oriana Skylar Mastro, "China's Agents of Chaos," *Foreign Affairs,* November/December 2024, https://www.foreignaffairs.com/united-states/china-agents-chaos-russia-mastro?utm _medium=newsletters&utm_source=twofa&utm_campaign=The%20New%20Battle %20for%20the%20Middle%20East&utm_content=20241025&utm_term=EWZZZ 003ZX.
142 "Chinese President Xi Jinping to U.S. State Secretary Antony Blinken During Beijing Visit: China, U.S. Should Be Partners, Not Rivals; I Propose Mutual Respect, Win-Win Cooperation," MEMRI #11082, April 2024, https://www.memri.org/tv/xi-jinping-meets-antony-blinken-beijing-partners-not-rivals.
143 "What the First Known Survivor of China's Forced Organ Harvesting Reveals: David Matas," American Thought Leaders, *The Epoch Times*, September 7, 2024, https://www .theepochtimes.com/epochtv/what-the-first-known-survivor-of-chinas-forced-organ -harvesting-reveals-david-matas-5719889?utm_source=Morningbrief&src_src=Morning brief&utm_campaign=mb-2024-09-08&src_cmp=mb-2024-09-08&utm_medium =email&est=AAAAAAAAAAAAAAAAY%2B0peBILkJLo77wDvWRKH%2Fp0zle% 2FQzAkSnnTu5OdEYzwv2cm.

Note: Peiming Cheng is the first known survivor of China's state-run organ harvesting campaign. Mr. Cheng was imprisoned for eight years and tortured for practicing Falun Gong and then in 2004 he was forced to undergo surgery, which removed part of his liver and left lung. Chinese officials acknowledged they operated on Cheng without his consent. The video with this article features international human rights lawyer David Matas who investigated the forced organ harvesting from Falun Gong in China.

144 Tony Munroe, et al, "China, Russia Partner up against West at Olympics Summit," Reuters, February 4, 2022, https://www.reuters.com/world/europe/russia-china-tell-nato-stop-expansion-moscow-backs-beijing-taiwan-2022-02-04/.

145 "The West Will No Longer Be Able to Divide Russia and China and Try to Dominate Eurasia," MEMRI, Special Dispatch No. 11352, article in Russia's *Izvestia*, "A Turning Point Visit," by Oleg Karpovich, May 17, 2024, https://www.memri.org/reports/russian-foreign-ministry-diplomatic-academy-pro-rector-west-will-no-longer-be-able-divide.

146 "Russia China Xi and Putin Pledge Deepened Cooperation, But Major Breakthroughs Prove Illusive," Worldview, STRATFOR, May 16, 2024, https://worldview.stratfor.com/situation-report/russia-china-xi-and-putin-pledge-deepened-cooperation-major-break throughs-prove?id=030c4e7823&e=f60ad9ba4b&uuid=05719960-bce7-4064-9b66-cd742d23c016&mc_cid=6e4f76c47e&mc_eid=f60ad9ba4b.

147 Linus Höller, "'Dual-use' Case: Russian Attack Drone Maker Evades Western Scrutiny," *Defense News*, September 23, 2024, https://www.defensenews.com/global/europe/2024/09/23/dual-use-case-russian-attack-drone-maker-evades-western-scrutiny/.

148 "China, Russia: Chinese Factory Producing Attack Drones for Russia," Worldview, Stratfor.com, September 25, 2024, https://worldview.stratfor.com/situation-report/china-russia-chinese-factory-producing-attack-drones-russia.

149 Andrea Kendall-Taylor and Richard Fontaine, "The Axis of Upheaval: How America's Adversaries Are Uniting to Overturn the Global Order," *Foreign Affairs*, Vol. 103, Issue 3, May/June 2024, https://www.foreignaffairs.com/china/axis-upheaval-russia-iran-north-korea-taylor-fontaine.

150 Hal Brands, "The Battle for Eurasia," *Foreign Policy*, June 4, 2023, https://foreignpolicy.com/2023/06/04/russia-china-us-geopolitics-eurasia-strategy/.

151 Munir Ahmed, "Moscow and Beijing Announce Further Cooperation during International Group Meeting in Pakistan," October 16, 2024, Associated Press, Moscow and Beijing announce further cooperation during international group meeting in Pakistan | AP News.

152 "China's Xi Jinping Highlights Europe's Divisions ahead of Expected Putin Visit," CNN, May 12, 2024, https://keyt.com/news/national-world/cnn-world/2024/05/12/chinas-xi-jinping-highlights-europes-divisions-ahead-of-expected-putin-visit/.

153 Ibid.

154 Ibid.

155 Ibid.

156 Ibid.

157 Michael Robbins, et al, "America Is Losing the Arab World," *Foreign Affairs*, July/August 2024, https://www.foreignaffairs.com/united-states/america-losing-arab-world?utm_medium=newsletters&utm_source=twofa&utm_campaign=Sleepwalking%20Toward%20War&utm_content=20240614&utm_term=EWZZZ003ZX.

158 "BRICS: Bloc Creates Partner Status, Extends Status to 13 Countries," Worldview, STRATFOR, October 24, 2024, https://worldview.ranenetwork.com/content/situation-report/brics-bloc-creates-partner-status-extends-status-13-countries?id=030c4e7823.

159 "Global Triggers: Why these Five Big Issues Could Cause Significant Problems in 2024," The Conversation.com, January 3, 2024, https://theconversation.com/global-triggers -why-these-five-big-issues-could-cause-significant-problems-in-2024-219371.

160 Jai Hamid, "Nearly 20 More Countries Set to Permanently Ditch Dollar in 2024," msn .com, accessed August 31, 2024, https://www.msn.com/en-us/money/markets/nearly-20 -more-countries-set-to-permanently-ditch-dollar-in-2024/ar-AA1mqNGx#:~:text=The %20global%20financial%20landscape%20is%20on%20the%20cusp,a%20significant %20departure%20from%20the%20long-standing%20USD-dominated%20system.

161 Ibid.

162 Alexander Gabuev, "Why China Is Sabotaging Ukraine," *Foreign Affairs*, June 14, 2024, https://www.foreignaffairs.com/china/why-china-sabotaging-ukraine-peace-agreement ?utm_medium=newsletters&utm_source=fatoday&utm_campaign=India%20Steps%20 Back%20From%20the%20Brink&utm_content=20240614&utm_term=FA%20Today %20-%20112017.

163 Hamid, *op. cit.*

164 Joe Biden, "Remarks by President Biden on the United Efforts of the Free World to Sup- port the People of Ukraine," White House, March 26, 2022, https://www.whitehouse .gov/briefing-room/speeches-remarks/2022/03/26/remarks-by-president-biden-on-the -united-efforts-of-the-free-world-to-support-the-people-of-ukraine/.

165 "Joint Russia-China Statement: 'The Russian Side Reaffirms Its Support for The One-China Principle… And Opposes Any Forms of Independence of Taiwan'," MEMRI, Special Dispatch No. 9755, February 7, 2022, https://www.memri.org/reports/joint-russia -china-statement-russian-side-reaffirms-its-support-one-china-principle-and.

166 Ibid.

167 Ibid.

168 Jan Jekielek, "The Real Battleground with China is Ideological—And America Needs to Counterattack, says John Lenczowski," American Thought Leaders, *The Epoch Times*, September 21, 2024, https://www.theepochtimes.com/epochtv/the-real-battleground -with-china-is-ideological-and-america-needs-to-counterattack-says-john-lenczowski -5727917?utm_source=Morningbrief&src_src=Morningbrief&utm_campaign=mb-2024 -09-23&src_cmp=mb-2024-09-23&utm_medium=email&est=AAAAAAAAAAAAAAAA Y%2B0peBILkJLo77wDvWRKH%2Fp0zle%2FQzAkSnnTu5OdEYzwv2cm.

169 Ibid.

170 Ibid.

171 Ibid.

172 Ibid.

173 Ibid.

174 Ibid.

175 Ibid.

176 Ibid.

177 "List of Eurasian Countries by Population," Wikipedia, accessed August 31, 2024, https:// en.wikipedia.org/wiki/List_of_Eurasian_countries_by_population.

178 Hal Brands, "The Battle for Eurasia," *Foreign Policy*, June 4, 2023, https://foreignpolicy.com /2023/06/04/russia-china-us-geopolitics-eurasia-strategy/.

179 Ibid.

180 Koh Ewe, "Is Southeast Asia Leaning More Toward China? New Survey Shows Mixed Results," *Time*, April 2, 2024, https://time.com/6962557/china-us-asean-southeast-asia-rivalry-survey/.

181 Ibid.

182 "In Munich, Guterres Calls for New Global Order That Works for All," UN News, United Nations, February 16, 2024, https://news.un.org/en/story/2024/02/1146622.

183 Kim Tong-Hyung, "Before His Summit with North Korea's Kim, Putin Vows They'll Beat Sanctions Together," June 18, 2024, https://www.latimes.com/world-nation/story/2024-06-18/before-his-summit-with-north-koreas-kim-putin-vows-theyll-beat-sanctions-together.

184 "Russia, North Korea: Russia Ratifies Defense Treaty with North Korea," Worldview, STRATFOR, October 24, 2024, https://worldview.ranenetwork.com/content/situation-report/russia-north-korea-russia-ratifies-defense-treaty-north-korea?id=030c4e7823&e=f60ad9ba4b&uuid=5d9370ef-bef7-4c5a-a0c0-3f78f520a1f7&mc_cid=b4cd277f70&mc_eid=f60ad9ba4b.

185 "North Korea, Ukraine: North Korean Troops Supporting Russia's War against Ukraine, Zelensky Says," Worldview, STRATFOR, October 17, 2024, https://worldview.ranenetwork.com/content/situation-report/north-korea-ukraine-north-korean-troops-supporting-russias-war-against-ukraine?id=030c4e7823 Note: In October 2024, the *Wall Street Journal* cited Ukrainian presidential advisor Mykhailo Podolyak as stating that as many as four hundred North Korean engineers were helping Russians operate North Korean missiles. North Korea has a history of providing troops for overseas conflicts and in particular in the current situation, Ukrainian President Volodymyr Zelensky contends that Pyongyang is assisting Russia by staffing factories in Moscow's Far East.

186 Anders Hagstrom, "North Korea Has Sent Troops to Russia, Pentagon Confirms," Fox News, October 23, 2024, https://www.foxnews.com/world/north-korea-has-sent-troops-russia-pentagon-confirms Note: In October 2024, US Defense Secretary Lloyd Austin confirmed the movement of North Korean troops to Russia, which he labeled a "very, very serious issue." Further, John Kirby, the White House National Security communications director, said, "We assess that between early to mid-October, North Korea moved at least 3,000 soldiers into eastern Russia." He speculated, "After completing training, these soldiers could travel to western Russia and then engage in combat against the Ukrainian military."

187 "Joint Russia-China Statement: 'The Russian Side Reaffirms Its Support for the One-China Principle... And Opposes Any Forms of Independence of Taiwan'," Op. Cit.

188 David Brunnstrom and Michael Martina, "Japan Minister Calls for New World Order to Counter Rise of Authoritarian Regimes," Reuters, January 5, 2023, https://www.reuters.com/world/japan-minister-calls-new-world-order-counter-rise-authoritarian-regimes-2023-01-05/.

189 Ibid.

190 Bryan H. Druzin, "How to Destroy the Liberal International Order," 34, *Duke Journal of Comparative & International Law* 1-37 (2024), https://scholarship.law.duke.edu/djcil/vol34/iss1/1.

191 Ibid.

192 Brands, *op. cit.*

193 "Famous Quotations and Quotes about Learning from History," age-of-the-sage.org, accessed August 31, 2024, https://www.age-of-the-sage.org/philosophy/history/learning_from_history.html.

194 Lester B. Pearson, azquotes, accessed August 31, 2024, https://www.azquotes.com/quotes /topics/world-war-i.html.

195 Hemandh Viswanath, "The Legacy of First World War: A Critical Evaluation of Its Causes Results and Consequences," *International Journal of Law, Management & Humanities*, Vol 1, Issue 3, 2021, https://heinonline.org/HOL/LandingPage?handle=hein.journals/ijlmhs 11&div=109&id=&page=.

196 "A black and white photo of a group of soldiers," National Library of Scotland, Unsplash, accessed September 6, 2024, https://unsplash.com/photos/a-black-and-white-photo-of-a -group-of-soldiers-Dp8q5tVxz1Y.

197 CPI Inflation Calculator, accessed August 31, 2024, https://www.in2013dollars.com/us /inflation/1914?amount=1.

198 Viswanath, *op. cit.*

199 David T. Zabecki, "Military Developments of World War I," *International Encyclopedia of First World War*, accessed August 31, 2024, https://encyclopedia.1914-1918-online.net /article/military_developments_of_world_war_i.

200 Aaron Gillette, "Why Did They Fight the Great War?" November 2006, Vol. 40, Nu. 1, https://www.jstor.org/stable/30036938?ab_segments=0%2Fbasic_search_gsv2%2Fcontrol.

201 Ibid.
202 Ibid.
203 Ibid.
204 Ibid.
205 Ibid.
206 Ibid.
207 Ibid.
208 Ibid.
209 Ibid.
210 Ibid.

211 John Keiger, "Thinking the Causes of World War I," *Journal of International Relations and Sustainable Development*, No. 1, Autumn 2014, https://www.jstor.org/stable/10.2307/48573432.

212 Ibid.
213 Ibid.
214 Ibid.
215 Ibid.
216 Ibid.
217 Ibid.
218 Ibid.
219 Ibid.
220 Ibid.
221 Ibid.
222 Ibid.
223 Ibid.
224 Ibid.
225 Ibid.
226 Ibid.
227 Ibid.

228 Martin H. Levinson, "Mapping the Causes of World War I to Avoid Armageddon Today," *ETC: A Review of General Semantics*, Vol. 62, No. 2, April 2005, https://www.jstor.org/stable/42580167.

229 Ibid.

230 Ibid.

231 Ibid.

232 Ibid.

233 Ibid.

234 Ibid.

235 Ibid.

236 Ibid.

237 Ibid.

238 Ibid.

239 Ibid.

240 "Dwight D. Eisenhower," azquotes, accessed August 31, 2024, https://www.azquotes.com/quote/598077?ref=world-war-ii.

241 Robert Citino, "From War to War in Europe: 1919-1939," National World War Two Museum, May 24, 2018, https://www.nationalww2museum.org/war/articles/war-war-europe-1919-1939.

242 Peggy T. Berman and Brigid O'Hara-Forster, "Part 2: Road to War Every Time a Hitler Threat Ended in Compromise, Hitler Won," *Time*, August 28, 1989, https://web-p-ebscohost-com.pentagonlibrary.idm.oclc.org/ehost/detail/detail?vid=3&sid=e02452d7-a3ca-4b07-b897-d7e7e1589e24%40redis&bdata=JnNpdGU9ZWhvc3Qtb Gl2ZQ%3d%3d#AN=57899841&db=mth.

243 Ibid.

244 Berman, *op. cit.*

245 Daniel Hansen, "a wooden building with a sign in front of it," Unsplash, accessed September 12, 2024, https://unsplash.com/photos/a-wooden-building-with-a-sign-in-front-of-it-cysGdUBt9aM.

246 Ibid.

247 Ibid.

248 Ibid.

249 Ibid.

250 Ibid.

251 Ibid.

252 Ibid.

253 Ibid.

254 Ibid.

255 Ibid.

256 Ibid.

257 Ibid.

258 Ibid.

259 Ibid.

260 Ibid.

261 Ibid.

262 Ibid.

263 Ibid.
264 Ibid.
265 Ibid.
266 Ibid.
267 Ibid.
268 Ibid.
269 Ibid.
270 Ibid.
271 Ibid.
272 Ibid.
273 Mark Carwright, "The Causes of WWII," *World History Encyclopedia*, March 26, 2024, https://www.worldhistory.org/article/2409/the-causes-of-wwii/.
274 Ibid.
275 "Dawes Plan," Wikipedia, accessed August 31, 2024, https://en.wikipedia.org/wiki/Dawes _Plan. "In 1924, the US' Dawes Plan temporarily resolved the German reparations issue. It se-up a staggered schedule for Germany's payment of war reparations, provided for a loan to stabilize the German mark and end the occupation of the Ruhr. Initially, the plan resulted in a brief economic recovery in the late 1920s. However, it was replaced by the Young Plan in 1929, which was an attempt to settle the issues related to the war reparations."
276 Carwright, *op. cit.*
277 Ibid.
278 Ibid.
279 Ibid.
280 Ibid.
281 Ibid.
282 Ibid.
283 Ibid.
284 Ibid.
285 Ibid.
286 Ibid.
287 Ibid.
288 Ibid.
289 Franklin D. Roosevelt, "Declaration of War," Educational Video Group, Inc., accessed August 31, 2024, https://www.speeches-usa.com/Transcripts/004_roosevelt.html.
290 "United States Declaration of War on Germany (1941)," Wikipedia, accessed August 31, 2024, https://en.wikipedia.org/wiki/United_States_declaration_of_war_on_Germany _(1941).
291 John A. Vasquez, "The Causes of the Second World War in Europe: A New Scientific Explanation," *International Political Science Review* (1996), Vol. 17, No. 2, 161-178, https://www.jstor.org/stable/1601301.
292 Ibid.
293 Ibid.
294 Ibid.
295 Ibid.
296 Ibid.
297 Ibid.

298 Ibid.

299 Ibid.

300 Ibid.

301 Ibid.

302 Ibid.

303 Vasquez attributes the finding that alliances among major states "are followed by war within five years" to two sources: J. David Singer and Melvin Small (1966b), "National Alliance Commitments and War Involvement, 1815–1945," Peace Research Society (International) Papers, 5: 404–422 and Jack S. Levy, "Alliance Formation and War Behavior: An Analysis of the Great Powers, 1495–1975." *Journal of Conflict Resolution*, December 1981, Vol. 25, No. 4, https://www.jstor.org/stable/173911.

304 Ibid.

305 Ibid.

306 Ibid.

307 Ibid.

308 "Michael G. Ignatieff," quotemaster.org, accessed August 31, 204, https://www.quote master.org/q74383d7da8e870f4f2c4bd495d69aad9.

309 Oliver O'Donovan, "War by Other Means," Cambridge Core, Cambridge University Press, June 5, 2012, https://www.cambridge.org/core/books/abs/just-war-revisited/war-by -other-means/A164B9DFFEF79EABFA01FE5DF831D4C8.

310 Vony Razom, "a tank that is on fire in a field," Unsplash, https://unsplash.com/photos /a-tank-that-is-on-fire-in-a-field-AdLby5JN9HU.

311 John A. Vasquez, "The Causes of the Second World War in Europe: A New Scientific Explanation," *International Political Science Review* (1996), Vol. 17, No. 2, 161–178, https:// www.jstor.org/stable/1601301.

312 "Global Military Spending Surges amid War, Rising Tensions and Insecurity," *op. cit.*

313 Ibid.

314 Ibid.

315 Noah Robertson, "How Russia Surprised the West and Rebuilt Its Force: 'They've Grown Back,'" Defensenews.com, May 21, 2024, https://www.defensenews.com/global/europe /2024/05/21/theyve-grown-back-how-russia-surprised-the-west-and-rebuilt-its-force/?utm _source=sailthru&utm_medium=email&utm_campaign=dfn-special-report and Eric Schmitt, "September was Deadly Month for Russian Troops in Ukraine, U.S. Says," New York Times, October 10, 2024, https://www.nytimes.com/2024/10/10/us/politics/russia -casualties-ukraine-war.html.

316 Ibid.

317 "Global Military Spending Surges amid War, Rising Tensions and Insecurity," *op. cit.*

318 Ibid.

319 "DOD Releases 2023 Report on Military and Security Developments Involving the People's Republic of China," US Department of Defense, October 19, 2023, https://www .defense.gov/News/Releases/Release/Article/3561549/dod-releases-2023-report-on-military -and-security-developments-involving-the-pe/.

320 "Commission on National Defense Strategy," July 2024, www.rand.org/nsrd/projects/NDS -commission.

321 Ibid.

322 "Global Military Spending Surges amid War, Rising Tensions and Insecurity," *op. cit.*

323 Frank Fang, "China's Satellite Fleet Poses Threats to US Troops in Potential Pacific Conflict: Space Force Intel Chief," *The Epoch Times*, May 6, 2024, https://www.theepochtimes.com/us/chinas-satellite-fleet-poses-threats-to-us-troops-in-potential-pacific-conflict-space-force-intel-chief-5644099?utm_source=Morningbrief&src_src=Morningbrief&utm_campaign=mb-2024-05-07&src_cmp=mb-2024-05-07&utm_medium=email&est=AAAAAAAAAAAAAAY%2B0peBILkJLo77wDvWRKH%2Fp0zle%2FQzAkSnnTu5OdEYzwv2cm.

324 Nick Robertson, "China Expanding Its Nuclear Arsenal: Report," *The Hill*, June 16, 2024, https://thehill.com/policy/defense/4725132-china-expanding-its-nuclear-arsenal-report/?utm_campaign=dfn-ebb&utm_medium=email&utm_source=sailthru.

325 Christopher Woody, "Chin's Newest Military Base abroad Is Up and Running, and There Are More on the Horizon," Breakingdefense.com, July 12, 2024, https://breakingdefense.com/2024/07/chinas-newest-military-base-is-up-and-running-and-us-officials-see-more-of-them-on-the-horizon/?utm_campaign=dfn-ebb&utm_medium=email&utm_source=sailthru.

326 Ibid.

327 Ellen Ioanes, "Japan's Plan to Ramp up Military Spending, Explained," *Vox*, January 15, 2023, https://www.vox.com/world/2023/1/15/23555805/japans-military-buildup-us-china-north-korea

328 Ibid.

329 Ibid.

330 Ibid.

331 Joe Saballa, "Philippines Oks $35B 'Re-Horizon 3' Military Modernization Plan," January 30, 2024, https://www.thedefensepost.com/2024/01/30/philippines-military-modernization-plan/.

332 "Global Military Spending Surges amid War, Rising Tensions and Insecurity," *op. cit.*

333 Ibid.

334 Vasquez *op. cit.*

335 Dawes Plan, *op. cit.*

336 Carwright, *op. cit.*

337 Ibid.

338 Heading, *op. cit.*

339 Ibid.

340 Ibid.

341 Ibid.

342 Dmitri Alperovitch, "Taiwan Is the New Berlin," *Foreign Affairs*, May 15, 2024, Dmitri Alperovitch: Taiwan Is the New Berlin (foreignaffairs.com).

343 Ibid.

344 Ibid.

345 Ibid.

346 Ibid.

347 MacKinnon, *op. cit.*

348 Ibid.

349 John A. Vasquez, "The Causes of the Second World War in Europe: A New Scientific Explanation," *International Political Science Review* (1996), Vol. 17, No. 2, 161–178, https://www.jstor.org/stable/1601301.

350 Ibid.

351 Ibid.

352 Biden, *op. cit.*

353 Robert E. Kelly and Paul Poast, "The Allies Are Alright: Why America Can Get Away with Bullying Its Friends," *Foreign Affairs*, February 22, 2022, https://www.foreignaffairs.com /articles/united-states/2022-02-22/allies-are-alright.

354 Ibid.

355 Ibid.

356 "German Territorial Losses, Treaty of Versailles, 1919," *Holocaust Encyclopedia*, United States Holocaust Memorial Museum, accessed September 17, 2024, https://encyclopedia. ushmm.org/content/en/map/german-territorial-losses-treaty-of-versailles-1919 Note: The Treaty of Versailles imposed punitive territorial provisions on Germany. Berlin was forced to return Alsace-Lorraine to France, Belgium receive Eupen and Malmedy; the industrial Saar region; Denmark received Northern Schleswig; Czechoslovakia received the Hultsch-in district; and Memel, a strip of land in East Prussia along the Baltic Sea. All tolled, Germany forfeited 13 percent of its territory and one-tenth of its population.

357 Ibid.

358 Winston Churchill, "I Have Watched This Famous Island…, 1938," speech delivered in the House of Commons, March 24, 1938, https://www.nationalchurchillmuseum.org /i-have-watched-this-famous-island.html.

359 "Neville Chamberlain," Wikiquote, accessed August 31, 2024, https://en.wikiquote.org /wiki/Neville_Chamberlain.

360 Churchill, *op. cit.*

361 James Cleverly, "Our Position on China: Foreign Secretary's 2023 Mansion House speech," UK's Foreign, Commonwealth & Development Office, April 25, 2023, https:// www.gov.uk/government/speeches/our-position-on-china-speech-by-the-foreign-secretary.

362 Adolf Hitler, "Speech before his generals," der-fuehrer.org, August 22, 1939, https:// der-fuehrer.org/reden/english/39-08-22.htm.

363 Ibid.

364 "Alvin Toffler," brainyquote.com, accessed August 31, 2024, https://www.brainyquote.com /quotes/alvin_toffler_378556.

365 Sergey Koznov, "a sci fi robot with a camera attached to it," Unsplash, https://unsplash.com /photos/a-sci-fi-robot-with-a-camera-attached-to-it-0ssP48DNVS0.

366 Alex Roland, "War and Technology," February 2009, https://www.fpri.org/article/2009 /02/war-and-technology/.

367 Ibid.

368 Ibid.

369 Ibid.

370 Ibid.

371 Ibid.

372 Ibid.

373 Ibid.

374 Ibid.

375 Ibid.

376 Ibid.

377 Ibid.

378 Ibid.

379 Ibid.

380 Mark T. Esper, Secretary of Defense Remarks for DOD Artificial Intelligence Symposium and Exposition, Department of Defense, September 9, 2020, https://www.defense.gov /News/Speeches/Speech/Article/2341130/secretary-of-defense-remarks-for-dod-artificial -intelligence-symposium-and-expo/.

381 Colin Demarest, "Inside the Next Era of Warfare: How Tech is Reshaping the Battlefield," *World*, July 10, 2024, https://www.axios.com/2024/07/10/us-military-future-weapons-ai -warfare

382 Ibid.

383 Mark A. Milley, "Strategic Inflection Point," *Joint Forces Journal*, 3rd Quarter 2023, https:// ndupress.ndu.edu/JFQ/Joint-Force-Quarterly-110/Article/Article/3447159/strategic -inflection-point-the-most-historically-significant-and-fundamental-ch/.

384 Ibid.

385 Ibid.

386 Ronald Reagan, "January 5, 1967: Inaugural Address (Public Ceremony)," Ronald Reagan Presidential Library and Museum, https://www.reaganlibrary.gov/archives/speech/january -5-1967-inaugural-address-public-ceremony.

387 Colin Clark, "Gen. Hyten On The New American Way of War: All-Domain Operations," BreakingDefense.com, February 18, 2020, https://breakingdefense.com/2020/02/gen-hyten -on-the-new-american-way-of-war-all-domain-operations/.

388 Ibid.

389 Ibid.

390 Ibid.

391 "The Future of the Battlefield," *Global Trends 2040*, US Office of Director of National Intelligence, March 2021, https://www.dni.gov/index.php/gt2040-home/gt2040-deeper -looks/future-of-the-battlefield.

392 Ibid.

393 Ibid.

394 Ibid.

395 Artificial intelligence (AI) is intelligence exhibited by machines, particularly computer systems that are equipped to perceive their environment and use learning and intelligence to take actions.

396 "The Future of the Battlefield," *op. cit.*

397 Ibid.

398 Ibid.

399 Ibid.

400 Ibid.

401 Ibid.

402 Ibid.

403 Ibid.

404 Ibid.

405 Ibid.

406 Ibid.

407 Ibid.

408 "The dark web is the World Wide Web content that exists on darknets: overlay networks that use the Internet but require specific software, configurations, or authorization to

access. Through the dark web, private computer networks can communicate and conduct business anonymously without divulging identifying information, such as a user's location. The dark web forms a small part of the deep web, the part of the web not indexed by web search engines, although sometimes the term *deep web* is mistakenly used to refer specifically to the dark web." "Dark Web," Wikipedia, accessed September 1, 2024, https://en.wikipedia.org/wiki/Dark_web.

409 "The Future of the Battlefield," *op. cit.*
410 Ibid.
411 Ibid.
412 Ibid.
413 Holly Ellyatt, "Fear of World War III Should Stop Global Disputes, Russia's Putin Says," CNBC, June 7, 2018, https://www.cnbc.com/2018/06/07/russias-vladimir-putin-holds-annual-phone-in.html.
414 Alex Shuper, "a man standing in the middle of a destroyed city," Unsplash, accessed September 12, 2024, https://unsplash.com/photos/a-man-standing-in-the-middle-of-a-destroyed-city-zz2vRUBE_yg.
415 German Gorraiz Lopez, "Is World War III Inevitable?" *Global Research*, March 18, 2024, https://www.globalresearch.ca/world-war-iii-inevitable/5852423.
416 Elliott Davis Jr., "Fears about WWIII Are Growing Amid Russia-Ukraine War, Survey Finds," *US News*, September 29, 2022, https://www.usnews.com/news/best-countries/articles/2022-09-29/survey-fears-about-world-war-iii-are-growing-amid-russia-ukraine-war.
417 Marissa Lundeen, "Concern about World War III on the Rise, Research Indicates," *Daily Universe*, March 16, 2023, https://universe.byu.edu/2023/03/16/professors-weigh-in-on-the-possibility-of-world-war-iii/.
418 Robert A. Johnson, "Predicting Future War," Parameters 44(1) Spring 2014, US Army War College Press, https://press.armywarcollege.edu/parameters/vol44/iss1/8/.
419 Ibid.
420 Ibid.
421 Ibid.
422 Bret Stephens, "This Is How World War III Begins," *New York Times*, March 16, 2022, https://www.nytimes.com/2022/03/15/opinion/russia-ukraine-world-war-iii.html.
423 Ibid.
424 Ibid.
425 Scott Anderson, "What's the Quickest Path to World War III?" *New York Times*, April 2, 2024, https://www.nytimes.com/2024/04/02/books/review/the-return-of-great-powers-jim-sciutto-up-in-arms-adam-e-casey.html.
426 Ibid.
427 Helene Cooper, "China Isn't Ready to Pick Up Phone after Balloon Incident," *New York Times*, February 7, 2023, https://www.nytimes.com/2023/02/07/us/politics/china-balloon-austin.html.
428 "Polish Leader Urges Nord Stream Patrons to 'Keep Quiet' as Pipeline Mystery Returns to Spotlight," Associated Press, August 17, 2024, https://apnews.com/article/poland-nord-stream-gas-pipelines-tusk-russia-46ca2fb3f287570820564d1d5b6a8e29.
429 Colin Demarest, "Oceans Can No Longer Protect America," Axios, June 7, 2024, https://www.axios.com/2024/06/07/space-weapons-cyber-warfare-us-defense?utm_campaign=dfn-ebb&utm_medium=email&utm_source=sailthru.

430 Ibid.
431 Carlos Lozada, "A Look Back at Our Future War with China," *New York Times*, July 23, 2023, https://www.nytimes.com/2023/07/18/opinion/china-usa-relations-books-war.html.
432 Ibid.
433 Ibid.
434 David Betz, "The Future of War Is Civil War," *Social Sciences* 2023, 12(12), 646; Social Sciences | Free Full-Text | The Future of War Is Civil War (mdpi.com).
435 Ibid.
436 Ibid.
437 Ibid.
438 Ibid.
439 Leo Glasgow, "World War III Has Already Begun," UWire, March 5, 2024, https://cornellsun.com/2024/03/15/glasgow-world-war-iii-has-already-begun/.
440 Ibid.
441 Ibid.
442 Ibid.
443 Chris Nesi, "Germany Preparing for Russia to Start World War 3, Leaked War Plans Reveal," *New York Post*, January 15, 2024, https://nypost.com/2024/01/15/news/germany-preparing-for-russia-to-start-world-war-3/.
444 Ibid.
445 Ibid.
446 Ibid.
447 Adam R. Seipp, "Visionary Battle Scenes": Reading Sir John Hackett's *The Third World War, 1977–85*," *Journal of Military History* 83:4 (October 2019).
448 Ibid.
449 "The United States and the First World War," World War I Memorial, National Park Service, accessed September 3, 2024, https://www.nps.gov/wwim/wwioverview.htm#:~:-text=The%20United%20States%20suffered%2053%2C402%20battle%20deaths%20in,I%2C%20in%20less%20than%20six%20months%20of%20fighting. Note: The American Expeditionary Forces arrived in France June 1917. However, it didn't have its first major action until May 28, 1918, as the 1st Division fought the Germans at Cantigny. In September 1918, American forces launched the Meuse-Argonne Offensive, which lasted 47 days and claimed 26,000 American lives. The armistice was signed on November 11, 1918, which ended the fight. All tolled, the US suffered 53,402 battle deaths in less than six months of fighting with another 63,114 died from accidents and disease.
450 "The Cost of U.S. Wars Then and Now," Norwich University, accessed September 1, 2024, https://online.norwich.edu/online/about/resource-library/cost-us-wars-then-and-now.
451 "American War and Military Operations Casualties: Lists and Statistics," Congressional Research Service, RL32492, Updated July 29, 2020, https://crsreports.congress.gov/product/pdf/RL/RL32492.
452 John F. Kenndy, azquotes.com, accessed September 1, 2024, https://www.azquotes.com/quotes/topics/preparing-for-war.html.
453 George Washington, acquotes.com, accessed September 1, 2024, https://www.azquotes.com/quote/307721?ref=preparing-for-war.
454 "Commission on National Defense Strategy," *op. cit.*

455 Michael Peck, "These Are the Top 26 National Security Threats Facing America," The National Interest, States News Service, January 3, 2019, https://nationalinterest.org/blog /buzz/these-are-top-26-national-security-threats-facing-america-40412.

456 Ibid.

457 Ibid.

458 Ibid.

459 "Commission on National Defense Strategy," *op. cit.*

460 "Military and Security Developments Involving the People's Republic of China," Report to Congress Pursuant to the National Defense Authorization Act for Fiscal Year 2000, Public Law 106-65, October 2023, https://www.defense.gov/News/Releases/Release /Article/3561549/dod-releases-2023-report-on-military-and-security-developments -involving-the-pe/.

461 Seth G. Jones, "China Is Ready for War," *Foreign Affairs*, October 2, 2024, https://www. foreignaffairs.com/china/china-ready-war-america-is-not-seth-jones?utm_medium =newsletters&utm_source=fatoday&utm_campaign=Where%20Will%20Israel%E2 %80%99s%20Multifront%20War%20End?&utm_content=20241002&utm_term=N.

462 Ibid.

463 Ibid.

464 "China's 'Aggressive Behaviour' in South China Sea Must Be Challenged, US Navy Offi-cial Says," Reuters, August 27, 2023, https://www.reuters.com/world/chinas-aggressive -behaviour-south-china-sea-must-be-challenged-us-navy-official-2023-08-27/.

465 Aaron-Matthew Lariosa, "Chinese Maritime Safety Officers Beat Vietnamese Fishermen During South China Sea Interdiction, Say Officials," USNI news, October 7, 2024, https://news.usni.org/2024/10/07/chinese-maritime-safety-officers-beat-vietnamese -fishermen-during-south-china-sea-interdiction-say-officials?utm_campaign=dfn-ebb&utm _medium=email&utm_source=sailthru.

466 Ibid.

467 Jim Gomez, "US Missile System Will Remain in Philippines Despite China's Alarm," As-sociated Press, September 25, 2024, US missile system will remain in Philippines despite China's alarm (defensenews.com).

468 Ibid.

469 "Military and Security Developments Involving the People's Republic of China," *op. cit.*

470 Anders Corr, "China Versus the US in Space: Do the Americans Have What It Takes?" *Epoch Times*, September 6, 2024, https://www.theepochtimes.com/opinion/china-versus -the-us-in-space-do-the-americans-have-what-it-takes-5719004?utm_source=Morning brief&src_src=Morningbrief&utm_campaign=mb-2024-09-07&src_cmp=mb-2024-09 -07&utm_medium=email&est=AAAAAAAAAAAAAAAAY%2B0peBILkJLo77wDv WRKH%2Fp0zle%2FQzAkSnnTu5OdEYzwv2cm.

471 Ibid and Fisher, *op. cit.*

472 Ibid.

473 Ibid.

474 "Russia Launches Massive Naval Drills with China," Associated Press, September 10, 2024, https://www.defensenews.com/global/europe/2024/09/10/russia-launches-massive -naval-drills-with-china/?utm_source=sailthru&utm_medium=email&utm_campaign =dfn-dnr.

475 Ibid.

476 Ibid.
477 Chris Summers, "China Publicly Test-Fires ICBM for First Time in Decades," The Signal, September 25, 2024, https://www.msn.com/en-us/news/world/china-publicly-test-fires-icbm-for-first-time-in-decades/ar-AA1rcLrn#:~:text=China%20has%20test-fired%20an%20intercontinental%20ballistic%20missile%20into,target%20and%20was%20in%20line%20with%20international%20law.
478 Ibid.
479 Peck, *op. cit.*
480 Yuliya Talmazan, "Russia Is Ready for Nuclear War, Putin Warns the West," NBC News, March 13, 2024, https://www.nbcnews.com/news/world/russia-ready-nuclear-war-putin-warns-west-rcna143119.
481 John Irish. et al, "Macron's Ukraine Troop Talk Shakes up NATO Allies," Reuters, February 28, 2024, https://www.reuters.com/world/europe/macrons-ukraine-troop-talk-shakes-up-nato-allies-2024-02-27/.
482 Katrina Manson and Tony Capaccio, "Russia's Bid for an Orbiting Nuclear Weapon Highlights a New Space Race," Bloomberg.com, February 17, 2024, https://www.msn.com/en-us/money/other/russia-s-bid-for-an-orbiting-nuclear-weapon-highlights-a-new-space-race/ar-BB1ir9k8.
483 Rudy Ruitenberg, "France Plans Low-orbit Demonstrator That Can Target Other Satellites," *Defense News*, September 17, 2024, https://www.defensenews.com/global/europe/2024/09/17/france-plans-low-orbit-demonstrator-that-can-target-other-satellites/?utm_source=sailthru&utm_medium=email&utm_campaign=dfn-space. Note: This article indicates that "France plans to launch a maneuverable satellite into low Earth orbit in the next two years that can target other satellites, something French Space Command said is necessary to show the country can take action to protect its space assets." It appears that satellite will have a laser to "target other satellites."
484 Liselotte Odgaard, "Russia and China's Cooperation in the Arctic Is a Rising Nuclear Threat," *Politico*, October 3, 2024, Russia and China's cooperation in the Arctic is a rising nuclear threat – POLITICO.
485 Ibid.
486 Ibid.
487 "Commission on National Defense Strategy," *op. cit.*
488 Peck, *op. cit.*
489 Farnaz Fassihi, "A Look at Iran's Military Capabilities," *New York Times*, April 12, 2024, https://www.nytimes.com/2024/04/12/world/middleeast/iran-israel-military-weapons.html.
490 Ibid.
491 Ibid.; "Iran: Tehran Sends Russia Ballistic Missiles for Use in Ukraine," Worldview, stratfor.com, September 6, 2024, https://worldview.stratfor.com/situation-report/iran-tehran-sends-russia-ballistic-missiles-use-ukraine?id=030c4e7823&e=f60ad-9ba4b&uuid=f9ef3c06-4e43-497b-b484-9c2bebf508ce&mc_cid=0fbaa7f568&mc_eid=-f60ad9ba4b.
492 "Israel's Netanyahu Claims Iran Lied about Nuclear Weapons Program," CBS News, April 30, 2018, https://www.cbsnews.com/news/israel-netanyahu-claims-iran-lied-about-nuclear-weapons-program/.
493 "North Korea's Military Capabilities," Council on Foreign Relations, June 28, 2022, https://www.cfr.org/backgrounder/north-korea-nuclear-weapons-missile-tests-military

-capabilities#:~:text=It%20has%20the%20world%E2%80%99s%20fourth-largest%20military%2C%20with%20more,is%20believed%20to%20possess%20chemical%20and%20biological%20weapons.

494 "Commission on National Defense Strategy, July 2024," *op. cit.*

495 "Department of Defense Releases the President's Fiscal Year 2024 Defense Budget, US Department of Defense, March 13, 2023, https://www.defense.gov/News/Releases/Release/Article/3326875/department-of-defense-releases-the-presidents-fiscal-year-2024-defense-budget/.

496 National Defense Budget Estimates for FY25, Office of the Under Secretary of Defense [Comptroller], April 2024

497 "Department of Defense Releases the President's Fiscal Year 2025 Defense Budget," US Department of Defense, March 11, 2024, https://www.defense.gov/News/Releases/Release/Article/3703410/.

498 "How Much Does the US Spend on the Military?" USA Facts Team, August 1, 2024, https://usafacts.org/articles/how-much-does-the-us-spend-on-the-military/#:~:text=In%202023%2C%20the%20US%20military%20spent%20approximately%20%24820.3,the%20entire%20federal%20budget%20for%20that%20fiscal%20year.

499 "How Many People Are in the US Military? A Demographic Overview," USA Facts Team, February 21, 2024, https://usafacts.org/articles/how-many-people-are-in-the-us-military-a-demographic-overview/.

500 "An Assessment of U.S. Military Power," Heritage.com, January 24, 2024, https://www.heritage.org/military-strength/assessment-us-military-power/conclusion.

501 Ibid.

502 John Torcasio, "gray f22 raptor," Unsplash, https://unsplash.com/photos/gray-f22-raptor-ElMr-GeVni4.

503 "An Assessment of U.S. Military Power," *op. cit.*

504 Ibid.

505 Ibid.

506 Ibid.

507 Ibid.

508 Ibid.

509 Ibid.

510 "Battle of the Aleutian Islands," History, June 20, 2020, https://www.history.com/topics/world-war-ii/battle-of-the-aleutian-islands. Note: "In the Battle of the Aleutian Islands (June 1942–August 1943) during World War II (1939–45), U.S. troops fought to remove Japanese garrisons established on a pair of U.S.-owned islands west of Alaska. In June 1942, Japan had seized the remote, sparsely inhabited islands of Attu and Kiska, in the Aleutian Islands."

511 A. Wess Mitchell, "America Is a Heartbeat Away from a War It Could Lose," *Foreign Policy*, November 16, 2023, https://foreignpolicy.com/2023/11/16/us-russia-china-gaza-ukraine-world-war-defense-security-strategy/.

512 "How Much U.S. Debt Does China Own?" The Investopedia Team, July 27, 2024, https://www.investopedia.com/articles/investing/080615/china-owns-us-debt-how-much.asp Note: The two leading foreign creditors at Japan, which holds about 3 percent of total US debt, and China, which holds about 2.6 percent of our debt.

513 Stephen Wertheim, "World War III Begins with Forgetting," *International New York*

Times, December 6, 2022, https://www.nytimes.com/2022/12/02/opinion/america
-world-war-iii.html.

514 Ibid.

515 Ibid.

516 J. C. McManaway, "America Must Prepare," Vital Speeches of the Day, EBSCO Publishing, May 30, 1940, https://www.ibiblio.org/pha/policy/1940/1940-05-30a.html.

517 Ibid.

518 Roger Wicker, "Senator Wicker Unveils Major Defense Investment Plan," US Senate, May 29, 2024, Senator Wicker Unveils Major Defense Investment Plan - U.S. Senator Roger Wicker (senate.gov).

519 John G. Ferrari and Todd Harrison, "Our Military Can't meet Its Mission if We Underfund It," The Hill, June 5, 2024, Our military can't meet its mission if we underfund it (thehill.com).

520 "Commission on National Defense Strategy," *op. cit.*

521 Wicker, *op. cit.*

522 "George Washington," azquotes.com, accessed September 1, 2024, https://www.azquotes
.com/quote/307721?ref=preparing-for-war.

523 "Deterrence," azquotes.com, accessed September 1, 2024, https://www.azquotes.com
/quotes/topics/deterrence.html.

524 Hermeus, "an artists rendering of a space shuttle in flight," Unsplash, https://unsplash
.com/photos/an-artists-rendering-of-a-space-shuttle-in-flight-BKSAYomTaaE.

525 "Deterrence," Cambridge.org, accessed September 1, 2024, https://dictionary.cambridge
.org/dictionary/english/deterrence.

526 Michael J. Mazarr et al, "What Deters and Why," RAND Corporation, November 20, 2018, What Deters and Why: Exploring Requirements for Effective Deterrence of Interstate Aggression | RAND.

527 George Washington, Fifth Annual Address to Congress, Mount Vernon Library, December 13, 1793, https://www.mountvernon.org/library/digitalhistory/past-projects/quotes
/article/if-we-desire-to-avoid-insult-we-must-be-able-to-repel-it-if-we-desire-to-secure
-peace-one-of-the-most-powerful-instruments-of-our-rising-prosperity-it-must-be-known
-that-we-are-at-all-times-ready-for-war.

528 "Big Stick Ideology," Wikipedia, accessed September 1, 2024, https://en.wikipedia.org
/wiki/Big_stick_ideology.

529 "Gambling and Vice in the State Capital," *Brooklyn Daily Eagle*. 1900-04-01. p. 39, as cited in "Big Stick Ideology," Wikipedia, accessed September 1, 2024, https://en.wikipedia
.org/wiki/Big_stick_ideology,

530 Victor Davis Hanson, "The Corrections," *National Review*, July 18, 2003, https://www
.nationalreview.com/2003/07/corrections-victor-davis-hanson/.

531 Sarah Pruitt, "Why Did Japan Attack Pearl Harbor?" History, May 13, 2020, https://
www.history.com/news/why-did-japan-attack-pearl-harbor.

532 Gerald Baker, "When Biden Says 'Don't,' America's Adversaries Do," *Wall Street Journal*, April 15, 2024, https://www.wsj.com/articles/when-biden-says-dont-americas-adversaries
-do-foreign-policy-deterrence-e3b65ecd.

533 Ibid.

534 Ibid.

535 Ibid.

536 "National Security Strategy," The White House, October 2022, https://www.whitehouse
.gov/wp-content/uploads/2022/11/8-November-Combined-PDF-for-Upload.pdf and
Michael J. Mazarr and Ivana Ke, "Integrated Deterrence as a Defense Planning Concept,"
RAND Corporation, June 4, 2024, https://www.rand.org/pubs/perspectives/PEA2263-1
.html#document-details.

537 Ibid.

538 Ibid.

539 Ibid.

540 "National Defense Strategy," Department of Defense, October 27, 2022, https://media
.defense.gov/2022/Oct/27/2003103845/-1/-1/1/2022-NATIONAL-DEFENSE
-STRATEGY-NPR-MDR.PDF.

541 "Commission on National Security Strategy," op. cit.

542 Ibid.

543 Ibid.

544 Ibid.

545 Mazarr, op. cit.

546 Hansen, op. cit.

547 "The Keys to Preventing Conflict between Countries," World Economic Forum, November 23, 2018, https://www.weforum.org/agenda/2018/11/how-to-prevent-conflict/.

548 "Colin Powell," azquotes.com, accessed September 1, 2024, https://www.azquotes.com
/quotes/topics/preparation.html.

549 "Dwight D. Eisenhower," goodreads.com, accessed September 1, 2024, https://www.good
reads.com/quotes/53952-neither-a-wise-nor-a-brave-man-lies-down-on#:~:text=%E2%80
%9CNeither%20a%20wise%20nor%20a%20brave%20man%20lies,to%20run%20over
%20him.%E2%80%9D%20%E2%80%95%20Dwight%20D.%20Eisenhower.

550 Ibid.

551 Jeremy Black, "Civilians in Warfare," History Today, May 2006, Vol. 56, Issue 5, https://
www.historytoday.com/archive/civilians-warfare-1500-1789.

552 Ibid.

553 Ibid.

554 Ibid.

555 Ibid.

556 Ibid.

557 Black, op. cit.

558 Ibid.

559 Ibid.

560 "Thirty Years War," History.com, August 21, 2018, https://www.history.com/topics/european
-history/thirty-years-war.

561 Ibid.

562 Ibid.

563 Ibid.

564 Ibid.

565 Ibid.

566 Ibid.

567 "Civilian Casualties of World War Two," History Learning, accessed September 1, 2024,
https://historylearning.com/world-war-two/civilian-casualties-of-world-war/.

568 "London at War," *History Today*, September 1985, pp. 61–62.
569 Ibid.
570 "Chislehurst Caves," Wikipedia, accessed September 1, 2024, https://en.wikipedia.org/wiki/Chislehurst_Caves.
571 "London at War," *op. cit.*
572 Matthew Hughes, "When Soldiers Kill Civilians," *History Today*, February 2010, Vol. 60, Issues 2, https://www.historytoday.com/archive/when-soldiers-kill-civilians-battle-saipan-1944.
573 Ibid.
574 Ibid.
575 Ibid.
576 Ibid.
577 Ibid.
578 Ibid.
579 Ibid.
580 Ibid.
581 Vsevolod Konstantinov, "The Impact of the Russian-Ukrainian War and Relocation on Civilian Refugees," *Journal of Loss & Trauma*, Vol. 28, Issue 3, July 6, 2022, https://www.tandfonline.com/doi/full/10.1080/15325024.2022.2093472.
582 Ibid.
583 Ibid.
584 Ibid.
585 David R. Meddings (2001), "Civilians and War: A Review and Historical Overview of the Involvement of Non-combatant Populations in Conflict Situations," *Medicine, Conflict and Survival*, 17:1, 6–16, DOI: 10.1080/13623690108409551 To link to this article: https://doi.org/10.1080/13623690108409551.
586 Ibid.
587 Ibid.
588 Ibid.
589 Ibid.
590 Ibid.
591 Ibid.
592 Jon Henley, "Sweden Distributes 'Be Prepared for War' Leaflet to all 4.8M Homes," *The Guardian*, May 21, 2018, https://www.theguardian.com/world/2018/may/21/sweden-distributes-be-prepared-for-war-cyber-terror-attack-leaflet-to-every-home?__twitter_impression=true&__twitter_impression=true.
593 Ibid.
594 Ibid.
595 Ibid.
596 Ibid.
597 Ibid.
598 Piotr Wilk, "woman wearing gillie suit holding sniper rifle," Unsplash, https://unsplash.com/photos/woman-wearing-gillie-suit-holding-sniper-rifle-KfXWIkOk4hI.
599 "Disaster Preparedness, Response, and Recovery," Substance Abuse and Mental Health Services Administration, accessed September 1, 2024, https://www.samhsa.gov/disaster-preparedness.

600 Vint Cerf, "U.S. Critical Infrastructure at Risk of Increasing Cyberattacks. Here's What You Need To Know," *Forbes*, June 4, 2024, https://www.forbes.com/sites/vintcerf/2024 /06/04/harden-critical-infrastructure-against-foreign-cyber-attacks-us-agencies-warn/.

601 James Conca, "How to Defend against the Electromagnetic Pulse Threat by Literally Painting Over It," *Forbes*, September 27, 2021, https://www.forbes.com/sites/jamesconca /2021/09/27/the-electromagnetic-pulse-threatcant-we-just-paint-over-it/ and "Electromagnetic Pulse (EMP) Protection and Resilience Guidelines for Critical Infrastructure and Equipment," National Coordinating Center for Communications, February 5, 2021, https://www.cisa.gov/sites/default/files/publications/19_0307_CISA_EMP-Protection -Resilience-Guidelines.pdf.

602 "The State of U.S. Strategic Stockpiles," Council on Foreign Relations, March 2, 2023, https://www.cfr.org/backgrounder/state-us-strategic-stockpiles.

603 C. Forrester and C. Judy, "Managing Mass Fatalities: A Toolkit for Planning," HHS.gov, accessed September 1, 2024, https://asprtracie.hhs.gov/technical-resources/resource/634 /managing-mass-fatalities-a-toolkit-for-planning.

604 Rob Orrison, "Militia, Minutemen, and Continentals: The American Military Force in the American Revolution," Prince William County Historic Preservation Division, April 30, 2021, https://www.battlefields.org/learn/articles/militia-minutemen-and-continentals -american-military-force-american-revolution.

605 10 U.S. Code § 246 - Militia: composition and classes, https://www.law.cornell.edu/uscode /text/10/246.

606 "Prohibiting Private Armies at Public Rallies," *Georgetown Law, Institute for Constitutional Advocacy & Protection*, Third Edition, September 2020, https://www.law.georgetown.edu /icap/wp-content/uploads/sites/32/2018/04/Prohibiting-Private-Armies-at-Public-Rallies.pdf.

607 "Following January 6th Anniversary Senator Markey and Congressman Raskin Introduce Legislation to Stop Private Paramilitary Activity," US Senator Edward Markey Press Release, January 11, 2024, https://www.markey.senate.gov/news/press-releases/following-january -6th-anniversary-senator-markey-and-congressman-raskin-introduce-legislation-to -stop-private-paramilitary-activity#:~:text=%E2%80%9CThe%20Preventing%20Private %20Paramilitary%20Activity,mechanisms%20to%20reinforce%20its%20prohibition.

608 "Preparedness Actions," FEMA, accessed September 1, 2024, https://orders.gpo.gov/icpd /ICPD.aspx#Preparedness%20Actions.

609 "Disaster Planning, Response, and Recovery for Organizations Serving People Experiencing Homelessness," CDC, accessed September 1, 2024, https://www.emergency.cdc.gov /homeless/index.asp.

610 "Prevention of Communicable Diseases after Disaster: A Review," *Journal of Research in Medical Sciences*, July 2011; 16(7): 956–962, National Library of Medicine, https://www .ncbi.nlm.nih.gov/pmc/articles/PMC3263111/.

611 "Food Security in Times of Armed Conflict: What You Need to Know," International Committee of the Red Cross, March 8, 2023, https://www.icrc.org/en/document/food -security-in-armed-conflict-what-you-need-know.

612 "William Glasser," brainyquote.com, accessed September 1, 2024, https://www.brainy quote.com/quotes/william_glasser_381943.

613 Jamie Ballard, "Most Americans Think There Will Be Another World War within the Next Decade," YouGov, March 21, 2024, https://today.yougov.com/politics/articles /48981-most-americans-think-another-world-war-within-the-next-decade.

614 "UN Chief: 2 Billion People Live in Conflict Areas Today," Associated Press, March 31, 2022, https://www.voanews.com/a/un-chief-2-billion-people-live-in-conflict-areas-today /6509020.html.

615 Mary Kekatos, "Physical and Mental Health Toll on People Trapped in War Zones as Israel Conflict Continues," ABC News, October 10, 2023, https://abcnews.go.com/Health /physical-mental-health-toll-people-trapped-war-zones/story?id=103829906.

616 Ibid.

617 Ibid.

618 Anthony Galloway, "More Than 400 Million Children Living in War Zones: Report," *The Sydney Morning Herald*, February 13, 2020, https://www.smh.com.au/politics/federal /more-than-400-million-children-living-in-war-zones-report-20200212-p53zz3.html.

619 Ibid.

620 Ibid.

621 Ibid.

622 "Syrian Refugees Share Stories of Survival and Suffering in Lebanon," PBS, February 5, 2016, https://www.pbs.org/newshour/show/syrian-refugees-share-stories-of-survival-and -suffering-in-lebanon#transcript.

623 Ibid.

624 Ibid.

625 "13 Powerful Refugee Stories from Around the World," Globalgiving.org, https://www .globalgiving.org/learn/listicle/13-powerful-refugee-stories/.

626 Ibid.

627 Ibid.

628 Ibid.

629 Ibid.

630 Ibid.

631 Ibid.

632 Avalon Hester, "Life in an Active War Zone: Fallbrook Missionary Describes What Life is Like for Those That Remain in Ukraine," *Village News* intern, August 18, 2023, https:// www.villagenews.com/story/2023/08/10/community/life-in-an-active-war-zone-fallbrook -missionary-describes-what-life-is-like-for-those-that-remain-in-ukraine/73879.html.

633 Ibid.

634 Ibid.

635 Paul Adams, "A Rare Glimpse of Daily Life in Occupied Ukraine," British Broadcasting Corp., October 3, 2022, https://www.bbc.com/news/world-europe-63076570.

636 Ibid.

637 Ibid.

638 Ibid.

639 Ibid.

640 Ibid.

641 Ibid.

642 Ibid.

643 Ibid.

644 Ibid.

645 Mikkel Thorup, "World War 3 Where Will Be Safe in a Global Conflict?" Expat Money blog, November 25, 2023, https://expatmoney.com/blog/world-war-3-where-will-be-safe -in-a-global-conflict.

646 Ibid.
647 Ibid.
648 Ibid.
649 Ibid.
650 Ibid.
651 Ibid.
652 Caspian Dahlström, "brown wooden house in the woods," Unsplash, https://unsplash .com/photos/brown-wooden-house-in-the-woods-MtrThdtctqo.
653 Ben White, "Woman sitting on brown bench while reading book," Unsplash, https:// unsplash.com/photos/woman-sitting-on-brown-bench-while-reading-book-vtCBruWoNqo.
654 "World Watch List: Trends," Open Door, accessed September 1, 2024, https://www.open doors.org/en-US/persecution/persecution-trends/.
655 "Darlene Deibler Rose: Life as a Missionary and World War II POW in the Presence of God," *Anchored in Christ*, accessed September 1, 2024, https://www.kevinhalloran.net /darlene-deibler-rose-life-as-a-missionary-and-world-war-ii-pow-in-the-presence-of-god/.
656 Ibid.
657 Ibid.
658 Ibid.
659 Ibid.
660 Ibid.
661 Ibid.
662 Kenneth Robb Kersey, "Faith in Jesus Sustained 'POW' in Vietnam," godsotherways.com, May 12, 2015, https://www.godsotherways.com/stories/2015/5/12/pow-sustained-by-gods -power.
663 Ibid.
664 Ibid.
665 Ibid.
666 Ibid.
667 Ammar Cheikhomar and Henry Austin, "Caught in the Middle: Christians Suffer amid Syria's Civil War," NBC News, August 11, 2013, https://www.nbcnews.com/news/world /caught-middle-christians-suffer-amid-syrias-civil-war-flna6C10893411.
668 Ibid.
669 Ibid.
670 Ibid.
671 "Ukrainian Christian Groups Face Violent Crackdown from Russian Forces," PBS, April 10, 2024, https://www.pbs.org/newshour/show/ukrainian-christian-groups-face-violent -crackdown-from-russian-forces.
672 Ibid.
673 Ibid.
674 Ibid.
675 Ibid.
676 Ibid.
677 Ibid.
678 Ibid.
679 Ibid.
680 Ibid.

681 "What Does the Bible Say About War?" Christian Bible Reference Site, accessed September 1, 2024, https://www.christianbiblereference.org/faq_war.htm.
682 Ibid.
683 Ibid.
684 John MacArthur, "What Does the Bible Say about War? Is There Ever a Just Reason for It?," Grace to You, July 17, 2009, https://www.gty.org/library/questions/QA65/What-does-the-Bible-say-about-war-Is-there-ever-a-just-reason-for-it.
685 Ibid.
686 Ibid.
687 Ibid.
688 Ibid.
689 William K. Harrison Jr., "May a Christian Serve in the Military?" Officers' Christian Fellowship, updated January 2, 2020, May A Christian Serve in the Military? - Officers' Christian Fellowship (ocfusa.org).
690 Ibid.
691 Ibid.
692 Ibid.
693 Ibid.
694 Ibid.
695 Dennis Phelps, "The Message Hidden in Your Pocket: Psalm 33," Preaching, accessed September 1, 2024,https://www.preaching.com/sermons/the-message-hidden-in-your-pocket-psalm-33/.
696 Interview with William Boykin on March 4, 2020.
697 Ibid.
698 "Harry S. Truman," quotefancy.com, accessed September 1, 2024, https://quotefancy.com/harry-s-truman-quotes.
699 "William Tecumseh Sherman," azquotes.com, accessed September 1, 2024, https://www.azquotes.com/quote/270116.
700 Billy Graham, "10 Quotes from Billy Graham on the End Times," The Billy Graham Library, April 8, 2021, https://billygrahamlibrary.org/blog-10-quotes-from-billy-graham-on-end-times/.
701 Pisit Heng, "brown-rock-formation-during-daytime," Unsplash, https://unsplash.com/photos/brown-rock-formation-during-daytime-ci1F55HaVWQ.
702 Robert L. Maginnis, *Alliance of Evil*, (Crane, MO: Defender, 2018), pp. 305ff.
703 Email from Dr. Michael Heiser, February 21, 2018.
704 Ibid.
705 Ibid.
706 Michael Heiser, "The Naked Bible: Biblical Theology, Stripped Bare of Denominational Confessions and Theological Confessions," YouTube, uploaded January 12, 2015, https://youtu.be/zgwWP1WbeZA.
707 Ibid.
708 Ibid.
709 "Biblical Hermeneutics—What Is It?" compellingtruth.org. Accessed March 17, 2018, https://www.compellingtruth.org/biblical-hermeneutics.html.
710 "Russian Orthodox Patriarch Warns of End Time Apocalypse," The Trumpet.com, December 5, 2017, https://www.thetrumpet.com/16611-russian-orthodox-patriarch-warns-ofend-time-apocalypse.

711 Michael Heiser, *The Unseen Realm*, (Lexham Press, 2015), pp. 364–366.

712 "Does the Bible Say Anything about Russia in Relation to the End Times?" Got Questions, accessed May 15, 2018, https://www.gotquestions.org/Russia-end-times.html.

713 David R. Reagan, "America the Beautiful? The United States in Bible Prophecy," Lamb & Lion Ministries. Accessed March 17, 2018, http://christinprophecy.org/articles/theunited-states-in-bible-prophecy/.

714 H. G. Wells, Brainyquote, accessed November 12, 2024, https://www.brainyquote.com/quotes/h_g_wells_161934.

715 Thibault Dandre, "a couple of men wearing virtual reality headsets," Unsplash, accessed September 7, 2024, https://unsplash.com/photos/a-couple-of-men-wearing-virtual-reality-headsets-HPL40k7Xaf0.

716 Peter Aitken, "Dogs of War: Britain's New Robots Aiding Ukraine, Terrorizing Russia as Drones Continue Dominating Battlefield," Fox News, August 25, 2024, https://www.foxnews.com/world/dogs-war-britains-new-robots-aiding-ukraine-terrorizing-russia-drones-continue-dominating-battlefield.

717 David Majumdar, "Russia's Armata T-14 Tank vs. America's M-1 Abrams: Who Wins?" *National Interest*, September 11, 2015, https://nationalinterest.org/blog/the-buzz/russias-armata-t-14-tank-vs-americas-m-1-abrams-who-wins-13825.

718 Carla Bleiker, "Russia's Hypersonic Missiles—What You Need to Know," DW, March 10, 2023.

719 "DOD Releases 2023 Report on Military and Security Developments Involving the People's Republic of China," *op. cit.*

720 Sandra Erwin, "Russia, China Catching up to U.S. in Space Weaponry, New Report Finds," SpaceNews, April 2, 2024, https://spacenews.com/russia-china-catching-up-to-u-s-in-space-weaponry-new-report-finds/.

721 Annika Burgess, "With More 'Unfriendly Behaviour' and New Weapons, the World Is Preparing for War in Space," ABC News (Australia), May 20, 2024, https://www.abc.net.au/news/2024-05-21/space-weapons-how-the-world-is-preparing-for-war-in-space/103634106.

722 Adrian Willings, "32 Interesting and Incredibly Futuristic Weapons and Modern Fighting Vehicles," pocket-lint.com, March 20, 2023, https://www.pocket-lint.com/gadgets/news/142272-28-incredible-futuristic-weapons-showing-modern-military-might/.

723 Ibid.

724 Ibid.

725 Ibid.

726 Ibid.

727 Ibid.

728 Ibid.

729 Ibid.

730 Ibid.

731 Ibid.

732 Ibid.

733 Ibid.

734 Ibid.

735 Janes, accessed August 25, 2024, https://www.janes.com. /about https://customer-janes-com.pentagonlibrary.idm.oclc.org/CountryIntelligence/Countries/Country_501/military.

736 "DOD Releases 2023 Report on Military and Security Developments Involving the People's Republic of China," *op. cit.*

737 "Global Firepower 2024," accessed August 25, 2024, https://www.globalfirepower.com/.

738 "Missiles of the World," CSIS, August 25, 2024, https://missilethreat.csis.org.

739 Michael Afonso, "gay warship on body of water," Unsplash, accessed September 7, 2024, https://unsplash.com/photos/gray-warship-on-body-of-water-BQgAYwERXhs.

740 "Home Prep Guide: What You Need to Last 2 Weeks in an Emergency," *Epoch Times*, October 12, 2024, https://www.theepochtimes.com/article/a-guide-to-home-preparedness-5740113?utm_source=Morningbrief&src_src=Morningbrief&utm_campaign=mb-2024-10-13&src_cmp=mb-2024-10-13&utm_medium=email&est=AAAAAAAAAAAAAAAAY%2B0peBILkJLo77wDvWRKH%2Fp0zle%2FQzAkSnnTu5OdEYzwv2cm.

741 Josue Michel, "the back of a vehicle with luggage in the back," Unsplash, accessed September 7, 2024, https://unsplash.com/photos/the-back-of-a-vehicle-with-luggage-in-the-back-uw_kd2djWic.

742 "Home Prep Guide: What You Need to Last 2 Weeks in an Emergency," *op. cit.*

Made in United States
Cleveland, OH
06 February 2025

14081913R00204